AGRICULTURAL PRODUCTION

AND THE ECONOMIC DEVELOPMENT

OF JAPAN 1873-1922

STUDIES OF THE EAST ASIAN INSTITUTE

COLUMBIA UNIVERSITY

AGRICULTURAL PRODUCTION AND THE ECONOMIC DEVELOPMENT OF JAPAN 1873-1922

JAMES I. NAKAMURA

PRINCETON UNIVERSITY PRESS

PRINCETON, NEW JERSEY

1966

The East Asian Institute at Columbia University

THE EAST ASIAN INSTITUTE was established by Columbia University in 1949 to prepare graduate students for careers dealing with East Asia, and to aid research and publication on East Asia during the modern period. The research program of the East Asian Institute is conducted or directed by faculty members of the University, by other scholars invited to participate in the program of the Institute, and by candidates for the Certificate of the Institute or the degree of Doctor of Philosophy. Some of the products of the research program are published as Studies of the East Asian Institute. The faculty of the Institute, without necessarily agreeing with the conclusions reached in the Studies, hope with their publication to perform a national service by increasing American understanding of the peoples of East Asia, the development of their societies, and their current problems.

The faculty of the East Asian Institute are grateful to the Rockefeller Foundation and the Ford Foundation for the financial assistance which they have given to the program of research and publication.

This book is one of the Studies of the East Asian Institute, Columbia University. Other books in the series are:

The Ladder of Success in Imperial China by Ping-ti Ho. New York, Columbia University Press, 1962; John Wiley, 1964.

The Chinese Inflation, 1937-49 by Shun-hsin Chou. New York, Columbia University Press, 1963.

Reformer in Modern China: Chang Chien, 1853-1926 by Samuel Chu. New York, Columbia University Press, 1965.

Research in Japanese Sources: A Guide by Herschel Webb with the assistance of Marleigh Ryan. New York, Columbia University Press, 1965.

Society and Education in Japan by Herbert Passin. New York, Bureau of Publications, Teachers College, Columbia University, 1965.

To Tetsuko
and
To My Mother

FOREWORD

To BE able to introduce a fundamental book on the economic development of Japan is a rare privilege indeed. Since the nineteenth century Japan has stood out as the one non-Western country which has successfully modernized; and increasingly Asian and African states, anxious to reform their traditional societies, have been looking to Japan for the secrets of success.

Certain of these secrets, however, have long resisted analysis. Japan's development has been replete with unresolved economic and social paradoxes. In the agricultural sector, for example, a sudden spurt in land area and yield per unit area (and therefore total production) occurred in the mid 1880's. Why then was there no corresponding transfer of labor and capital into agriculture during that period? Moreover, since reported staple food production continued to rise rapidly at more than twice the population growth, why did staple food imports rise? If production increased remarkably from 1878 to 1922, why was there not a more rapid transformation of social and political relations, as might be suggested by Japan's postwar transformation?

Dissatisfied with the various hypotheses offered, Professor Nakamura undertook the arduous task of reexamining the sources of the government statistics. After years of painstaking research in the original records, he found convincing evidence that the government figures were seriously distorted by the practice of various forms of land tax evasion. Using several ingenious methods, he then reconstructed a more reliable series of agricultural production figures, showing that the median growth rate of agriculture in the early period was not 2.4 per cent per year as previously believed, but probably no more than about 1.0 per cent.

This is a revolutionary finding, for it dispels much of the mystery which surrounded Japan's miraculous "take-off" in the Meiji period. The truth seems to be more complex, but more understandable—more complex in that the explanations for Japan's growth hereafter must be sought not only in the modern period itself, but also in the preceding three centuries of the Tokugawa era, when the preconditions for economic growth were being formed; and more understandable in that Japan's economic development seems to be less unique and more in accord with the pattern of development of other advanced countries than had previously been suspected.

This is a major work by a new economic development specialist in the field of Japanese studies. James Nakamura received his advanced degrees from Columbia University: the B.S. in 1952, and the Ph.D. in economics in 1964. The present work is a revised version of his dissertation. After extensive research experience, partially supported by Ford Foundation fellowships, and teaching at the City University of New York, Hunter College, and Adelphi College, he accepted a post at Columbia jointly in the Department of Economics and the East Asian Institute, where he offers graduate instruction in comparative economic development, emphasizing the economy of Japan.

JAMES WILLIAM MORLEY
Director, East Asian Institute

Tokyo
July 1965

PREFACE

JAPAN's economic growth has almost invariably been described in superlatives. Some of the features so described are indeed impressive. Her early growth has been estimated to be the most rapid of any economically developed nation. She is said to have used capital with most remarkable efficiency (i.e., had the lowest marginal capital-output ratio of any nation). Almost universal acceptance has also been given the proposition that agriculture played an unusually important role by increasing output at a remarkable rate and providing labor and saving to other sectors. The above conclusions have led many economists to argue that the Japanese experience would provide a useful model for the underdeveloped countries of the world.

Because this book challenges the validity of all of the above propositions and many others, it is bound to arouse controversy since most scholars have long accepted the foregoing propositions.

Due to its controversial nature let me state here what the book is—and is not. It has three basic objectives: first, to demonstrate that Japanese government statistics seriously understate the value of production in the early Meiji era and thereby to criticize previous estimates of Meiji national product which accepted these statistics with little or no modification; second, to work out new estimates of the growth rate of the Japanese economy and, more particularly, the growth rate of Japan's agricultural production from 1873-77 to 1918-22; and finally, to examine some of the implications of the new findings. Although my estimates corrected insofar as possible for understatement provide indices and growth rates of agricultural production (and to a limited extent for the economy as a whole), I do not and cannot claim that the figures are definitive. It is unlikely, however, that any definitive estimate of production can ever be made in view of the paucity of reliable data and the conflicting evidence that appear to exist. The character of my estimates is such that they are measures of the trend in agricultural production, not measures that accurately indicate short-term changes or the absolute level of the value of output.

Nevertheless, these estimates are probably the best that can be made given the present state of knowledge of Japanese production. This study, therefore, is an attempt to set straight insofar as it is possible the statistical record of growth mostly in the agricultural sector of the Meiji era. The conclusion that government statistics seriously understate actual production in early Meiji will receive broader support than my revised estimates of production.

The conclusions drawn in this book are dependent on the existence of government statistics. The best description of those statistics in the English language is, of course, Professor Kazushi Ohkawa's (with associates) in the *Growth Rate of the Japanese Economy Since 1878*. I should note also that four other books have been invaluable in my study: William W. Lockwood's *Economic Development of Japan*, Thomas C. Smith's *Agrarian Origins of Modern Japan*, Takeo Ono's *Meiji zenki tochi seido shiron* [A treatise on early Meiji land system], and the Ministry of Finance's compendium of official documents, *Meiji zenki zaisei keizai shiryō shūsei* [Collection of financial and economic materials of early Meiji].

I was not always aware that these serious statistical misstatements existed. They came to my attention in 1955 in Japan where I had gone to study the effect of government agricultural policies on the economic development of Japan. Owing to the near impossibility of using existing estimates of agricultural production with confidence until more reliable estimates could be worked out, a decision to switch to a study of agricultural production was made.

This book has turned out to be more than an analysis of Meiji production statistics. It is hoped that the nature of the materials in it will be useful to specialists in Japanese area studies, to economists and other scholars interested in the study of underdeveloped economies, and to economists interested in the theory of economic development. One of the important minor themes in the book is a study of the effect of land tax evasion practices of the Tokugawa and Meiji periods on production records. Another minor but significant study is one of the calorie consumption needs of the Japanese in early Meiji. In the appendices I have included two separate studies. One is a study of the Land Tax Reform Act of 1873 and the Land Tax Law of 1884 because the attempt to seek tax equity through these laws provided the villages with the incentive to underreport production. The other is on the land improvement policy of the government giving a concrete picture of how little economic assistance the government provided agriculture outside of Hokkaidō until about 1910.

The citations of Japanese references are given in the following form. Book (including monograph) titles are italicized and only the first letter is in caps. Journal names are italicized and the first letter of each word is in caps. Titles of journal articles are placed within quotes. Laws and regulations are identified by their Japanese legal designation, number, and date of passage. English translations are given only for titles of books and articles. Japanese names are given in the Western form— first names first—to avoid confusion for Western readers.

A great many people—too many for memory to hold—have contributed to the writing of this book. Among them are a number to whom a special debt of gratitude is owed.

Professor Arthur R. Burns of Columbia University, my sponsor, and Professor Harry T. Oshima, now of the University of Hawaii, who was largely responsible for my original decision to begin a study of agriculture's role in Japanese economic development, have given me guidance and encouragement at virtually every stage in the preparation of this book. Professor Herschel Webb of Columbia University, who along with Professor Burns read and criticized the entire manuscript, has also given me the benefit of his experience and knowledge for an extended period. Their advice and suggestions which have made the exposition clearer and the text more readable are profoundly appreciated.

Professors Alan H. Gleason, International Christian University; William W. Lockwood, Princeton University; and Hugh T. Patrick, Yale University, read the entire manuscript and offered invaluable criticism and comment which have helped to clear up some of the errors in fact and analysis. I am deeply indebted to them and particularly to Professor Gleason for detailed comment. I am also grateful for the criticisms and suggestions of Columbia University Professors Harold Barger, Donald B. Keesing, Peter B. Kenen, James W. Morley, and William S. Vickrey, and of Dean Jerome B. Cohen of the City University of New York.

I am indebted to many people who made my year of research in Japan profitable and comfortable. Professor Shigeto Tsuru, who was then Director of the Institute of Economic Research at Hitotsubashi University, made available to me office space and the resources of the Institute. I learned about Japanese agriculture and economy from Professor Kazushi Ohkawa and other distinguished economists, including Professors Mataji Umemura and Shozaburo Fujino of Hitotsubashi University, Mr. Tsutomu Noda, now of the Economic Planning Board, and Professor Kenzo Hemmi of Tokyo University who was then research associate at the National Research Institute of Agriculture. During this period I was given the privilege of attending meetings of research and study groups headed by Professor Ohkawa, and was also given unstinting advice and help from him and members of his groups. Since then Professors Hemmi, Ohkawa, and others have read and criticized selected chapters of this book. I have also had the opportunity to discuss it with Professor Ohkawa on a number of occasions in America. Furthermore, I have had the benefit of discussions with Professor Hemmi and Dr. Kokichi Asakura of the Bank of Japan (whose work on financial institutions is a landmark in early Meiji economic research) in 1963 in New York. In the summer of 1964 in Tokyo, enlightening and pleasant conversations were held with Professors Toshio Furushima and Kenzo Hemmi of Tokyo University, Kunio Niwa of Gifu University, and Shigeru Ishikawa of Hitotsubashi University.

I wish to acknowledge my debt to the Ford Foundation for making it possible for me to undertake and continue this study of the Japanese economy. Its assistance included area study fellowships for graduate study at Columbia University and a year in Japan in 1955-56 to collect materials for a doctoral dissertation, and a dissertation fellowship for faculty members in 1962-63 during which time I was on leave from Adelphi

College. This book is the outgrowth of that dissertation. In the past year the East Asian Institute of Columbia University has provided unusually favorable research conditions for which I am most grateful.

Parts of this book were presented at two conferences during the summer of 1963: Conference on the Modernization of Japan, Estes Park, Colorado, June 24-29, 1963; and Conference on Land and Tax Reform in Less Developed Countries, Milwaukee, Wisconsin, August 26-28, 1963. I am grateful for the criticisms offered at these conferences. The Colorado Conference was particularly valuable since it brought together experts on Japan's modern development.

I am also deeply indebted to the staff of the East Asian Library, particularly Miss Miwa Kai, who through many years have been of great assistance in guiding me through the library's resources. I have reserved my final tribute for my wife, Tetsuko, who did almost all of the typing and helped in countless ways, not the least of which was by an understanding tolerance for the intolerances of one who often had little confidence in what he was attempting to do.

I am acutely aware of the possible errors and other inadequacies for which I am personally and solely responsible, and I beg the readers' indulgence.

JAMES I. NAKAMURA

September 1965
New York

CONTENTS

TABLES

xix

FIGURES

xxiii

AGRICULTURAL PRODUCTION
AND THE ECONOMIC DEVELOPMENT
OF JAPAN 1873-1922

Abbreviations of Documentary Sources

DNSS   Ministry of Finance, *Dai nihon sozei shi* [Annals of taxation in Japan], 3 vols. and supplement. Tokyo, 1926.

MAF Yearbook Ministry of Agriculture and Forestry, Agriculture and Forestry Economics Bureau, Statistics Section, *Statistical Yearbook of the Ministry of Agriculture and Forestry.*

MZS   Meiji Zaisei Shi Hensankai, *Meiji zaisei shi* [History of Meiji public finance], 15 vols. Tokyo, 1904-05.

MZZKSS   Ministry of Finance, *Meiji zenki zaisei keizai shiryō shūsei* [Collection of financial and economic materials of early Meiji], 21 vols. Tokyo, 1932-36.

NNHS   Nōgyō Hattatsu Shi Chōsakai, *Nihon nōgyō hattatsu shi* [History of Japan's agricultural development], general editors, Seiichi Tōbata and Toshitarō Morinaga, 10 vols. and 2 supplementary vols. Tokyo, 1953-59.

NRT   Ministry of Agriculture and Forestry, Agriculture and Forestry Economics Bureau, Statistics Section, *Nōsakumotsu ruinen tōkeihyō: ine* [Historical statistics of the Ministry of Agriculture and Forestry, 1868-1953]. Tokyo, 1955.

NRTHI   Ministry of Agriculture and Forestry, Agriculture and Forestry Economics Bureau, Statistics Section, *Nōsakumotsu ruinen tōkeihyō: ine, 1881-1956* [Agricultural crop statistics: rice, 1881-1956]. Tokyo, 1957.

Tōkei nenkan Statistical yearbook of Japan from 1882 to present, published by various government offices under differing Japanese names.

CHAPTER 1

Introduction, Summary, and Conclusion

Introduction

ACCURATE DATA on the volume of production is basic to the study of the economic growth of any nation. It is the foundation upon which all empirical propositions about economic growth must necessarily be based. However, of almost all available economic data, those relating to growth—especially at an early stage of economic development—are the weakest. This weakness is inevitable. Except in the post-World War II period, nations at an early period of economic development have seldom, if ever, been sufficiently interested in improved statistical reporting to compile reliable statistics. Even if the desire had existed, the nature of production in a preindustrial society makes accurate counting almost impossible. Finally, an economist investigating long-term growth tends to push his studies back in time as far as availability of records permits and this usually means that data of dubious reliability are used.

Japan offers no exception to the rule that early records are of questionable reliability. Scholars and Japanese government officials have warned against the uncritical use of these data.[1] The most authoritative of such warnings appears in the second volume of the *Tōkei nenkan*[2] as follows: "It is extremely diffi-

---

[1] Among others, the following scholars may be named: William W. Lockwood, *The Economic Development of Japan* (Princeton, 1954), pp. 82-85, *passim*; Kazushi Ohkawa, *et al.*, *The Growth Rate of the Japanese Economy Since 1878* (Tokyo, 1957), pp. 6, 74; Yasuo Kondō, *Nihon nōgyō no tōkeiteki bunseki* [Statistical analysis of Japanese agriculture] (Tokyo, 1953), pp. 1-25, *passim*; Yuzo Yamada, ed., *Nihon kokumin shotoku suikei shiryo* [Materials for the estimation of national income] (Tokyo, 1951), p. 1, *passim*.

[2] The full titles of this publication are *Tōkei nenkan* (1882-84), *Nihon teikoku tōkei nenkan* (1885-1936), *Dai nihon teikoku tōkei nenkan*

cult to obtain reliable statistics because people, fearing increased taxes, conceal the truth and because [land and crop]
measurement techniques have not been sufficiently improved."[3]
This quotation is translated from the introduction to the section
on agricultural statistics. The inference that may be drawn
from the quote is that the tendency was to understate production to prevent an increase in taxes. This tendency is, of course,
almost universal. Reasonably accurate production statistics can
only be expected if the estimation of production is undertaken
independently of tax administration by disinterested and
trained specialists.[4]

Notwithstanding the warnings, all existing estimates[5] of
Japanese national and sectoral income of the Meiji Era are
based on government statistics without major adjustments for
errors. Regarding agricultural production with which this study
is concerned, considerable differences exist in the results obtained by different investigators owing to methodological and
other variations; however, they are all characterized by rapid
growth during the period from around 1880 to 1920. This
growth can be regarded as a result of reported increases in two
variables: the area planted to crops and the yield per unit area
of various crops.

Two American scholars, Harry T. Oshima and William W.
Lockwood, have shown more than usual skepticism of Japanese
statistics. Oshima, an expert on the economic statistics of
underdeveloped countries, has done pioneering work in the
estimation and evaluation of their statistics. Among other
things he has long pointed out the unavoidable biases that do,

---

(1937-40), and *Nihon tōkei nenkan* (1949—). All are cited as *Tōkei
nenkan.*

[3] *Tōkei nenkan,* Vol. 2, p. 41.

[4] For probable understatement of rice production in certain Asian
countries, see V. D. Wickizer and M. K. Bennett, *The Rice Economy of
Monsoon Asia* (Stanford, 1941), Chapter IX.

[5] Three well-known studies may be mentioned (cited in the order of
publication): Y. Yamada, *op.cit.*; Bruce F. Johnston, "Agricultural Productivity and Economic Development in Japan," *Journal of Political
Economy,* LIX, 6 (December 1951); Ohkawa, *et al., op.cit.*

and the deliberate distortions that may, appear in them.[6] In respect to Japanese statistics, Oshima has stated in an article and a book review[7] his conviction that previous studies overstate the growth rate of the Japanese economy. Lockwood in his classic study of Japan's economic development[8] has been most cautious in the use of Meiji statistics. In many instances he has not used early Meiji data, and in others he has noted his reservations about their reliability.[9]

Although previous investigators have hesitated to adjust official statistics because they believed they would be forced to rely on dubious statistical and analytical procedures, in the postwar years, particularly in the last decade, new studies have made available data that reduce the range of probable errors that may be expected from correction of government statistics. These studies have been made by government (Ministry of Agriculture and Forestry[10]) and private (both Western[11] and

[6] "National Income Statistics of Underdeveloped Countries," *Journal of American Statistical Association*, LII (June 1957), 162-77. See also his "A Critique of National Income Studies of Selected Asian Countries" (unpublished Ph.D. dissertation, Columbia University, New York, 1956).

Serious misgivings about the reliability of food production and consumption statistics of less developed nations are stated in M. K. Bennett, *The World's Food* (New York, 1954), pp. 189-212.

[7] "Notes on an Alternative Method of Estimating the National Income and Expenditure of Japan, 1881," *Keizai Kenkyū*, VIII, 3 (July 1957), 243-51; and review of Ohkawa *et al., op.cit.*, in *American Economic Review*, XLVIII, 4 (September 1958), 685-87.

For a short comment on Oshima's article, see Chapter 6, p. 127n.

[8] *Op.cit.*

[9] *Ibid.*, pp. 82-89 including Tables 2 and 3; pp. 111-21, including Tables 8, 9, 10; p. 130, Table 11; pp. 101, 128-29, 133-37, 462-63.

[10] The Ministry of Agriculture and Forestry ascertained that under-measurement continues to exist in land area records. Kōichi Hatanaka, "Kōchi tōkei no kakuritsu" [Establishment of reliable arable land statistics] *Nōrin Tōkei Chōsa* VII, 10 (October 1957), 14.

[11] An outstanding Western study of Tokugawa period agricultural productivity including studies of understatement of production is Thomas C. Smith, *Agrarian Origins of Modern Japan* (Stanford, 1959). Albert C. Craig also discusses agricultural productivity and understatement of production in his *Chōshu in the Meiji Restoration* (Cambridge, 1961), Chapter I. The relatively high productivity of the Tokugawa agriculture

Japanese[12]) researchers in respect to arable land measurement and yield estimation for both the Meiji era and the Tokugawa period. In particular, Tokugawa period studies have made imperative a reexamination of Japanese production data.

Two basic propositions will be tested by an examination of agricultural production data through 1922. They are: (1) *land tax evasion practices caused a serious understatement of agricultural production*; and (2) *the degree of understatement decreased over time.*

Should these propositions be supported by historical evidence, the implications of such a finding would be of immense economic significance. It is immediately apparent that such a finding would affect the growth rate of agricultural (and, indeed, of total) production in Japan during a highly important period of growth. It would also arouse a great deal of interest among economists concerned with economic growth for a variety of reasons. Because Japan, as the only non-Western nation to have developed a modern industrial economy, has often been held up as a model for less developed nations, a change in the structure of that model is surely important. Since one of the aspects of Japan's growth that has attracted much attention is the apparent speed with which she emerged out of backwardness, serious reservations about that speed must perforce excite interest.

---

may also be inferred from E. S. Crawcour, "Changes in Japanese Commerce in Tokugawa Period," *Journal of Asian Studies*, XXII, 4 (August 1963), 387-400.

[12] There have been innumerable books and articles by Japanese scholars relating to agriculture, the level of agricultural production, and understatement of production in the Tokugawa period. One of the many outstanding volumes in this field is that of Toshio Furushima, *Kinsei nihon nōgyō no tenkai* [Development of Tokugawa agriculture] (Tokyo, 1963). Mention is made of understatement of Meiji era agriculture in Kunio Niwa, *Meiji ishin no tochi henkaku* [Land reform of the Meiji Restoration] (Tokyo, 1962), pp. 427-29. A treatise on Meiji financial institutions which supports the view that agricultural productivity was high in early Meiji is Kōkichi Asakura, *Meiji zenki nihon kinyū kōzō shi* [History of the structure of early Meiji finance] (Tokyo, 1961). There are other works (too numerous to list here) that provide important new Tokugawa evidence. A number of them have been cited elsewhere.

Perhaps more important still would be the implications that any new finding about Japan's agricultural production would have on the relation between the agricultural sector and economic development. Because the agricultural sector has been the dominant one in all nations at the beginning of economic development, upon it devolves the major part of the responsibility for generating the surplus necessary for sustained growth. Much has been written about the role of agriculture in Japanese economic development with existing estimates of agricultural production as data for the analysis.[13] A substantial change in that data would raise questions about current views on that role. And indeed if existing estimates are found to overstate the growth rate of Japanese agriculture, a reexamination of much that has been proposed about the process of Japan's growth is called for.

The opportunity and incentive to underreport production were provided landowners in various land valuation legislation and statistical reporting practices of the Meiji era. The first opportunity came with the basic Meiji land tax legislation enacted in 1873.[14] It revised the land tax system from a harvest tax assessed as a proportion of the harvest in rice, or its equivalent in money, to a land value tax assessed as a proportion of the land value. The land value was conceptually the market value of land, but owing to the difficulty of obtaining the market value for most land units, the value was determined by

[13] Some Western language studies may be mentioned: Johnston, "Agricultural Productivity and Economic Development in Japan," *op.cit.*; Bruce W. Johnston, "Agricultural Development and Economic Transformation," *Food Research Institute Studies*, III, 3 (November 1962); Ohkawa, *et al.*, *op.cit.*; Kazushi Ohkawa, "Economic Growth and Agriculture," *Annals of the Hitotsubashi Academy*, VII, 1 (October 1956); Kazushi Ohkawa and Henry Rosovsky, "The Role of Agriculture in Modern Japanese Economic Development," *Economic Development and Cultural Change*, IX, 1, Part 2 (October 1960); Bruce F. Johnston and John W. Mellor, "The Role of Agriculture in Economic Development," *American Economic Review*, LI, 4 (September 1961); Gustav Ranis, "The Financing of Japanese Economic Development," *Economic History Review*, XI, 3 (April 1959).

[14] Discussion of the provisions in the land tax law is based on Appendix A.

capitalizing at the prevailing interest rate the gross value of production less the national land tax, the local surtax on the national land tax, and the costs of seeds and fertilizers. The value of production in turn was determined by the area of cultivated land, the yield per unit area, and the price level. A significant feature of the law directing the cadastral survey was that the measurement of land and the estimation of the yield per unit area were delegated to the landowners and the villages subject to check by Finance Ministry officials. The survey report submitted by the village required for each lot the inclusion of the area, the total physical harvest, and the land value.

Village participation in and control of land measurement, yield estimation, and land valuation was necessary at this early stage in the emergence of Japan as a modern society. Most landowners were then not capable of independently understanding government directives and filing reports. The filing of uncoordinated reports would also be unwise if underreporting was to be a general village practice as it turned out to be. Independent reporting could lead to highly divergent reports on area, yield, and valuation—a discrepancy that tax officials would be apt to detect and question. Thus, if underreporting and undervaluation were to take place, consistency was desirable, and it could only be achieved if the village maintained control over the survey.

That the village was engaged in aiding and abetting the mass evasion of the land tax may seem strange to those in countries where the taxing authority on property is usually the local community. Today in Japan the tax on real property is also a local rather than a national tax. But in Japan of the Meiji era the land tax was primarily a national tax as already noted. The tax on one hand was a direct burden on the village, and on the other, was of problematic and indirect benefit to the villagers. Under these circumstances, reducing the village burden would immediately and directly benefit the villagers. Nevertheless, had it not been for Tokugawa period attitudes and practices, the villages might not have engaged in this mass promotion of land tax evasion. In the Tokugawa period the village had been held responsible for the delivery of taxes in kind or money even though the tax was assessed on a lot basis. If there were unregistered fields, undermeasurement of land, or underreporting of yields, the total village tax would be lower and the village would be better off as a result. Thus the village tended to maintain a collective silence on these transgressions.

A report by Keichō Ario, who participated in both land surveys as an official, supports the contention that undermeasurement occurred and that the village was involved in the undermeasurement:[15]

> Land had to be measured first, and this was a very difficult undertaking. To save on expenses, the people were directed to measure their own land and report the measurements. But the landowners were not familiar with measurement techniques; and it was impossible for the government officials to measure each plot of land. Thus, men in their middle years who seemed suitable for the purpose were selected and trained by government officials. However, when measurement is entrusted to the people, they, bent on minimizing taxes by understating the area, rarely do an honest job. Even when they understood the procedure, they pretended not to, and submitted crude figures. On inspection it was clear that the measurements were incorrect, and the people were required to repeat the measurement. Remeasurement led to more trouble and time consumption. . . .

Although the land survey was conducted under the supervision of tax officials, and all survey reports were subject to review by officials responsible to the national tax office, it is clear that some amount of understatement was expected and *tolerated.* The best evidence of toleration is the law itself which permitted the acceptance of reported land values which, in the judgment of the officials, did not understate the market value by more than 10 per cent.[16] How flexible the judgment of the

[15] Translated from Keichō Ario, *Hompō chiso no enkaku* [A history of Japan's land tax] (Privately printed by the monthly conference of the Hypothec Bank of Japan, 1914), p. 73.

[16] *Dajōkan fukoku 272 bessatsu chihōkan kokoroesho* (July 28, 1873), Article 6.

officials was is a debatable point, but some flexibility was the rule as will be evident from a later discussion of specific tax evasion practices.

There were three practices that understated the arable land area: concealment, misclassification[17] (see Chapter 2) and undermeasurement (see Chapter 3). Concealment was largely eliminated during the land survey of the 1880's, but misclassification and undermeasurement continue to exist even today. Undermeasurement remains since once an area is recorded in the land register it does not change. The opportunity for further undermeasurement exists only for lots that have been reclaimed or are being remeasured.

The underreporting of yield (see Chapter 4), the fourth tax evasion practice, can continue indefinitely for all arable land as long as incentive remains and an annual estimation of production is made. The incentive to underreport yield continued to exist because the land valuations were not fixed once and for all by the land tax act of 1873. In 1874 an amendment to the 1873 act provided for a quinquennial revaluation of land beginning in 1880 to conform with changing market values.[18] In fact, periodic revaluations were never carried out, and the amendment was abolished in 1884, because it became clear that such revaluations would be costly and time-consuming, and provoke political friction. However, land revaluations did take place under special legislation. Whether the yield actually helped determine the new values is a moot point, but as long as the possibility existed that it might, the landowners and villages did have incentive to underreport yield.

In revising production statistics, ideally the area planted and yield per unit area statistics should be corrected, where required, for all agricultural crops. This is impossible, however. Official data for all crops are not available even today, and in the early Meiji era production data were collected only for the most important crops. Even when official data are available, the bases on which a revision can be made are either nonexistent

[17] Misclassification refers to concealment of arable land by classifying it as land of a different class in the government land register.
[18] *Dajōkan fukoku 53* (May 12, 1874).

or not sufficiently reliable for individual crops with the exception of paddy rice. For these reasons many of the revisions were based on assumptions guided by judgment built on historical evidence and understanding of agricultural techniques and practices.

The model for the estimation of production is a simple one. The value of agricultural production (V) is taken to be the sum of the values of paddy rice production (V_1) and of all other agricultural production (V_2). V_1 is equal to the product of the output of rice (O_1) and the price of rice (P_1). Analogously, $V_2 = kO_2P_2$, where k is a constant coefficient,[19] O_2 is a production index, and P_2 is a price index of all agricultural commodities except paddy rice. O_1 is equal to the product of the area planted to rice A_1 and the yield per unit area of rice (H_1). Analogously, $O_2 = A_2H_2$ where A_2 is the index of the area put into all other agricultural production and H_2 is a yield index. Therefore, the value of agricultural production in time period t is $V_t = (P_1A_1H_1)_t + k(P_2A_2H_2)_t$.

Since the objective was to obtain the value of production in constant yen, the procedure, in practice, involved the determination of three basic sets of figures. They were (1) the construction of two quinquennial indices of area planted; (2) the construction of two quinquennial indices of yield per unit area; and (3) the estimation of base year (1913-17) values of paddy rice production and of other agricultural production. Actually, the area planted adjustment was made in two steps. One adjustment was for concealment prior to the land survey of the 1880's. The other was the adjustment for undermeasurement. Given the above sets of figures the value of agricultural production in constant yen and the growth rate of agricultural production can be obtained.

The estimation problem would have been simpler if the understatement were related functionally to some known time series. However, it is unlikely that any such relationship of sufficient reliability can be uncovered. Therefore, the over-

[19] The constant (k) is the value of agricultural production less rice in the base year; it, therefore, relates the index of the value of production (O_2P_2) to the actual value of production (V_2).

riding consideration in using the method developed here was that it permitted the correction of area planted and yield statistics.

Summary of Chapters 2 to 7

My corrected agricultural production indices and growth rates differ fundamentally from previous estimates. The corrected index of total agricultural production increases by 44 per cent over a 35-year span from 1878-82 to 1913-17; in contrast, the previously accepted index constructed by Kazushi Ohkawa and his associates increases by 136 per cent over the same period. The Ohkawa growth rate of 2.4 per cent per year is more than twice the 1.0 per cent median growth rate of the corrected value.[20] Both the total percentage increase and the annual growth rate are transformed from the exceptional to the average. Comparisons are also made with the production indices and the growth rates of Bruce F. Johnston and Saburo Yamada. The growth rate estimates of the two are, respectively, 1.9 and 1.8 per cent per year. The Johnston figure is probably an understatement of the growth implicit in government statistics. The Yamada rate is lower than the other two because it incorporates some adjustments for understatement of production.

Ohkawa, Yamada, and corrected values of agricultural production at 1913-17 prices are compared in Figure 1-1. The corrected value is considerably higher in all five-year periods, but most conspicuously so in the first period. The corrected value in 1878-1882 is 80 per cent higher than the Ohkawa value and 43 per cent higher than the Yamada value.

The reduction in the growth rate of agricultural production also lowers the growth rate of the economy as a whole. By correcting the agricultural production figure in the Ohkawa estimate of value of production for the economy without altering the Ohkawa estimate for nonagricultural production, we

---

[20] For summary purposes, the median growth rate of agricultural production of 1.0% per year will be used for computation of changes in production. I conclude in Chapter V that the rate probably ranged between 0.8 to 1.2% per year.

FIGURE 1-1

COMPARISON OF OHKAWA, YAMADA, AND CORRECTED VALUES OF
AGRICULTURAL PRODUCTION AT 1913-17 PRICES

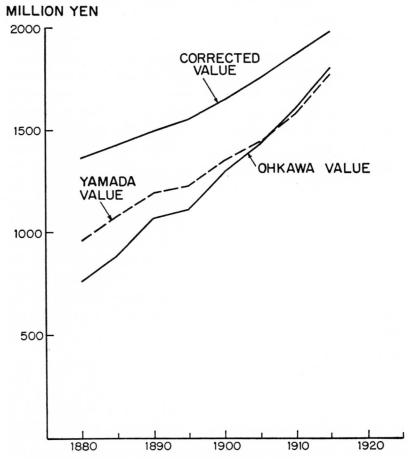

SOURCES: Corrected value: Table 5-7, Column (3).
Ohkawa value: Table 6-1. Column (3).
Yamada value: Table 6-2. Column (2).

obtain a 2.8 per cent growth rate for the economy. Since
nonagricultural production was also seriously understated, the
growth rate of the economy is estimated to be substantially less
than 2.8 per cent per year in contrast to the Ohkawa estimate
of 4.0 per cent.

The corrected estimates are primarily based on a close study of land tax evasion practices which were responsible for the serious understatement of agricultural production in the official statistics of the Meiji era and which caused this understatement to be substantially greater in the earlier part of the 45-year period under study. The understatement is corrected by adjusting upward the area planted to crops and the crop yield per unit area. Other historical evidence not previously examined for this purpose are presented in support of our estimates. The main reason for the differences between the corrected estimates and all previous estimates is that the latter are computed from uncorrected government statistics with the exception of the Yamada estimate which makes a partial correction.

It has also been argued in this book that calorie consumption, labor force, and capital formation were understated in the Meiji era and that the understatement was greater in the earlier years as it was in the case of agricultural production. The understatement of calorie consumption follows almost necessarily from the underreporting of agricultural production. Incomplete statistical reporting, particularly conspicuous in the earlier years, helps to account for the understatement of the labor force and capital formation. It may be inferred that many other variables consistently followed the pattern of understatement indicated here.

From the above findings, conclusions are drawn that challenge previous thinking about the pattern of Japanese economic development. One implication of this study is that too much uncritical reliance may also have been placed in government statistics of present developing economies and in those of the early developmental years of economically developed countries.

The corrected estimates are found to be in greater harmony with other economic conditions of the period under study than are previous estimates. We find that the per capita calorie supply computed from government food production statistics was totally inadequate to feed the early Meiji population. My estimate of agricultural production brings per capita calorie supply up to more plausible levels. I also determine that previous estimates of the growth rate of agricultural production, which are roughly double the annual growth rate of population of 1.0 per cent, can scarcely be reconciled with increasing food imports. A number of other improbable relationships including those relating to volumes of inputs and outputs are also pointed out. If previous views on the relationships of inputs and outputs are correct, they would make Japanese agricultural production of the 1880's independent of the three basic short-term variables, land supply, labor supply, and capital formation. In each of these cases the conclusions that agricultural output increased at a rate ranging between 0.8 and 1.2 per cent and that no sudden spurt occurred in agricultural production provide more probable and consistent relationships.

Explanations of resource flow from agriculture to nonagriculture and saving in agriculture offered here differ significantly from those of analysts who believe that both came primarily from a rapid increase in agricultural production. In respect to resource flow, my findings favor the contention that previously untapped resources were made available to the nonagricultural sector. At the end of the Tokugawa period, institutional and other restraints had caused more resources to be tied to the agricultural sector than would have been the case in their absence. When the restraints were removed following the Meiji Restoration, a more efficient allocation became possible.

In regard to saving in the agricultural sector, the previous contention that it increased owing to the rapid growth of agricultural production is no longer tenable. In fact, a question arises as to whether that sector was saving. It is argued here that it did save in early Meiji because measures associated with land reform caused a revolutionary transfer of income from the Tokugawa ruling class to the landowners, a transfer made possible because the agricultural sector was producing a substantial surplus above subsistence. This was a transfer to a class with a lower average propensity to consume. Therefore, I conclude that in the first decade or so of the Meiji era the nation's propensity to save out of current income rose to a higher level. This contention is contrary to the previous belief that Japan's early economic development took place with relatively little capital. Evidence indicates that most of the landowners' savings were transferred out of agriculture.

The conclusions drawn in this book also cast serious doubt on previous propositions on the relationship of capital to output. It is argued that the Meiji marginal capital-output ratio is not necessarily the lowest in the world for any stage in economic development as previously indicated.

Conclusion

We have obtained a model of Japan's economic development whose parameters are shown to be much more like those in the development of the economically advanced countries of the West than indicated previously; that is, Japan's development was much less unique than previously believed. Let us note some of the similarities with Western development. (1) Much of the groundwork for growth had been laid before modern industrialization began. These included the development of a national transportation and communications system, a national market, banking institutions, and an entrepreneurial spirit; the achievement of national unity and a remarkably high literacy rate; and the maintenance of independence from foreign domination. (2) The level of per worker output was at a relatively high level at the end of the Tokugawa period, due in part to the maintenance of a long period of peace; high enough in any case to make possible a very substantial income redistribution early in the Meiji era. (3) Growth was preceded by far-reaching institutional changes (in Japan modeled after those of the West) that established the incentive base and broke down barriers to resource mobility. (4) Growth occurred at a time when considerations of social justice—which make it difficult to give priority to growth policies—were regarded with less concern than they are now by the masses of the people. (5) Scientific methods were applied to production and other problems. (6) The finding, that the growth of agricultural production in Japan was not as rapid as previous estimates indicate, brings it in line with rates of increase in other basically traditional agricultural societies at comparable periods in development. (7) The finding that the growth rate of the economy as a whole was seriously overstated and input was seriously understated constitutes reassurance for economists (and other social scientists) that there was nothing magical about Japan's growth; Japan too required great effort and heavy sacrifices to achieve modest rates of growth.[21]

Judging from the above factors, the Japanese experience confirms the principle that discontinuities do not occur in nature short of a major catastrophe exogenous to the system such as wars and natural calamities of overwhelming magnitude. It is perhaps *a propos* to suggest at this point that the frequently noted stability of the Japanese social and political systems of the Meiji era should be partially attributed to the relatively slow development of the Japanese economy. A rapid economic change probably would have had a sharper impact on noneconomic institutions, as indeed postwar developments in Japan appear to indicate.

In brief, if it is true that labor, capital formation, and production statistics understate or misrepresent reality as I have argued, then most generalizations in respect to such important economic variables as the rate of growth, output per worker and unit of capital, capital-output ratio, capital intensity, income and price elasticities of demand and supply, import-output and export-output ratios, and the like require reexamination. A few of them have been discussed here.

Despite its similarity to Western patterns of growth, Japan's was not a carbon copy of that of Western nations (which were hardly carbon copies of each other for that matter). Whereas economic development in the West occurred largely under laissez-faire capitalism, the Japanese industrial development, although taking place under an implanted capitalistic system, had many more elements of planning and conscious guidance than was true in the West at that time. Japan, quite consciously and rationally, adopted the Western model of economic development because it was the only model tested by time that had been found to be conducive to growth.[22] This conscious

[21] For other less tangible respects in which the Japanese experience had parallels elsewhere, see: Robert N. Bellah, *Tokugawa Religion* (Glencoe, Illinois, 1957); Everett E. Hagen, *On the Theory of Social Change* (Homewood, Illinois, 1962).

[22] Although I have generalized about *a* "Western model," the late George Sansom has quite correctly stated that Japan exercised a conscious choice from among *several* Western models in selecting Western

planning is one feature which sets her apart from her Western predecessors with rare exceptions.

Two other features of Japan's economic development may be regarded as a departure from the norm. One was the relative rapidity and ease with which the revolutionary Meiji socio-economic reforms were effected. The second, which is a consequence of the socioeconomic reforms but merits mention in its own right because of its importance, was the expropria-tion of the feudal rights and income of the samurai by the Meiji rulers who were members of the same ruling class. This was an unquestionably heroic measure in view of samurai restiveness and their tendency to resort to assassination to gain their ends.

The Meiji oligarchs played a key role in the socioeconomic transformation.[23] Let us enumerate some of the important changes that were wrought. The samurai class (out of which most of the oligarchs emerged) were stripped of feudal privi-leges and income rights. This forced the samurai to enter the mainstream of economic activity, and many assumed positions of leadership (for which they were eminently suited by train-ing and formal education) in fields that were essential to economic development. Of even greater importance, fresh outlets were provided for the energies of other creative ele-ments by abolishing feudal institutions, including privileges, rights, restraints, and obligations, and replacing them with new ones based on Western models. These reforms, the founda-tion for changes in national economic behavior, caused the

---

institutions believed to be important in Japan's modernization. (*Western World and Japan* [New York, 1951], p. 311.) Sansom was referring to social and political as well as economic institutions. I refer only to the latter and lump them all under a single classification for simplicity, since their essential features were shaped by a capitalistic market system.

[23] The oligarchs' contribution was not a one-shot affair. As the domi-nant force in the government until the end of the Meiji era, they directed national policy consistently toward the twin goals of military power and economic performance. In respect to the latter, their principal policies were directed toward building the industrial sector—frequently at the expense of the agricultural sector—and the nation's capacity to import.

Japanese to save, invest, and innovate at a higher rate than before. Without them growth could not have taken place.

The principal victims of the revolution were members of the ruling class as stated above. The new rulers correctly saw that rewards must necessarily go to (1) those who would thereby contribute most to Japan's growth;[24] and (2) those whose support they needed for political stability. The oligarchs also perceived the need to place the superior knowledge and training of the samurai into productive effort: for example, the program for the economic rehabilitation of the samurai was geared to this goal. The fact is that the oligarchs did induce, goad, or beguile this potentially reactionary class (or at least a large part of it) into taking a progressive role in the nation's growth—and this constituted one of their most striking achievements.

Although the main objective of this book has been to demonstrate that the economic growth rate of the Japanese economy has been seriously overstated, the growth that actually took place was still a substantial one, comparable to those in the West. That growth can be explained by (1) the moderate increases in the quantity and productivity of land and labor; (2) an increase in the average propensity to save due to the income redistribution effect of land reform; and (3) the reallocation of resources (primarily labor) that took place following the lifting of feudal restrictions on mobility. The reallocation of labor resources probably occurred over a number of years since complementary capital resources cannot be made available on short notice.

It has been generally believed that Japan's economic development provides invaluable guidelines to present developing nations in planning their emergence from an economically backward condition. The conclusion here that Japan's development was closer to the Western model than had been previously believed may lead some readers to conclude that the Japanese

[24] By more richly rewarding those who helped Japan grow, a new elite was created that was not necessarily distinguishable from the old in personnel but was indisputably different in function.

experience is no longer as useful as a model for the developing economies. Such a conclusion would not be warranted. If the findings in this book give a truer picture than those of other scholars of the pattern of changes that occurred in Japan, they would tend to correct false conclusions and hopes about what can happen elsewhere. This reappraisal of Japan's development, for instance, does not support the hope that growth can occur with little investment, and can be accompanied by a substantial rise in consumption as implied by previously computed growth rates. The process of modern economic growth, no matter where it takes place and under what economic system, is accompanied by changes that are similar in most important respects. For this reason, in many aspects of development, the experience of all economically advanced nations can provide useful lessons to the developing economies.[25]

If the preconditions and conditions of the Japanese experience were substantially different from those of a present developing nation, a detailed comparative study and much ingenuity will be required to extract lessons from Japan's experience. It has been argued, for example, that even Japanese agricultural development is a less useful model for Asian nations than generally believed since it (primarily in reference to paddy rice culture) was at a considerably more advanced stage than is the case in many Asian nations today.[26] Furthermore, because Japan benefited from the relatively low rate of population growth of 0.9 per cent (which may have been influenced partly by Tokugawa attitudes toward population control) and had a relatively high rate of saving, she was able to depend

[25] For fuller discussion of the lessons provided by the Japanese experience, see, among others, Lockwood, op.cit., passim; Martin Bronfenbrenner, "Some Lessons of Japan's Economic Development, 1853-1938," Pacific Affairs, XXXIV, 1 (Spring 1961); Hugh T. Patrick, "Lessons for Underdeveloped Countries from the Japanese Experience of Economic Development," Indian Economic Journal, IX, 2 (October 1961); Takekazu Ogura, ed., Agricultural Development in Modern Japan (Tokyo, 1963). My views do not necessarily agree with theirs.

[26] Shigeru Ishikawa, "Nihon no keiken wa tekiyō kanō ka" [Is the Japanese experience applicable?] Keizai Kenkyū, XIV, 2 (April 1963), 114-22.

almost entirely on domestic sources of saving.[27] Developing nations today with rates of population growth in excess of 2 per cent and relatively low rates of saving probably cannot rely solely on domestic sources of capital if their per capita growth rate is to increase at an acceptable rate.

The Japanese experience, however, differed from that of the Western economies in many important respects, at least in degree where not in kind. Growth was assured within twenty years after the Meiji Restoration, following the clearing of the institutional barriers against resource mobility and acquisition of new knowledge and the attainment of political stability which was severely tested for the last time by the Matsukata deflation. Her development from a feudal to an industrial economy of the 1930's was crowded into a shorter span of years. Production continued to increase without a serious break except for the decline accompanying defeat in World War II, whereas Western nations suffered a serious slowdown of growth in the interwar period. The annual rate of growth accelerated over time—less than 2.8 per cent to 1920, 3 to 5 per cent in the interwar period, and double the latter in the postwar years. The record of early growth has generally been more fully documented in Japan than among the advanced economies. Further, the people of many developing nations may be more receptive to the Japanese experience because a greater element of national direction is evident in it. For these reasons, and because Japan is a non-Western state, her experience may be more helpful and attractive to the developing nations than that of Western states.

Finally, this study serves as a warning that Meiji era economic statistics have to be used with the greatest circumspection and that any attempt to give numerical values to complex variables (capital-output ratio, capital intensity, labor productivity, and the like) can cause a compounding of already serious errors. This study also suggests that the statistics of many other countries during their early development can bear reexamination lest they too seriously misstate what actually took place.

[27] Japan's dependence on foreign capital did not reach important proportions until after the Sino-Japanese War. (See Chapter 7, p. 155n.)

CHAPTER 2

The Concealment of Arable Land

TWO FORMS of concealment of arable land[1] existed during the period under study. One form was the practice of concealing land from official notice by not registering it. The second form was concealment by misclassification as another land class, almost always as land of a less valuable class to minimize taxes. Clearly, concealment by not registering, if successful, meant that no taxes would be paid for the land involved. Most of this chapter will be devoted to this form of concealment which will be designated simply as *concealment*. The other form will be designated as *misclassification*.

Concealment by Failure to Register

In 1872 before the Meiji cadastral survey began, the area of arable land as reported by the various provinces was 3,234 thousand *chō*.[2] This area cannot be compared with any subsequent area data because it was based on provincial measures of area which were not always uniform. In the 1870's a cadastral survey was undertaken by the Meiji government to put in order the chaotic land records of the Tokugawa period. The government believed that all previously concealed land would be registered and that all misclassified land would be properly

---

[1] The Japanese use three terms for concealed land: *onden*, *kirisoe*, and *kirihiraki*. *Onden* refers to concealed arable land and as such is the generic term; *kirisoe* refers to an addition to a preexisting registered cultivated field that is not reported to the government; *kirihiraki* refers to a cultivated field reclaimed from undeveloped land that is not reported to the government.

[2] Ministry of Finance, *Meiji zenki zaisei keizai shiryō shūsei* [Collection of financial and economic materials of early Meiji] (21 vols., Tokyo, 1932-36), Vol. 7, p. 346. This reference will be cited henceforth as *MZZKSS*.

One *chō* is equal to 2.45 acres.

reclassified as a result of the survey. There was basis for this belief. Registration of land was accompanied by the issuance of a land ownership certificate which was legal proof of ownership. Without such a certificate legal property transfer could not take place, and where transfer was effected without a certificate, both the land and the payment were subject to confiscation by the government.[3] It was believed that the above procedures would lead to a proper classification of misclassified land. To encourage voluntary disclosure during the survey period, the government took great pains to assure the landowners that action would not be taken against them for previous concealment.[4] In 1881 after the completion of land surveys for arable land, the area of arable land totaled 4,486 thousand *chō*.[5] Despite the inducements offered it became evident that in some areas the landowners followed the practice of Tokugawa peasants and grossly underreported their land holdings in the first Meiji land survey by concealment, misclassification, and undermeasurement.

To eliminate concealed land and to reclassify misclassified land,[6] a second land survey was undertaken in the years 1886

---

[3] *Okurashō 25* (February 24, 1872), Article 12.

[4] *Okurashō 159 besshi: chiken watashikata kisoku* (October 31, 1872), Article 21; *Dajōkan fukoku 315* (September 10, 1873); *Dajōkan fukoku 67* (May 12, 1876).

To those who are familiar with Western property rights, it would seem that the landowner would be loath to underreport his holdings because he would thereby lose claim to a part of his land. But to the early Meiji era landowner, property rights existed if they were acknowledged by the community. People in the villages were familiar with which plot of land was farmed by whom, where the boundaries lay, and what land rights attached to whom. Under these circumstances, the conception of legal property rights could not be quickly assimilated. Meiji Japan was not atypical in this respect. One source states ". . . in many traditional societies what may be called the public memory, often assisted by a high degree of publicity, ceremony and even ritual, is in itself a form of record which may take the place of a written record." Food and Agriculture Organization of the United Nations, *Cadastral Surveys and Records of Rights in Land: An FAO Land Tenure Study* (Rome: Food and Agriculture Organization, 1953), p. 26.

[5] Statistical Appendix: Table 1C.

[6] The Finance Ministry was less concerned with undermeasurement.

to 1889.[7] During this survey the pressures on the landowners to comply with the law were greater than during the first Meiji land survey. New legal pressure was applied through the Land Tax Law of 1884 which imposed fines for concealment of land and made land taxes payable retroactively to 1873 or covering the delinquent period, whichever was less.[8] To encourage disclosure the fine was waived when voluntary disclosure occurred.[9] A second force of great importance was the growing appreciation of the value of official recognition of property ownership. A third, and probably the most important, factor that forced compliance was an 1884 regulation[10] which revised the land register forms including land maps. Up to that time the form of the records including the maps was left largely to the discretion of the villages. It was said that the records and maps were in utter confusion and that the maps were not only inaccurate in respect to area and configuration, but some lots were not mapped and others were duplicated. In extreme cases east and west were said to have been inverted.[11] Since reasonably accurate maps were required for every lot, and each lot was probably inspected by tax officials to check the accuracy of the map and land register records, concealment became difficult.

If there had been concealment or misclassification of arable land as a means to evade land taxes, and if the second survey did in fact cause the official emergence of such land, the area of registered arable land would show a rise during the period required to complete the survey—a rise not reasonably attributable to any other cause. The time series which provide the information desired are the Taxed Paddy Field Area, and

[7] *MZZKSS*, Vol. 7, p. 401. Before the second land survey some areas, where the underreporting of land area was excessively high, had already been resurveyed. (*Ibid.*)

[8] *Dajōkan fukoku 7 bessatsu: chiso jōrei* (March 15, 1884), Article 25. An amendment in 1889 made the taxes retroactive for only three years. (*Hōritsu 30* [November 29, 1889], Article 25.)

[9] *Dajōkan fukoku 7 bessatsu: chiso jōrei* (March 15, 1884), Article 29.

[10] *Okurashō tasshi 89* (December 16, 1884).

[11] *MZZKSS*, Vol. 7, pp. 401-03.

the Taxed Upland Field Area.[12] Arable land previously concealed but registered for the first time or reclassified as arable
land during the second Meiji land survey would be included
in one of the two series as a rule.[13] The sum of the two is the
Taxed Arable Land Area. Hokkaidō data will be excluded from
the series because the land survey of 1886-1889 did not apply
to Hokkaidō, and because land development in that prefecture
owing to government subsidization and its undeveloped state
in the nineteenth century was different from that in the rest of
Japan.

Between 1885 and 1890 the Taxed Arable Land Area changed
from 4,514 thousand *chō* to 5,030 thousand, an increase of 516
thousand *chō* as shown in Table 2-1. Relatively, the gain was
11.4 per cent. This increase is not even remotely approached in
any other five-year period. In the next 30 years from 1890 to
1920, the absolute increase was 223 thousand *chō*, or a gain of
4.4 per cent.

Columns (2) and (4) of Table 2-1 reveal an interesting
contrast. The five-year (1885-1890) change in paddy field area,
4.3 per cent, is considerably less than that of upland fields, 21.6
per cent. Nevertheless, for paddy fields this change is more
than twice as large as the change in any other five-year period,
and is about 4.4 times larger than the average five-year change
of 0.97 per cent in the subsequent 30-year period. If the hypothesis, that the change is attributable to the registration or
reclassification of previously concealed land, is valid, the difference between the percentage changes in the area of paddy
fields and upland fields can be ascribed to the much greater
attention paid to the measurement and registration of paddy
fields by the government during the land survey of 1873-1879.

[12] The Taxed Paddy Field appears in the *Tōkei nenkan* as *Minyū
yūsochi, ta*; and the Taxed Upland Field as *Minyū yūsochi, hata*. Where
Okinawa data are included in the *Tōkei nenkan* figures, they have been
deducted from the above series. Okinawa data are excluded in conformity with the present practice in Japan.
[13] A small portion of such land which had been recently reclaimed may
well have continued to be taxed as undeveloped land, since such land
was technically undeveloped until the lapse of a stipulated period of time.

TABLE 2-1

PERCENTAGE CHANGES IN THE AREA OF TAXED ARABLE LAND,
EXCLUDING HOKKAIDŌ, 1880-1920

Period	Paddy field (1000 chō)	Five year % change from previous period	Upland field (1000 chō)	Five year % change from previous period	Arable land (1000 chō)	Five year % change from previous period
	(1)	(2)	(3)	(4)	(5)	(6)
1880	2623	–	1847	–	4470	–
1885	2640	0.6	1874	1.5	4514	1.0
1890	2752	4.3	2278	21.6	5030	11.4
1895	2748	−0.2	2288	0.5	5036	0.1
1900	2761	0.5	2283	−0.2	5044	0.2
1905	2819	2.1	2317	1.4	5136	1.8
1910	2837	0.6	2321	0.2	5158	0.4
1915	2866	1.1	2302	−0.8	5168	0.2
1920	2912	1.6	2341	1.7	5253	1.6

SOURCES: Columns (1), (2), and (3) taken from Statistical Appendix: Tables 1A, 1B, 1C, respectively.

Owing to this greater attention, landowners were unable to conceal or misclassify paddy fields as readily as upland fields. Moreover, concealment or misclassification was also less feasible because as a rule water rights had to be obtained for paddy fields.

A breakdown in Table 2-2 of the 1885-1890 change into yearly percentage changes shows that most of the change was concentrated in the two-year period between 1886 and 1888 with the greatest change occurring between 1887-1888. The pattern is similar for both paddy fields and upland fields. The concentration in 1886-1888 occurred because surveys were completed during these two years in almost all prefectures. An examination of the period between 1880 and 1922 reveals that, except for a single two-year interval, the annual change for every other year is less than 1.0 per cent per annum for paddy fields and arable land and 1.2 per cent or less for upland fields.[14] As for the two-year interval between 1891 and 1893 the paddy field area increased by about 8 per cent. But this change is

[14] Statistical Appendix: Table 2.

TABLE 2-2

ANNUAL PERCENTAGE CHANGE IN TAXED PADDY FIELDS, UPLAND FIELDS,
AND ARABLE LAND, EXCLUDING HOKKAIDŌ, 1884-1890
(unit=per cent)

From end of year	To end of year	Paddy fields	Upland fields	Arable land
		(1)	(2)	(3)
1884	1885	0.0	0.1	0.0
1885	1886	0.5	0.4	0.4
1886	1887	1.7	4.9	3.0
1887	1888	2.9	14.5	7.8
1888	1889	−0.9	0.8	−0.2
1889	1890	0.0	0.0	0.0

SOURCE: Statistical Appendix: Table 2.

preceded by a drop in area of 8 per cent in 1891. The decrease in 1891 occurred because the arable land in three prefectures—Mie, Gifu, and Aichi—failed to be recorded owing to a severe earthquake in those provinces. Mie Prefecture was returned to the series in 1892, and the other two prefectures were returned in 1893, accounting for the increases in the two years.[15] It can also be noted that where unusual changes occur in upland field area, they are preceded by offsetting changes except between 1886 and 1888.[16]

A prefectural breakdown of the change from 1885 to 1890 indicates even more clearly that the change in the area of arable land was almost totally attributable to registration of previously concealed land or to reclassification of misclassified land. The change in area tended to be concentrated in certain prefectures. The five-year change in the Taxed Paddy Field Area for the ten prefectures with the highest percentage changes is 74 thousand *chō*,[17] which is 66 per cent of the 112

[15] In 1890 the Taxed Arable Land Area of the three prefectures was 348 thousand *chō*. (Computed from data in *Tōkei nenkan*, Vol. 10, p. 23.) The decrease in area of the nation's Taxed Arable Land from 1890 to 1891 was 348 thousand *chō*, down from 5,030 thousand *chō* to 4,682 thousand *chō*. (Statistical Appendix: Table IC.)

[16] Statistical Appendix: Table 2.

[17] The ten prefectures are listed in Table 2-3. The paddy field area for

thousand chō[18] change which occurred for the nation. In 1890 the ten prefectures accounted for about 25 per cent of the area of taxed paddy fields.[19] Relatively, the same prefectures averaged a 12.2 per cent increase in the five-year period as shown in Table 2-3 in contrast with the national increase of 4.3 per cent. The changes in the ten prefectures ranged from 5.9 to 34.9 per cent. A breakdown of the five-year change into annual changes brings out another interesting fact. The change is concentrated in a single year in every prefecture. For Kyoto Prefecture the concentration occurs in 1886, for Yamaguchi, 1887, and for all others, 1888.[20]

The change in the area of taxed upland fields likewise tends to be concentrated in certain prefectures and the change in each prefecture tends to be concentrated in a single year. Ex-

---

the ten prefectures in 1885 was 606 thousand chō, and 680 thousand chō in 1890. (*Tōkei nenkan*, Vol. 6, pp. 15-18; Vol. 10, pp. 23-25.)

[18] Computed from Statistical Appendix: Table 1C.

[19] The total area was 2,752 thousand chō. (*Ibid.*)

[20] The same pattern exists in other prefectures.

TABLE 2-3

ANNUAL TAXED PADDY FIELD AREA INCREASES IN TEN PREFECTURES WITH
HIGHEST PERCENTAGE INCREASES FROM 1885 TO 1890
(unit=per cent)

Prefectures	1885-1886 (1)	1886-1887 (2)	1887-1888 (3)	1888-1889 (4)	1889-1890 (5)	1885-1890 (6)	1890-1920 (7)
Yamaguchi	0.0	34.8	0.2	1.2	−1.3	34.9	2.0
Kyoto	16.4	1.9	0.3	−1.0	0.1	18.0	−2.5
Kagoshima	−0.4	0.6	10.1	1.2	0.5	12.1	5.2
Kumamoto	0.0	0.4	11.2	0.1	0.1	11.8	10.7
Okayama	−0.2	2.3	7.8	0.3	0.2	10.5	6.0
Fukuoka	0.0	0.0	13.6	−7.0	4.1	9.9	9.9
Miyazaki	−2.2	0.8	8.4	1.5	0.6	9.0	11.5
Oita	0.0	0.0	9.5	−2.2	0.4	7.6	10.9
Nagano	0.1	0.3	6.7	−0.3	0.0	6.8	11.5
Ibaragi	0.8	0.1	5.1	0.0	−0.1	5.9	6.2
Ten Prefectures	1.0	3.9	7.3	−1.0	0.6	12.2	7.2

SOURCE: Computed from *Tōkei nenkan*.

amining the data of ten prefectures whose upland field areas show the greatest percentage increases between 1885 and 1890, the upland field area of the ten is found to increase 178 thousand *chō*,[21] which accounts for 44 per cent of the national increase of 404 thousand *chō*.[22] In 1890 the Taxed Upland Field Area of the ten prefectures accounted for 20 per cent of the national area.[23]

The percentage increase in the upland field area of the ten prefectures is 64.9 in the five-year period as shown in Table 2-4 as against the national increase of 21.6. The increases in the ten prefectures ranged from 49.0 per cent to 98.0 per cent. In every prefecture except Gifu the change occurs almost entirely in a single year, and in Gifu the changes occur within two years, 1887-1889.

The evidence presented thus far strongly suggests that the increases in Taxed Arable Land Area from 1885 to 1890 were almost entirely fictitious. Could a substantial part of the change have been the consequence of reclamation or restoration of land ruined by natural calamities? Professor Shiroshi Nasu notes two estimates of additions to arable land area by reclamation from 1880 to 1885. One showed an annual increase of 9 thousand *chō*, the other, said to be the more reliable of the two, showed an annual increase of 2.5 thousand *chō*.[24] Even if the larger estimate is accepted, no more than about 20 thousand *chō* of land could have been expected to be added by reclamation in any two-year period. As for restoration of ruined land, there is no evidence of any unusual activity along this line.

Moreover, an appreciable real increase in the area of arable land is hardly conceivable without sharp increases in the labor force to reclaim land and to cultivate the added farmland. In

[21] The ten prefectures are listed in Table 2-4. The Taxed Upland Field Area of the ten was 275 thousand *chō* in 1885 and 453 thousand *chō* in 1890. (*Tōkei nenkan*, Vol. 6, pp. 15-18; Vol. 10, pp. 23-25.)

[22] Computed from Statistical Appendix, Table 1B.

[23] The national area minus Hokkaidō in 1890 was 2,278 thousand *chō*. (Statistical Appendix, Table 1B.)

[24] Shiroshi Nasu, *Aspects of Japanese Agriculture* (Mimeograph, New York, 1941), pp. 72-73.

TABLE 2-4

ANNUAL TAXED UPLAND FIELD AREA INCREASES IN TEN PREFECTURES WITH
HIGHEST PERCENTAGE INCREASES FROM 1885 TO 1890
(unit=per cent)

Prefectures	1885-1886 (1)	1886-1887 (2)	1887-1888 (3)	1888-1889 (4)	1889-1890 (5)	1885-1890 (6)	1890-1920 (7)
Kōchi	−0.6	99.7	0.7	−0.6	−0.4	98.0	13.5
Fukuoka	0.0	0.0	76.7	−2.0	0.6	74.3	−10.6
Ishikawa	0.1	67.1	0.6	1.1	0.2	70.4	−10.5
Miyazaki	−0.3	0.2	52.6	3.4	0.7	58.7	−4.5
Kagawa	0.3	0.0	56.8	0.2	0.3	58.2	−5.6
Ehime							
Tokushima	0.6	5.7	48.8	0.0	0.0	58.1	−12.7
Toyama	0.3	0.0	51.5	3.5	0.2	57.5	−12.3
Gifu	0.0	0.9	19.4	25.3	0.3	51.2	1.4
Yamaguchi	0.1	48.0	0.1	0.0	0.4	49.0	−4.1
Ten Prefectures	0.0	23.4	29.9	2.6	0.2	64.9	−3.1

SOURCE: Computed from *Tōkei nenkan.*

the prefectures discussed there is no evidence of related increases in the labor force in the relevant years.[25]

In the light of the foregoing discussion, it can be reasonably
concluded that the increase in Taxed Arable Land Area between 1885 and 1890 was not a result of real changes (except
negligibly) but rather the result of the registration of previously unregistered land or the proper classification of previously
misclassified land. It can also be concluded that the land
survey of the 1880's did successfully obtain the registration of
almost all previously unregistered land. It can be further stated
that this form of concealment, having been almost completely
eliminated, could never again present a serious problem,[26]

[25] Neither Irene B. Taeuber, *The Population of Japan* (Princeton, 1958),
nor Naotarō Sekiyama, *Kinsei nihon no jinkō kōzō* [Structure of Tokugawa period population] (Tokyo, 1958) shows evidence of population or
labor force movement that is related to increases in reported arable land
area. For a discussion of the agricultural labor force see Chapter 7, p.
140ff.

[26] That concealment was not completely eliminated even as late as
1929 can be inferred from the fact that in that year an Agriculture and

because once a lot is registered it is most unlikely to be stricken from the land register.

Concealment by Misclassification

Whereas a one-shot cure may be applied to unregistered land, misclassification can continue to occur as long as land class changes take place and the owners do not register the change. To adjust the arable land area for the biases introduced by this factor, it is necessary to obtain the extent of misclassification that existed after the land survey of the 1880's and the changes that occurred thereafter to 1922. This type of quantification is quite impossible. However, a conclusion may be drawn about the impact of misclassification with less information. If it can be determined that misclassification tended to increase or decrease, irrespective of its original extent, the direction of the bias introduced by this factor can be determined.

It may be reasonably assumed that most of the misclassification was eliminated as a result of the 1886-89 survey. This is an inference drawn from the great care with which the Finance Ministry conducted the survey. Owing to the importance of the project the Ministry divided the nation into districts over which special national tax officials, instead of prefectural officials, were placed. It also sought the full cooperation of the landowners. To this end tax officials dispatched by the national office were given the following instructions:[27] (1) to be courteous in giving instructions to the people; (2) to impress upon the people the seriousness of the government's objectives through the efforts of the county, district, town, and village heads; (3) to give instructions orally so that full understanding might be obtained; (4) to familiarize themselves thoroughly with local conditions so that national policies might be adapted for local application where they so required; (5) to conduct a

---

Forestry Ministry directive on the compilation of agricultural statistics contains a provision for the treatment of land for which land registers contain no record. (*Naikaku kunrei* 1 [April 24, 1929], Article 50, Clause 4.)

[27] *MZZKSS*, Vol. 7, pp. 404-05.

model survey before the landowners, so that they would become thoroughly familiar with the procedure; (6) to have
people submit their reports which would be checked to determine that everything was in order; and, finally, (7) to
ascertain that the documents were consistent with the facts by
checking them against the relevant lots.

There are other evidences of government concern. The
Finance Ministry directive[28] which served as the basis for the
second land survey provided that a national tax official would
be dispatched to a village to enforce a land survey if any reluctance to comply with the order was shown. In July 1886,
after the survey had started, the Finance Ministry issued confidential instructions[29] in response to the suspension of the
survey in some areas because of landowner resistance to its
objectives, advising national tax officials that the suspension
was evidence that people had not been sufficiently well briefed
on its importance. In 1888 the Revenue Bureau requested
police chiefs to send confidential reports to revenue office chiefs
when cases came to the attention of the police[30] in which prefectural tax officials failed to report land class changes or
concealed land. However, the terms in which the request was
made suggest that the Bureau was more interested in removing
misclassification and concealment, than in removing and
penalizing prefectural tax officials or in penalizing landowners.
The Bureau stated that because the officials' responsibilities
covered the land and records for hundreds of thousands to
over a million lots, they could easily have overlooked some lots.
This provided the basis for a graceful turnabout on the part of
tax officials, and also warned the police against pushing the
case if compliance was forthcoming. As for the landowners,
they were absolved from responsibility when they submitted
corrected reports and maps.[31]

[28] *Kunrei* 10 (February 1885). The *kunrei* is reprinted in *MZZKSS*,
Vol. 7, p. 401.
[29] *Ōkurashō naikun* [Confidential Instructions of the Finance Ministry]
(July 31, 1886). The instructions are reprinted in *MZZKSS*, Vol. 7, pp.
404-05.
[30] *Ibid.*, p. 406.
[31] When errors were found in the reports or maps, the standard

The final report of the Finance Ministry on the second land survey states that "errors were successfully reported and discrepancies between reality and land records were eliminated."[32] Although the reported success may have been partially bureaucratic rhetoric, great efforts appear to have been made to obtain good results. It is not unreasonable to assume that most of the misclassification was eliminated, particularly in view of the instructions for a lot-by-lot inspection of survey documents.

If some misclassification remained after the survey, it is probable that arable land misclassified as other land classes exceeded other land classes misclassified as arable land. This conclusion is drawn from the fact that the average value per *tan* of arable land was much greater than the average values of other classes of land except *takuchi*[33] as Table 2-5 reveals. More important still was the fact that the average value of paddy fields was greater than that of *takuchi*. There are five classes of land having sufficient area to have a significant effect on total misclassification, paddy fields, *takuchi*, upland fields, woodland, and *genya*.[34] These are given in the order of average value per *tan*. If the proposition that misclassification is a tax evasion practice is correct, paddy fields would tend to be misclassified as any of the other land classes, but the converse is not likely to take place; *takuchi* would tend to be misclassified as upland fields, woodland, or *genya* but not the converse; and so forth. It then follows that there would exist a tendency for arable land to be classified as other land classes, and the only offsetting misclassification is for *takuchi* to be classified as upland fields.[35] It is reasonable to assume in the absence of conflicting data that arable land misclassified as other land classes

---

practice was to make the landowners correct and resubmit them. This process was accompanied by strenuous efforts to convince the landowner that compliance was socially desirable. See *Ōkurashō naikun* in *ibid.,* p. 404.

[32] *Ibid.,* p. 401.

[33] See note to Table 2-5 for definition.

[34] See note to Table 2-5 for definition.

[35] Many paddy fields were undoubtedly classified as upland fields, but this does not affect the net misclassification of arable land.

TABLE 2-5

AREA AND VALUE PER TAN OF TAXED LAND, 1890

Land class	Average value per *tan*[a] Yen	Area 1000 *chō*
Paddy fields	40.254	2,752.1
Takuchi[b]	37.482	381.1
Salt fields	27.686	6.5
Cultivated land	27.059	5,029.9
Upland fields	11.118	2,277.8
Mineral spring sites, ponds, marshes, miscellaneous land classes	5.267	18.8
Woodland	0.333	7,304.8
Genya[b]	0.225	1,058.5

SOURCE: *Tōkei nenkan*, Vol. 10, pp. 22, 25.

NOTES: [a] The area and the average value per *tan* of cultivated land are computed from the source noted above.

[b] *Takuchi* which is usually translated as residential land includes commercial and industrial sites. Salt fields are fields on which salt is produced by evaporation. Woodland includes forests as well as small wooded areas. *Genya* is defined as undeveloped land which is not wooded but has other forms of wild vegetation on it. It is translated variously as meadow, pasture, plain, moor, wasteland, and wilderness.

tended to exceed the latter misclassified as the former. If this is a true statement, then the Taxed Arable Land Area would understate the actual arable land area, discounting other factors.

The discussion to this point indicates that misclassification either did not exist in significant degree after the land survey of the 1880's, or that, if it did, there was a preponderance of arable land misclassified as other land classes rather than the converse.

The question remains as to whether misclassification increased from the survey of the 1880's to 1920. Although failure to register land class changes was subject to penalty,[36] registra-

[36] The penalty for failing to register land class changes was 1.00 to 1.95 yen. (*Hōritsu 30* [November 29, 1889], Article 27.) In contrast the penalty for concealment of land was 4 to 40 yen. (*Ibid.*, Article 25.)

tion involved time-consuming paper work and expense, including the registration fee[37] and the additional land tax if the change increased the registered land value. It would seem that a landowner would be disposed to delay registration of a change when it meant an increase in tax burden in addition to other expenses. Where the land class change would reduce the tax burden, registration of the change could be expected.[38]

In the period following the turn of the century new forces emerged that tended to encourage registered conversions to arable land and discourage registration of conversions of arable land to *takuchi*. Registered conversions to arable land took place because arable land development was given subsidies,[39] tax relief,[40] or government loans, all of which would require official surveillance of the project. Almost all arable land reclamation and improvement took place under government auspices.

Best evidence that misclassification of the kind indicated above took place is provided by an analysis of what happened to *takuchi* soon after the turn of the century. In 1904 land tax per *tan* on rural *takuchi*[41] rose above that on paddy fields. The

[37] The fee for registration of change of land value was 1% of land value. (*Hōritsu* 27 [March 27, 1896], Article 5.)

[38] Conversions of arable land to public use would, of course, be a registered change.

[39] The earliest direct monetary subsidies for reclamation were granted by prefectures with the liberality of the grants differing among them. For a brief discussion see Seiichi Tōbata and Toshitarō Morinaga, eds., *Nihon nōgyō hattatsu shi* [History of Japan's agricultural development] (10 vols. plus 2 sup. vols., Tokyo, 1953-59), Vol. 5, pp. 312-13; Vol. 4, pp. 217-18. Gumma Prefecture, for example, enacted legislation in 1901 to bear 25% of the reclamation costs. (*Ibid.*, p. 218.)

Direct national subsidies became available only in 1919. (*Hōritsu* 42 [April 5, 1919].)

[40] Tax relief for arable land reclamation and improvement was provided in a great deal of legislation, including the land tax laws and the Arable Land Adjustment Law (known as the *Kōchi seiri hō* in Japanese). For a discussion of the latter see Appendix B.

[41] *Takuchi* were differentiated into urban and rural *takuchi*. A statistical differentiation is made in the *Tōkei nenkan* from 1898 to 1909. Urban *takuchi* were specially designated land characterized by a higher concentration of population, of commercial and industrial sites, of government offices, and other evidence of advanced urban development. (*Nihon*

average land tax per *tan* on paddy fields rose from 1.174 yen
to 1.525 from 1903 to 1904 owing to a tax increase. In the same
period the average per *tan* tax on rural *takuchi* increased from
0.973 yen to 1.771 yen.[42] Although *takuchi* area had increased
from 379 thousand *chō* in 1896 to 388 thousand *chō* in 1904,
in the next seven years (to 1911) the area declined to 378
thousand *chō*. It was not until 1921 that the area returned to
the 388 thousand level.[43] Because Japan was rapidly indus-
trializing at this time, increases in *takuchi* area could normally
have been expected. Since no other explanation can reasonably
be given for the reduction in *takuchi* area, it may be inferred
that owing to the tax rate changes conversions from arable land
to *takuchi* tended not to be registered; conversions from *takuchi*
to arable land tended to be registered; and arable land previously misclassified as *takuchi* tended to be reclassified as arable
land.

The evidence presented thus far indicates that the trend
established in 1904 would in time cause the area of other
classes of land misclassified as arable land to exceed the area
of arable land misclassified as other land classes. It can reasonably be assumed that the latter exceeded the former before 1904.
A study by the Crop Statistics Section of the Ministry of Agriculture and Forestry appears to vindicate the conclusion. In
1956 the net misclassification[44] of arable land as other land
classes was 174 thousand *chō*[45] in the nation (less Hokkaidō),
which is 3.5 per cent of the total registered arable land area.

What the net misclassification was around 1920 cannot be
estimated without making unwarranted assumptions. Because
the net misclassification was relatively minute in 1956, one

---

keizai shi jiten [Encyclopedia of Japanese economic history], 3 vols.,
Tokyo, 1940, Vol. 2, p. 1,009.)

[42] Tax data computed from *Tōkei nenkan*.

[43] Area data computed from *Tōkei nenkan*.

[44] The area of other land classes misclassified as arable land is deducted
to obtain the net figure.

[45] Computed from a mimeographed worksheet provided by Kōichi
Hatanaka of the Crop Statistics Section of the Ministry of Agriculture and
Forestry.

inference that may be made is that it was even smaller around 1920. Two reasons may be adduced in support of this inference; that is, the trend toward urbanization strengthened and subsidization of reclamation and arable land improvement increased from about the time of World War I.

In view of the uncertainty surrounding the area of misclassified land and the probable insignificance of the actual net misclassification around 1920, no attempt will be made to adjust the land area figures for this bias. It can be concluded, however, that since the Taxed Arable Land Area is used to estimate the upland field production, this failure to adjust will probably cause the increase in agricultural production to be greater than it would otherwise be (that is, it would tend to give an upward bias to the growth rate).

Relationship between Taxed Land Area and Area Planted to Crops

Earlier it was concluded that a very significant fictitious increase in Taxed Arable Land Area occurred as a result of the land survey of the 1880's. Such a change would not necessarily have caused changes in production statistics, or, more specifically, in the reported area planted to crops. Because the reported increase in the Taxed Arable Land Area was almost entirely fictitious, the actual production of agricultural crops can be assumed to have remained almost unchanged. However, if arable land was concealed before the survey as a means to minimize taxes, it is virtually certain that the area planted to crops on concealed land was not reported so that the concealment could be successful. When the concealment was eliminated in the 1880's, the need to prevent the discovery of concealment evaporated. Therefore, when the Taxed Arable Land Area increased as a result of the elimination of concealment, the reported area planted to crops can also be expected to have increased. We now turn to statistical evidence to determine whether the latter did increase as expected.

An examination of the reported area planted to paddy rice reveals a pattern of increase from 1885 to 1890 similar to that for Taxed Paddy Field Area, with, as a rule, only a slight lag.

Excluding Hokkaidō because its area planted to crops grew much more rapidly than for the rest of the nation, the area indices for the two classes of land from 1885 to 1890 with 1885 as the base year are shown in Table 2-6. The greater increase in the area planted to paddy rice can be attributed to the narrowing of the gap between the areas of the two classes of land by 27 thousand *chō* in the five-year period.

Even more revealing is a study of prefectural statistics. We take the ten prefectures with the highest percentage changes in the Taxed Paddy Field Area and compute for each the percentage changes in the area planted to paddy rice in the five-year period from 1885-1890. The results are shown in

TABLE 2-6

COMPARISON OF CHANGES IN TAXED PADDY FIELD AREA AND REPORTED AREA PLANTED TO PADDY RICE, EXCLUDING HOKKAIDŌ, 1885-1890

Year	Taxed paddy field area (1000 *chō*)	Index	Reported area planted to paddy rice (1000 *chō*)	Index
1885	2640	100.0	2572	100.0
1886	2652	100.5	2586	100.5
1887	2697	102.2	2606	101.3
1888	2776	105.2	2657	103.3
1889	2751	104.2	2693	104.7
1890	2752	104.2	2711	105.4

SOURCE: Statistical Appendix: Tables 1A, 3A.

Column (6) of Table 2-7. The percentage changes in the two classes of land area for each of the ten are closely related. If the ten prefectures are taken as a group to cancel out many of the random fluctuations that smaller universes are subject to, we find that the Taxed Paddy Field Area increased by 12.2 per cent and the area planted to paddy rice by 13.7 per cent. For the rest of the prefectures, excluding Hokkaidō, the increases were 1.8 and 2.9 per cent. For the nation as a whole, the changes were, respectively, 4.2 and 5.4 per cent. It is concluded that the changes in the two areas are closely related and that the actual area planted to rice probably changed very little in the five-year period from 1885 to 1890.

Estimation of Area Planted to Paddy Rice

The estimation of the actual area planted to paddy rice requires that the reported area planted to paddy rice be corrected for the years before the completion of the land survey of the 1880's. Although the survey was completed in 1888, and the Taxed Arable Land Area fully reflects the elimination of concealment in its 1888 area, the reported area planted to paddy rice apparently does not fully adjust until 1890. Therefore, the area planted to paddy rice will be revised for the years 1878 through 1890. The revised areas are obtained by extrapolating the reported area planted to paddy rice, excluding Hokkaidō, by use of a straight line least-squares trend line fitted to 1890-1910 data. The 1890-1910 period was selected because supply and demand conditions do not appear to have shifted significantly during this time,[46] and the 20-year period is long enough to provide a trend. Government statistics on the area planted to paddy rice, excluding Hokkaidō, from 1878 to 1917 and the straight line trend are charted in Figure 2-1. The charted government data show the sharp increase that occurred in area planted from 1886 to 1890.

Government data from 1890 to 1917 suggest a curvilinear, rather than a straight line trend, and indeed a curve showing a relatively greater increase in the latter half of the period under discussion would be consistent with some of the supply and demand conditions of the period. Early in the Meiji era (and in late Tokugawa period) a rice surplus was probably being produced.[47] Therefore, in view of the improvements in transportation and storage facilities that took place in early Meiji the need to increase supply may have been weak. Then in the 1890's demand appears to have caught up with supply as evidenced by the terms of trade turning in favor of rice as

[46] The impact of a growing shortage of domestically produced rice probably tended to increase paddy field area at a faster rate than previously after the turn of the century. Then a shortage of labor in agriculture owing to increased transfer of labor from the agricultural to the non-agricultural sector during World War I was probably an important factor in reversing the trend from around 1917.

[47] See Chapter 4, p. 100.

TABLE 2-7

COMPARISON OF PERCENTAGE CHANGES IN TAXED PADDY FIELD AREA AND REPORTED
AREA PLANTED TO PADDY RICE IN SELECTED PREFECTURES, 1885-1890

Prefecture	Paddy field area 1885 (1000 chō)	Paddy field area 1890 (1000 chō)	% change	Area planted 1885 (1000 chō)	Area planted 1890 (1000 chō)	% change
	(1)	(2)	(3)	(4)	(5)	(6)
Yamaguchi	58.6	79.0	34.8	51.7	78.1	50.9
Kyoto	40.3	47.6	18.1	38.6	45.7	18.3
Kagoshima	48.7	54.6	12.1	47.8	51.4	7.6
Kumamoto	58.1	65.0	11.9	60.3	65.8	9.1
Okayama	75.0	83.0	10.7	74.3	83.5	12.3
Fukuoka	96.9	106.5	9.9	96.1	107.5	11.9
Miyazaki	35.6	38.8	9.0	35.1	38.8	10.6
Oita	46.2	49.7	7.6	45.1	48.6	7.6
Nagano	65.5	70.0	6.9	61.9	67.6	9.2
Ibaragi	81.2	86.0	5.9	78.9	83.6	6.0
Ten prefectures	606.1	680.2	12.2	589.8	670.6	13.7
Nation less Hokkaidō	2641	2752	4.2	2572	2711	5.4
Nation less ten prefectures and Hokkaidō	2035	2072	1.8	1982	2040	2.9

SOURCE: Columns (1), (2), (3), and (4) computed from Ministry of Agriculture and Forestry, Agriculture and Forestry Economics Bureau, Statistics Section, *Nōsakumotsu ruinen tōkeihyō: ine, 1881-1956* [Agricultural crop statistics: rice, 1881-1956] (Tokyo, 1957).

against other commodities.[48] In response to this situation, from around the turn of the century direct money subsidization of agricultural land improvement began and the rate of reclamation of agricultural land started to increase.[49]

While a curved trend may be indicated by the 1890-1917 data, extension of the data to 1922 and later makes such a trend less evident, if not erroneous, because the rate of increase in the area planted to rice declines after 1917, and the area declines absolutely after 1920. It is also possible, contrary to the

[48] Kasaku Ōta, *Meiji-Taishō-Shōwa beika seisaku shi* [Rice value policy of Meiji, Taishō, and Shōwa Eras] (Tokyo, 1938), p. 8.

[49] See Appendix B for a discussion of agricultural land improvement policies.

FIGURE 2-1

AREA PLANTED TO PADDY RICE EXCLUDING HOKKAIDŌ AND
LEAST SQUARES TREND LINE

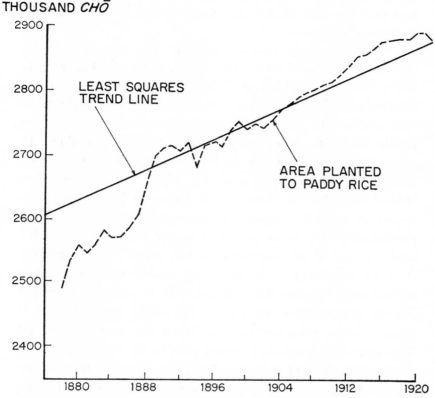

THOUSAND *CHŌ*

SOURCE: Statistical Appendix: Table 3A.
Trend equation: Yc = 2750 + 5.878X, based on 1890-1910
area.
Origin: 1900; X unit equals one year.

arguments presented above, that the area planted to rice may
have continued to rise fairly rapidly in early Meiji because rice
was one of the few commodities that had a ready cash market.
It is known that farmers needed more and more cash at this
time to pay taxes and to buy products that were becoming
increasingly available in rural markets.

Since evidence supporting a curved trend is not conclusive,
it was decided to select the straight line trend which has the

dual virtue of being simpler and more conservative in the sense
that it reduces the growth rate of agricultural production less
than a curved trend would. In practice, if the latter were used
the growth rate of agricultural production would be lower by
less than one-half of 0.1 percentage points. This is hardly a
significant difference.

The corrected five-year averages of area planted to paddy
rice during ten periods for the nation, for Hokkaidō, and for
the nation less Hokkaidō are shown in Table 2-8. A national
area index with a 1873-77 base period is also shown in the table.

In addition to paddy rice, a second crop is grown on many
paddy fields. If landowners deemed it desirable to adjust the
area planted to paddy rice to conform with the Taxed Paddy
Field Area, they probably tended to adjust the area planted to
second crops for the same reason. Between 1903 (when surveying of multiple cropping commenced) and 1922 the proportion of paddy fields grown to second crops fluctuated between 29 and 31 per cent with no clear trend.[50] The proportion
does not include green manure crops which cannot count as a
second crop because they are not a final agricultural output
but are planted to increase the yield of the original crop. If
green manure crops had been included the proportion would
have increased from 35 to 40 per cent in the 20-year period.[51]
For the purposes of this book it will be assumed that 30 per
cent of the area of paddy fields was grown to second crops
during the period from 1873 to 1922.[52]

[50] Computed from Nobufumi Kayō, ed., *Nihon nōgyō kiso tōkei* [Basic
statistics of Japanese agriculture] (Tokyo, 1958), p. 72.
It is probable that the percentage was fairly stable before 1903. An
increase in double cropping was mostly dependent on the drainage of
fields that were flooded the year around in that part of Japan where
double cropping was practiced. Although some drainage projects were
undertaken prior to the enactment of the Arable Land Adjustment Law
(see Appendix B), it is not until after the broadening of this law in 1909
to subsidize such projects that a significant increase in the drainage of
flooded land could have been expected.
[51] *Ibid.*
[52] Questions are raised about this assumption in this chapter, pp. 50-52.

TABLE 2-8

CORRECTED AREA PLANTED TO PADDY RICE AND INDEX,
FIVE-YEAR AVERAGES, 1873-1922

Period	National area less Hokkaidō (1000 *chō*)	Index 1873-77 = 100	Hokkaidō area (1000 *chō*)	National area (1000 *chō*)	Index 1873-77 = 100
	(1)	(2)	(3)	(4)	(5)
1873-1877	2603	100.0	0	2603	100.0
1878-1882	2632	101.1	0	2632	101.1
1883-1887	2662	102.3	1	2663	102.3
1888-1892	2699	103.7	2	2701	103.8
1893-1897	2712	104.2	4	2716	104.3
1898-1902	2745	105.5	11	2756	105.9
1903-1907	2779	106.8	19	2798	107.5
1908-1912	2820	108.3	36	2856	109.7
1913-1917	2867	110.1	54	2921	112.2
1918-1922	2890	111.1	83	2973	114.2

SOURCES: Column (1): The annual data for the five-year averages were obtained from two sources. The 1873-1889 areas were computed from the following estimating equation: $Yc = 2750 + 5.878X$ with 1900 as the origin and X unit equalling one year. The equation is a least-squares trend line based on 1890-1910 data. The 1890-1922 areas are from Statistical Appendix: Table 3.
Column (3): The annual data on which the five-year averages are based are from Statistical Appendix: Table 3.

Estimation of Area Planted to Dryland Crops

The construction of a corrected index of area planted to all other crops (that is, excepting rice) obviously poses a greater problem than that for the area planted to paddy rice. The area planted to all other crops includes all upland field areas including Hokkaidō and that part of paddy fields on which two crops are grown.[53] It has already been assumed that double cropping occurred on 30 per cent of the adjusted paddy field area.

With respect to upland fields we must determine whether the increase in registered upland field area affected the reported production of dryland crops. The problems in doing so are different and more difficult to resolve than those associated

[53] Double cropping of paddy rice in Kōchi Prefecture can be ignored as it was an insignificant part of the total double-cropped area.

with paddy fields. Almost all paddy fields were and are put into rice, and because of the established boundaries of paddy fields the problem of determining the acreage planted to each crop was probably not a difficult one for village statistical reporters. But on upland fields, serious estimation problems arise due to six circumstances that differentiated the planting pattern of these fields from that on paddy fields. On upland fields (1) many more varieties of crops were grown; (2) crops were more readily changed from year to year; (3) multiple cropping was more extensive and intensive; (4) new crops were being introduced; (5) all upland field crops were not surveyed and the number of crops surveyed was less in the earlier years; and (6) some land that was used in shifting agriculture[54] was classified as upland fields.

Given the conditions under which crops were raised on upland fields, accurate reporting would have required the measurement of the area planted to each crop. Such an undertaking would have required the services of many men and would also have aroused the suspicions of the farmers. The villages lacked the resources for the former and certainly did not wish to evoke the latter; moreover, they were not fully aware of the importance of accurate statistical reporting. For these reasons the estimations of the area planted to various crops on upland fields were probably no more than informed guesses at best. The Ministry of Agriculture and Forestry studies that were made between 1948 and 1952[55] reveal a high probability of error in reporting the area planted to crops. The ratio of reported area to that actually planted for the three principal grains other than rice (wheat, barley, and naked barley) was 78 per cent; for soy beans, 72; for rapeseed, 56; and for peanuts,

[54] Shifting agriculture is also known as slash and burn agriculture. The cycle of use as cultivated land of land used in shifting agriculture varied from a few years to many years, and because such land is typically located in remote mountain districts, tabulations of crops grown on these fields probably occurred erratically, if at all.

[55] Kōichi Hatanaka, "Waga kuni ni okeru sakuzuke to kōchi ni kansuru tōkei chosa no genkyō," [Present state of statistical reporting on crop area and arable land area in Japan], *Nōgyō Tōkei Kenkyū*, III, 3 (February 1956), 2n.

53. As was to be expected, the rate was highest for rice at 93 per cent because almost all paddy fields are grown to rice and the area of individual paddy fields is known except for the average undermeasurement of about 7 per cent.

There are 15 dryland crops for which data are available for 1884, 1892, 1902, and 1912. As generally unreliable as the area planted data may be, the increases shown by these crops between 1884 and 1892 for the nation, less Hokkaidō, appear to validate the contention that the planted area of upland fields tended to adjust to the Taxed Upland Field Area. The 15 crops can be divided into winter and summer crops.[56] The percentage changes in the eight-year period from 1884 to 1892 and in two following ten-year periods for the two classes of crops can be tabulated as shown in Table 2-9. The 15 per cent increase for summer crops, the 16 per cent increase for winter crops, and the total increase of 15 per cent, are sufficiently differentiated from subsequent percentage changes to warrant the conclusion that they were largely influenced by the increase in Taxed Upland Field Area. A distinction is made between winter and summer crops because a large part of the winter crops was grown on paddy fields. The years 1884 and 1892 were selected because they are the closest years to 1885 and 1890 for which data are available for the greatest number of crops.

Since the data on area planted to dryland crops are incomplete and rapid shifts in areas planted to specific crops occurred, area planted statistics cannot be used to construct an index of the actual area planted to dryland crops. The only other reasonable basis for estimating the planted area is by assuming that it is functionally related to the Taxed Upland Field Area. This area, excluding Hokkaidō, is almost a constant between 1889 and 1917 showing only a slow upward drift of 43 thousand *chō* in the 27-year period.[57] The area before 1889 was obtained by a least squares straight-line trend fitted to

[56] The 15 dryland crops consist of 4 winter crops: wheat, barley, naked barley, and rapeseed; and 11 summer crops: upland rice, sweet potatoes, white potatoes, foxtail millet, barnyard millet, proso millet, buckwheat, soybeans, indigo, cotton, and mulberry.

[57] Statistical Appendix: Table 1B.

TABLE 2-9

PERCENTAGE CHANGES IN REPORTED AREA PLANTED TO
FIFTEEN DRYLAND CROPS, SELECTED YEARS

	1884	1892	1902	1912
Summer crops (1000 *chō*)	1413	1619	1743	1835
% change from previous period	–	15	8	5
Winter crops (1000 *chō*)	1650	1911	1961	1910
% change from previous period	–	16	3	—3
Total dryland crops (1000 *chō*)	3063	3530	3704	3745
% change from previous period	–	15	5	1

SOURCE: Computed from Ministry of Agriculture and Forestry, Agriculture and Forestry Economics Bureau, Statistics Section, *Nōrinsho ruinen tōkeihyō, 1868-1953* [Historical statistics of the Ministry of Agriculture and Forestry, 1868-1953].

1889-1917 data as shown in Figure 2-2. Statistical Appendix: Table 1B, reveals a sharp decrease in Taxed Upland Field Area in 1891 and 1892. This is due to the failure to include data from Aichi and Gifu Prefectures in both years and from Mie in 1891, following a severe earthquake in the three prefectures. Because in these two years area planted reports were made by these prefectures and the reports are comparable to those of other years, a straight line interpolation of the national data using 1890 and 1893 areas as bases was made for these years.

Five-year averages and the index (1873-77 = 100) of the corrected arable land area on which dryland crops were grown are shown in Table 2-10. This area is the sum of the corrected upland field area, Hokkaidō upland field area, and 30 per cent of the corrected paddy field area. The total change in area from 1873-77 to 1918-22 was 955 thousand *chō*. Eighty per cent of this change can be attributed to the increase in the area of Hokkaidō upland fields.

It will be assumed for the purpose of this book that the index of the corrected area of dryland crop fields in Table 2-10 is also the *index of the corrected area planted to dryland crops* which is to be used to obtain the dryland crop production.

Two significant qualitative differences exist between the

FIGURE 2-2

TAXED UPLAND FIELD AREA EXCLUDING HOKKAIDŌ AND
LEAST SQUARES TREND LINE

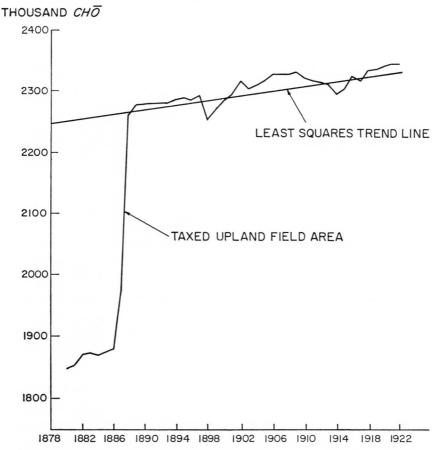

SOURCE: Statistical Appendix: Table 1B.
Trend equation: Yc = 2299 + 1.95X, based on 1889-1917 area.
Origin: 1903; X unit equals one year.

NOTE: The area for 1891 and 1892 given in Table 1B is not used because owing to a major earthquake three prefectures did not report their areas in 1891 and two did not report in 1892. Therefore, the 1891-92 area used here is a straight-line interpolation of 1890 and 1893 areas.

TABLE 2-10

CORRECTED AREA OF DRYLAND CROP FIELDS AND INDEX,
FIVE-YEAR AVERAGES, 1873-1922
(1000 *chō*)

Period	Corrected national upland field area less Hokkaidō	Hokkaidō upland field area	Corrected double cropped paddy field area	Corrected national area (1)+(2)+(3)	Index 1873-77=100 %
	(1)	(2)	(3)	(4)	(5)
1873-1877	2244	–	781	3025	100.0
1878-1882	2254	–	790	3044	100.6
1883-1887	2264	25	799	3063	101.3
1888-1892	2276	45	810	3130	103.5
1893-1897	2281	96	815	3192	105.5
1898-1902	2283	225	827	3335	110.2
1903-1907	2317	324	839	3480	115.0
1908-1912	2322	497	857	3676	121.5
1913-1917	2311	626	876	3813	126.1
1918-1922	2340	748	892	3980	131.6

SOURCE: Column (1): The annual areas on which the five-year averages are based
are obtained as follows: 1) the 1873-88 annual areas are computed from the
following least-squares trend equation: $Yc = 2299 + 1.95X$ with 1903 as
the year of origin and X units equal to one year; 2) annual areas for 1889-
1922 are from Statistical Appendix: Table 1B, except for 1891 and 1892
which are straight line interpolations of the national data between 1890 and
1893 to correct for the omission of data from three prefectures.
Column (2): Statistical Appendix: Table 3B.
Column (3): This is 30% of Table 2-8, Column (4).

upland fields of Hokkaidō and other regions of Japan. The first
difference is that Hokkaidō upland fields are almost entirely
grown to one crop per year whereas most upland fields in the
rest of the nation are grown to two or more crops. The same
difference exists between double-cropped paddy fields and
upland fields excluding Hokkaidō; double-cropped paddy fields
are also grown to one dryland crop per year.

The second difference between Hokkaidō and other upland
fields is that physical returns per unit of area in the northern
part of Japan tend to be lower on the average than for the
nation as a whole. The differences mean that a *chō* of Hokkaidō
upland field or of double-cropped paddy field produces less

dryland crops on the average than a *chō* of upland field in the rest of the country. Owing to this the index of the change in the total area of the three groups of dryland crop fields would appear to overstate the increase of the total area planted to dryland crops because the area of Hokkaidō upland fields and double-cropped paddy fields was growing more rapidly than the area of upland fields in the rest of the nation.

According to computations made from one set of government data the average upland field excluding Hokkaidō was grown to 1.84 crops in 1955.[58] This figure is probably an understatement because statistics were not collected for some minor crops; the surveyor cannot be present to observe developments on each field when three or four crops are grown and he probably tends to understate the area planted to crops; and there is a tendency to underestimate the area planted to crops when reports are based only on observation as they are for a number of crops.[59] In any case, a substantial qualitative difference is evident.

The overstatement of the increase is at least partially offset by two factors. It is probable that one factor was a tendency for the proportion of upland fields planted to more than one crop to increase in time as the following developments indicate. The area planted to more than one crop tended to move northward over time; land utilization was further intensified in upland fields, excluding Hokkaidō, as urbanization progressed, transportation improved, fertilizer use increased, and labor-saving innovations were introduced which saved labor use during peak labor input periods. The last point is particularly important because multiple cropping requires that sufficient labor time be available within a short period to harvest one crop, to prepare the same land for the next crop, and to plant the next crop. At least partially offsetting the above tendency toward more intensive land use was the fact that upland field reclamation, excluding Hokkaidō, tended to occur in the more sparsely settled northern regions of Japan where single cropping predominated.

[58] *MAF Yearbook*, Vol. 32 (1955), p. 166.
[59] *Ibid.*, p. 54.

The second factor which tends to reduce the overstatement is that the value of production from two-crop land is not necessarily twice that from one-crop land. The net value of total production from a given piece of land is determined by such factors as the latitude of its location, proximity to large population centers, the number of frost-free days, the number of days of rain and sun, and the like. It is known that the second crop taken from a two-crop field returns less to the cultivator than the first crop for many reasons. One important reason is that two crops take more out of the soil than one crop. A second is that the second crop is usually grown during a season when the growing conditions (e.g., hours of sunlight, the temperature, adverse weather conditions) tend to be poorer.

It is possible that a third offset factor exists. The assumption that double-cropped paddy fields remained constant at 30 per cent of the national paddy field area is open to question despite the apparent confirmation by the statistical evidence. More commercial fertilizers became available which checked soil depletion resulting from double cropping. Introduction of labor-saving innovations during peak labor demand periods also helped in making double cropping more feasible. In view of these developments it is possible that the proportion of paddy fields put into two crops tended to increase in the 45-year period. Moreover, the statistical evidence of a constant percentage is for the period after 1903, and assuming that the data are accurate, it is possible that during the 30 years prior to that date the proportion was smaller.[60]

Giving Hokkaidō upland fields and double-cropped paddy fields the same weight as upland fields in the rest of the nation assumes that the offset factors fully compensate for the bias that the weighting apparently introduced. Of the various assumptions made in estimating the planted area index, this one is most open to question and one in which a change in assumption can have the most serious effect on the growth

[60] For a qualification see p. 42n.

rate of agricultural production. If it is assumed, for example, that the product per *chō* from Hokkaidō upland fields is 50 per cent[61] of that of the rest of the nation, then an increase in dryland crop fields equivalent to 748 thousand *chō* of cultivated fields of the same quality as Hokkaidō fields would have had to take place to offset the bias introduced by the weighting. Such a development would require that the total area put into additional crops in both paddy fields and upland fields in the rest of Japan would have to increase by about 14 per cent if we assume that the second crop is equivalent in value to one crop in Hokkaidō.[62] An increase of 14 per cent might have taken place, but such a substantial rise is not very plausible. If multiple cropping had not increased at all and the production per *chō* of Hokkaidō upland fields and of double-cropped paddy fields is 50 per cent of that of upland fields in the rest of the nation, then the area of upland fields would be overstated by 430 thousand *chō* in 1918-22. If this were deducted from the corrected national upland field area, the upland field index for 1918-22 (base years 1873-77) would decline from 131.5 to 114.0. This difference would reduce the growth rate of agricultural production expressed in per cent by 0.13,[63] which is still not a very substantial difference in view of the tolerances with which we must necessarily work.

Although it is probable that multiple cropping did increase, on balance it seems reasonable to conclude that the index of the corrected area of dryland crop fields probably overstates the increase in the area planted to dryland crops due to the overwhelming weight of Hokkaidō upland fields in the increase. However, because of the uncertainties involved, no attempt will be made to refine the simple assumptions made in obtain-

[61] No reliable estimate can be obtained, but a crude estimate based on 1925 data indicates that the 50% figure may be a reasonable approximation.

[62] The increase in double-cropped paddy field area of 11% would also require an offset of about 50 thousand *chō*.

[63] This difference holds when the original growth rate was 1.03% per year assuming median paddy rice yields in the terminal periods of the study.

ing the area index, particularly since the bias introduced by the assumptions is likely to be on the conservative side—that is, apt to increase the growth rate of agricultural production rather than reduce it.

Summary

Two types of concealment of cultivated land existed at the beginning of the Meiji era: concealment by failure to register and concealment by misclassification. Both were village measures for reducing the reported cultivated land area of the village, particularly the area of paddy fields. These measures caused village production and, therefore, the tax levied on the village to be lower than if accurate reports were given.

The ultimate purpose of this chapter was to estimate the actual area planted to paddy rice and to dryland crops. This was accomplished in the case of the former crop by extrapolating what is believed to be the relatively more reliable area-planted data of 1890 to 1910 back to 1873 by using a linear least-squares trend line. For dryland crops, since the area-planted data were not reliable, independent estimates of three classes of land were made. The index was constructed by simply adding these together. Biases introduced by the methods used were also discussed.

CHAPTER 3

The Undermeasurement of Arable Land

UNDERMEASUREMENT of arable land was practiced, as already noted, as a means to minimize the land tax burden. It was an important factor in the understatement of agricultural production in that it caused an understatement of the area planted to crops. The objectives of this chapter are to ascertain that undermeasurement did exist during the Meiji era and to obtain undermeasurement indices for paddy and upland fields to offset the bias in production data introduced by undermeasurement.

Tokugawa and Early Meiji Undermeasurement

To understand arable land undermeasurement in Japan, a study of Tokugawa period land measurement practice is helpful. During that period not only was undermeasurement a common practice but it was also tolerated by the authorities. It provided a safeguard for the peasantry against over-zealous tax officials who had a "natural inclination to increase revenues in the belief that such action constituted loyal service to their lord."[1] One designation for the practice was *nawa-gokoro* which may be freely translated as the "spirit of magnanimity which tolerates the stretching of the measuring rope."[2] During the Tokugawa period, then, undermeasurement was not a tax evasion, but rather a tax alleviation, practice.[3]

The officially tolerated rate of undermeasurement was apparently not a firm figure, and considerable discretion was given to the land survey magistrate. However, "The usual

[1] Hiroshi Andō, *Tokugawa bakufu kenji yōryaku* [Outline of the provincial administration of the Tokugawa Shogunate] (Tokyo, 1915), p. 178.

[2] *Ibid.*

[3] In contrast, concealment was not tolerated but rather subject to severe punishment.

practice on land being measured for the first time was to permit
a 10 per cent undermeasurement of the length and a 20 per
cent undermeasurement of the width of a piece of land. Where
a field that had been surveyed in antiquity was being remeasured and it was believed appropriate to undermeasure the field,
the undermeasurement at times was 10 per cent for one side
and 10 or 20 per cent for the other."[4] Where a linear undermeasurement of 20 and 10 percent was permitted, the area
undermeasurement would be 28 per cent. There were other
practices[5] that caused further, though minor, undermeasurement.

What the precise undermeasurement was at the end of the
Tokugawa period cannot be known. That same undermeasurement was, of course, carried into the Meiji era up to the time
of the cadastral survey. A Ministry of Finance document[6] of
December 1873, states that it ranged from 20 to 30 per cent.
There are scattered records of undermeasurement for the Tokugawa period. One study[7] reveals an undermeasurement of 29
per cent on 52.731 *tan* of land held by a landlord in Kawachi
Province (now part of Osaka Prefecture).

One of the original purposes of the Meiji land survey of the
1870's was to obtain the correct measurement of land along
with the registration of concealed land and the reclassification
of misclassified land. However, in view of Tokugawa period
toleration, accurate measurement probably could not have been
attained unless the measurement had been undertaken by personnel from outside the village under strict instructions to
survey accurately. What actually happened, however, was that
the surveying was delegated to landowners and villages and
their measurements were subject to spot checks by tax officials.[8]
It is a matter of record that the registered arable land area
increased from 3,234 thousand *chō* in 1872 to 4,486 thousand

[4] *Ibid.*, pp. 177-78.

[5] These included an allowance for ridges between paddy fields (*aze-
giwa biki*) and the practice of dropping fractional amounts in both linear
and square measures. (*Ibid.*, pp. 176-77, 180.)

[6] *MZZKSS*, Vol. 7, p. 336.

[7] Furushima, *op.cit.*, p. 535, Table 35.

[8] Appendix A, p. 191.

chō in 1881. It is impossible to determine how much of this change can be attributed to correct measurement of undermeasured fields since a large part of the change can be attributed to the registration of concealed land and the reclassification of misclassified land.

While it is certain that a substantial reduction of undermeasurement occurred at this time it was by no means eliminated. In his account of the Meiji tax reform, Keichō Ario stated that during the survey of the 1870's, undermeasurement of up to 10 per cent was tolerated at first. Later the tolerance was reduced to 3.3 per cent.[9]

The range of undermeasurement turned out to be much greater than 3.3 to 10 per cent owing to the crude techniques of measurement used, the determination of landowners to gain maximum tax advantage, and the absence of a firm policy. In some areas undermeasurement was not tolerated at all, and in the case of a district (Chikugo) in Fukuoka Prefecture, the registered area was greater than the true area of arable land.[10] Cases of overmeasurement were rarities, however.[11] Cases of toleration in excess of 10 per cent were more frequent. In six districts in five prefectures undermeasurement was so great and the land records so poor as a rule that disputes arose over ownership. These districts were remeasured during the land survey of the 1880's and as a result the increase in the area of arable land was 30 per cent.[12] Resurveys were apparently to take place in other areas when the extent of undermeasurement was such that "one *tan* was recorded as 0.8 *tan* or as 0.7 *tan*."[13] Without systematic remeasurement of all land it is unlikely that errors of 20 to 30 per cent could always be detected. From the ambiguous account given by Ario it is probable that only flagrant undermeasurements were investigated by tax officials.

A Ministry of Finance report on land measurement of the land survey of the 1880's also attests to the survival of undermeasurement. The document states that owing to the crude techniques used in measurement during the cadastral survey of the 1870's, errors of measurement can be expected in every

---

[9] Ario, *op.cit.*, p. 76.   [10] *Ibid.*, p. 97.   [11] *Ibid.*, p. 98.
[12] MZZKSS, Vol. 7, p. 402.   [13] Ario, *op.cit.*, pp. 142-43.

parcel of land upon remeasurement.[14] However, it adds that the purpose of the land survey of the 1880's was not to correct these "small" errors.

Construction of Undermeasurement Index

The only reliable estimates of undermeasurement available are those made by sampling by the Crop Statistics Section of the Ministry of Agriculture and Forestry.[15] The survey undertaken in 1956 shows undermeasurement separately for paddy fields and upland fields. The ratio of the true area to the registered area will be called the undermeasurement index (UI).[16] The UI is, therefore, a device for computing the true area from the registered area. The national paddy field UI was found to be 1.069, the national upland field UI, 1.049.[17] The national arable land UI was 1.061. The Crop Statistics Section estimates were made by sampling 1,440 districts.[18] Interestingly, 324 of these districts had arable land UI of 1.10 or greater, and of these, 14 had UI of 1.30 or greater. These figures support the contention that there was considerable variation in the tolerance of undermeasurement during the land surveys of the Meiji era.

Although the UI of the 1950's may be known, this does not reveal what the UI was immediately after the survey of the 1880's nor what it was up to 1922. However, even if the numerical figure cannot be obtained, it may be possible to determine that the Crop Statistics Section estimate is the lower limit of what the UI could have been during the Meiji era. The rest of this chapter will attempt to demonstrate that the UI probably decreased over time.

[14] *MZZKSS*, Vol. 7, p. 402.

[15] Hatanaka, "Kōchi tōkei no kakuritsu," *op.cit.*, p. 14.

[16] The undermeasurement index will be represented by the symbol UI in this chapter only.

[17] Statistical Appendix: Table 4.

[18] The standard error of estimate is six thousand *chō*. (Hatanaka, *op. cit.*, p. 13.) The total undermeasurement (the difference between the true area and the registered area) was 303 thousand *chō* in 1956 out of an arable land area of 5,004 thousand *chō*. (From worksheet provided by Kōichi Hatanaka.)

If the original registered arable land area had remained unchanged—that is, if additions to the registered arable land area, deletions therefrom and measurements thereof had not occurred—the national arable land UI would have remained constant over time. But such changes have occurred and each one could have affected the UI. Precise relationships exist between the UI of each added or deleted field and the national arable land UI. If the areas of all additions and deletions made after the survey of the 1880's to the year 1956 were known, if the values of their respective UI's were also known, and if the results of any remeasurement that occurred were known, the value of the national[19] arable land UI at any given date would, of course, be known. But very little of the above information is available. Nevertheless, some logical relationships and useful data can be obtained.

The following logical relationships[20] are relevant: (1) Deletion of undermeasured land from the arable land area reduces the undermeasurement.[21] (2) Addition of undermeasured land to the arable land area increases the undermeasurement. (3) Accurate remeasurement of undermeasured arable land reduces the undermeasurement and also reduces the UI.[22] (4) If the

---

[19] Henceforth national arable land excludes Hokkaidō in this chapter unless otherwise specified.

[20] It will be assumed that overmeasurement does not exist. Overmeasured land is one on which the UI is less than unity.

[21] Undermeasurement as used here is the difference between the true area and the registered area; that is, it is the numerical value of the undermeasurement.

[22] The change in UI is determined by the following equation:

$$UI' = \frac{T + dT}{A + dA}$$

where UI$'$ = the undermeasurement index following a change in T, A, or both;

A = registered area of all land classified as arable land;

dA = change in A;

T = true arable land area (A plus the actual undermeasurement of all arable land);

dT = change in T.

When there is no change in the true and registered arable land area, dA and dT are, of course, zero. When a deletion occurs the two variables

UI of the addition or deletion is equal to the national arable land UI, the national UI will remain unchanged. (5) If the UI of the addition is less, or the UI of the deletion is greater, than the national UI, the new national UI will be less than the old one. (6) If the UI of the addition is greater, or the UI of the deletion is less, than the national UI, the new UI will be greater than the original one.

As far as deletions are concerned, the probability is that the UI of a deletion was on the average equal to the national arable land UI at the time it occurred. Therefore, deletions caused a reduction of undermeasurement but tended not to affect the UI. The total deletions from arable land area in the 15-year period from 1926 through 1940 including Hokkaidō was 544 thousand chō.[23] Assuming that the rate at which deletions took place was about equal over the entire period, the total deletions would exceed 2.3 million chō.[24] If the average UI over this period was 1.06 for arable land about 140 thousand chō of undermeasurement would have been eliminated.[25]

If it is assumed that an addition to arable land area was undermeasured and that its UI was equal to the national arable land UI at the time it was made, then the undermeasurement would have increased but the UI would have remained constant. Additions to the arable land area in the 15-year period from 1926 to 1940 including Hokkaidō was 702 thousand chō.[26] Given the above assumptions and assuming further that the

---

are negative, and when an addition occurs, they are positive. The term T/A is the national arable land UI prior to a change, and the term dT/dA is the UI of the addition or deletion from the national arable land area. The accurate remeasurement of an inaccurately measured arable land is a special case of an addition to or deletion from the registered arable land area. The true area in these cases obviously remains unchanged.

[23] MAF Yearbook, Vols. 3-17.

[24] This figure probably overstates the deletions. Such forces as increasing urbanization, increasing population, and increasing need of land for public purposes were probably stronger in 1926-40 than the average for the period.

[25] The figure is based on tenuous assumptions and can only be taken as a rough guide to what the decline in undermeasurement might have been.

[26] MAF Yearbook, Vols. 3-17.

rate of addition remained constant in the 66-year period from 1890 to 1956, the total additions would have exceeded 3.0 million *chō* and the undermeasurement added would be about 180 thousand *chō*[27] (assuming the UI was 1.06). In this event taking additions and deletions together the net gain in undermeasurement would have been 40 thousand *chō* and the UI would have remained constant.

The assumption that the UI of additions tended to be equal to the national arable land UI appears reasonable on three grounds. First, since the prevailing sentiment was for tolerance of undermeasurement, officials probably made little effort to eliminate it from additions.[28] Second, tax equity and harmony in the village would have been better maintained if additions had been undermeasured by the same percentage as existing arable land. (Owing to village supervision of land surveys, within a village the UI of each field surveyed during the land surveys would have tended to be uniform.) Third, a uniform UI for all arable land and *takuchi* would help in avoiding complications in drafting maps of the lots within the village. In the absence of empirical data, further discussion seems fruitless.

The final type of change that could have significantly affected the arable land UI is accurate remeasurement of arable land. If such land had been previously undermeasured, accurate measurement would cause the cultivated land UI to decline.

The remeasurement of land whose classification did not change was required as a rule when land was being adjusted under the provisions of the Arable Land Adjustment Law passed in 1899 and revised in 1909.[29] The law made possible a more orderly arrangement of fields, irrigation ditches and ponds, drains, ridges and paths between fields, and roads, and a concomitant construction or reconstruction of irrigation and

[27] Footnote 25, p. 58, applies to this figure.

[28] The law states that whenever a land class change is made a remeasurement is legally required. It is assumed that the authorities were more interested in social justice and convenience than in the letter of the law.

[29] For a discussion of the provisions, objectives, and the accomplishments of the Arable Land Adjustment Laws, see Appendix B.

drainage works where improvement required it. Under its good offices conversion to arable land and reclamation of wasteland and undeveloped land also took place. Clearly, such a project required the accurate measurement of all land holdings so that redistribution of fields could be equitably achieved as long as the rights of more than one owner or cultivator were involved.[30] Where only one owner or cultivator was involved, measurement was not necessary because the periphery of the area being adjusted was known.

Where undermeasurement exists, the need for accurate measurement tends to be a deterrent to land adjustment since the tax benefits accruing from undermeasurement should then be lost. This deterrent was first removed by a prior law passed in 1897 which provided that "when the landowners of an entire city, town, or village, or any part thereof, should in union rationally adjust their fields, the total assessed value prior to the adjustment of the district involved shall be appropriately redistributed to the adjusted fields."[31] Because the assessed value of the district does not change regardless of whether accurate measurement had changed the recorded area, the tax burden remains the same. In 1909 the valuation provisions were made even more generous. An increase in arable land area up to 20 per cent by reclamation or other means was allowed without an increase in total land value of the district.[32]

There were powerful inducements for landowners to participate in land adjustment projects. Some of the more important benefits realized from adjustment were:[33] 1) increase in area of arable land and irrigated land; 2) increase in land productivity; 3) improvement of the drainage system; 4) better utilization

[30] Accurate measurement does not necessarily mean correct measurement in terms of some standard unit of measure. A unit of measure longer or shorter than the standard, if consistently applied, would achieve accurate measurement of each lot in the adjustment project relative to other lots, which is all that is required for equity within the adjustment project.

[31] *Hōritsu* 39 (March 30, 1897).

[32] Appendix B, pp. 205-206, 206n, 207n.

[33] Appendix B, pp. 209-211.

of water; 5) increase in land value; 6) greater availability of credit owing to increase in land value; 7) increase in labor productivity; 8) increased rent on leased land; 9) greater convenience and time saving in transportation; and 10) more frequent and efficient use of animals in cultivation.

From the beginning of 1900 to the end of 1940, a total of 34,529 projects (adjustment districts) were approved.[34] The total original registered area of the projects was 1,238,295 *chō*. After remeasurement the total registered area of the same districts was 1,303,335 *chō*, an increase of 65,040. If land adjustment had not been sought and remeasurement had not occurred, the registered area would have remained 1,238,295 *chō*, and the absolute undermeasurement of the area would have remained greater by 65,040 *chō*. However, we are concerned only with cultivated land. Because an independent estimate of the undermeasurement of cultivated land cannot be obtained it will be assumed that the degree of undermeasurement of cultivated land in the adjustment districts is about the same as that estimated for all land in the districts. The assumption is tenable in view of the fact that cultivated land constituted 87.7 per cent of land in these districts indicating that most of the undermeasurement was accounted for by cultivated land.[35] Given this assumption the absolute preadjustment undermeasurement of cultivated land in these districts was 57.0 thousand *chō* (87.7 per cent times 65,040 *chō*), which means that the UI was 1.056.

The UI of 1.056 which was removed by remeasurement from 1900 to 1940 is less than the 1.061 UI of 1956. This seems to indicate that the UI may have increased over time. But such a conclusion is not warranted inasmuch as undermeasurement apparently was not removed from all adjustment districts. In each of three prefectures—Miyagi, Saga, and Ōita Prefectures —where a total of 112 thousand *chō* were adjusted, the preadjustment and postadjustment areas are identical. In Fuku-

[34] *MAF Yearbook*, Vol. 17, p. 6. Okinawa and Hokkaidō are excluded.
[35] Of the 1,303,335 *chō* of land in the adjustment districts, 957,795 *chō* were paddy fields, 184,800 were upland fields, and 160,740 *chō* were roads, canals, dikes, etc. (*Ibid.*)

shima and Nagasaki Prefectures out of 62 thousand *chō* adjusted, the postadjustment areas were a minute 3 *chō* and 5 *chō* greater than the preadjustment areas.[36] If these prefectures had been free of undermeasurement, it is likely that the two areas would have been equal. Since each of these prefectures had above average UI in 1956,[37] it is not conceivable that they should have been free of undermeasurement from 1900 to 1940. It is possible that varying degrees of undermeasurement were permitted to remain in the adjustment districts in other prefectures.[38] If it is assumed that the undermeasurements were not removed in only the above five prefectures, and that the UI's of the adjustment districts in these prefectures were equal to their respective prefectural UI's, then the preadjustment UI of all adjustment districts would have been greater than 1.061.

Weighing the effect of the three types of change—deletions, additions, and reclassification—on the arable land UI, on balance it seems more likely that the UI tended to decline from 1890 to 1956. However, it will be conservatively assumed that the Crop Statistics Section values of 1.069 and 1.049 for paddy field and upland field UI's remained constant from the land survey of the 1880's to 1922.[39]

One further assumption in the discussion should be made

[36] *Ibid.*

[37] Statistical Appendix: Table 4.

[38] One of the reasons that undermeasurement might not have been removed in some of the readjustment districts was the objection of tenants who feared a rise in rent. Therefore, to obtain their cooperation in a project from which landowners, tenants, and the community could be expected to reap broad benefits, the landowners and the prefectural (or district) authorities might have agreed to retain the existing undermeasurement in the registered area of the adjusted land. It is known that tenant objections aborted attempts to undertake land adjustment. (*NN HS.*, Vol. 6, pp. 165ff.) One method of carrying out a land adjustment without eliminating the undermeasurement is to use a linear measure whose length is greater than the standard unit by the proportion represented by the UI of the land to be adjusted.

[39] If the UI had decreased—or increased—over time the effect on the growth rate of agricultural production would have been almost negligible. A 1% change in UI of paddy fields or upland fields would have changed the growth rate by less than 0.03%.

explicit: that is, the UI values given above exclude Hokkaidō. Since the undermeasurement in Hokkaidō is uncertain, it will be assumed here that the undermeasurement in that prefecture is identical to that in the rest of the nation.

Summary

Undermeasurement was not only tolerated, but actually constituted a tax alleviation device during the Tokugawa period. It was carried over into the Meiji era until an attempt was made to obtain accurate land records through the land tax reform of the 1870's. Although the cadastral survey of the 1870's and the resurvey of the 1880's eliminated most of the undermeasurement, a significant amount of undermeasurement persists to this day.

The main problem in this chapter was to obtain an index to correct the undermeasurement so that a more accurate measure of the area planted to crops could be obtained. The correction factors are 1.069 for paddy fields and 1.049 for upland fields. This means that the area planted indices for the two classes of arable land are to be increased by 6.9 and 4.9 per cent respectively for the two classes of land. It is assumed that the undermeasurement remained constant after the land survey of the 1880's to 1918-22.

One consequence of the revisions made in Chapters II and III is the construction of what is probably the most reliable series presently available on the area of paddy fields, dryland crop fields, and land planted to dryland crops.

CHAPTER 4

The Underreporting of Yield[1]

THE RELATIONSHIP between crop yield per *tan* and the tax liability is more complex than that between land area and tax liability, since yield changes from year to year whereas land area does not. Owing to this, yield was linked to tax liability in two ways. First, it was an important variable in determining the value of land during the cadastral survey of the 1870's. The landowners were motivated to underreport yield at that time since the lower the yield reports on a given field the lower its valuation would tend to be. The second link to tax liability is that landowners were led to believe that subsequent yield reports would affect land value. It is not certain that subsequent reports actually did so, but believing that they did landowners did have incentive to underreport village yields in years following the cadastral survey. One of the two purposes of this chapter is to validate the hypotheses that yield was underreported and that the degree of underreporting diminished over time. The other purpose is to obtain corrected indices of yield per *tan* for paddy rice and dryland crops.

There is greater opportunity for underreporting yield than land area. The latter is subject to an irrefutable check: remeasurement. But estimated yield is a less certain quantity. Since accurate official records were not kept as a rule, if a farmer or a village insisted that a certain yield was normal, the

[1] It is a noteworthy point that Japan offers an opportunity for correction of agricultural yield per unit area data that may not be duplicated elsewhere. It is most probable that underreporting similar to that which took place in Japan occurred in many other countries for the same reason; namely, to escape taxes. But Japan may be unique in having preserved records that could be used for estimating the actual yield per unit area of paddy rice. If this is so, it can be attributed to the singular importance of rice in Japan's diet and the relatively useful records that had to be kept due to the need to control supply and tax payments.

tax officials had little basis to refute it[2] except to refer to Tokugawa period records.[3] As for annual village production reports after the cadastral survey, they were submitted by village statistical reporters who were either village officials or leading farmers who regarded appointment to the post as an honor. If reflection of policies favorable to landowners was desired in statistical reports, it could be expected regardless of which of the two was responsible for the reports.

The Incentive to Underreport Yield

The village incentive to underreport yield was probably strongest in early Meiji. The incentive arose from the likelihood that land might be revalued with yield as one of the determinants of value. The prospect of revaluation was present from 1874, when an amendment to the Land Tax Revision Act of 1873 provided for a quinquennial revaluation of land beginning in 1880. Revaluation did not occur under the provisions of the 1874 amendment as the planned 1880 revaluation was postponed to 1885; and the quinquennial revaluation policy was abandoned by the enactment of the Land Tax Law of 1884, which stipulated that existing land values would not be changed except when land class changes occurred.[4] It is possible that some weakening of incentive occurred about this time.[5]

The abandonment of quinquennial land revaluations, however, did not mean that revaluations did not occur thereafter. Four arable land revaluations did take place under special legislation.[6] The final one came in 1898-99 following the passage of a revaluation bill which in one form or another had been introduced annually in the Diet since its establishment in 1890. Paddy field value was largely determined by three variables: the interest rate, the price of rice, and the yield per *tan*. Of these three the landowners had some control over

[2] *MZZKSS*, Vol. 7, p. 366.
[3] It is possible that most yield figures used for land valuation were Tokugawa period figures. (See pp. 73, 76n.)
[4] Appendix A, p. 192.
[5] See pp. 67, 82.   [6] Appendix A, pp. 194-95.

yield and very little, if any, over the other two. Because the arable land revaluations were not completed until 1898-99, the landowners' incentive to underreport yield probably persisted until around the turn of the century. Therefore, if underreporting did take place, it can reasonably be expected to have lasted to about that time.

Most of the discussion to follow will center on paddy rice yield, for which data are more plentiful and reliable than for other crops. The paddy rice yields based on government statistics appear in Table 4-1 as five-year averages for periods from 1878-82 to 1918-22. It will be argued that all of these averages are understatements of the actual yield with the possible exception of the 1918-22 figure of 1.927 *koku* per *tan*. Because of the importance of the 1918-22 yield it may be desirable to obtain an average based on a longer time period. Over the 11-year period from 1915 to 1925 the average was 1.894 *koku*[7] per *tan*, which is slightly less than the 1918-22 average. The two can be rounded off to 1.9 *koku*.

An extremely important document on early Meiji harvest reports and land valuation was an explanatory message from the Ministry of Finance to the Cabinet setting forth the reasons

[7] One *koku* is equal to 4.96 bushels.

TABLE 4-1

PADDY RICE YIELDS IN KOKU PER TAN BASED ON GOVERNMENT STATISTICS, FIVE-YEAR AVERAGES, 1878-1922

Period	Yield per *tan*	% change from previous period	Period	Yield per *tan*	% change from previous period
	(1)	(2)		(1)	(2)
1878-1882	1.166	–	1903-1907	1.626	7.2
1883-1887	1.297	11.2	1908-1912	1.734	6.6
1888-1892	1.428	10.1	1913-1917	1.843	6.3
1893-1897	1.371	−4.0	1918-1922	1.927	4.6
1898-1902	1.516	10.6			

SOURCE: Computed from Statistical Appendix: Table 5. The yield per *tan* for 1878 is from Ministry of Agriculture and Forestry, Agriculture and Forestry Economics Bureau, Statistics Section, *Nosakumotsu ruinen tōkeihyō: ine, 1881-1956* [Agricultural crop statistics: rice, 1881-1956] (Tokyo, 1957), p. 182.

for introducing a land revaluation bill to the 1892 Diet.[8] It states that landowners did not report full harvests during the cadastral survey of the 1870's. It further states that the need for revaluation arises in part from the differences in the under-statement of yield in the various prefectures. For this reason the Ministry of Finance sought an interprefectural adjustment of yields—an adjustment that would be accomplished solely by reducing the yield for land valuation purposes from the yield reported during the cadastral survey.[9] This document also states that factors that tend to increase yield have been almost nonexistent since the land tax reform.[10] The inference to be drawn from the document is that production was substantially understated during the cadastral survey and up to the time the document was issued in 1892.

Another clear statement on the underreporting of yield as a factor in the unreliability of Japanese agricultural statistics was made by Jikei Yokoi in an address to the Imperial Agricultural Association in 1914.[11] He said:[12]

> Although there are statistics in Japan, they cannot be relied upon. The reason is that the reporting standards were established when harvests were first surveyed. At that time the village office fearing that taxes would be excessive if the true harvest were reported, reduced the figure by several tenths. ... In succeeding years, harvest reports were based on and tended to vary around the original reported harvests. ... However, in recent years, particularly since the Russo-Japanese War (1904-1905) conditions appear to have changed, and now the farmers want harvests to show an increase. One reason for this is that if the harvests (output per *tan*) remain constant, it would be inconvenient in at-tempting to gauge the effectiveness of agricultural improve-ments. Another is that they simply wish to give reports they

[8] *MZZKSS*, Vol. 7, pp. 412-15.
[9] *Ibid.*, p. 414.
[10] *Ibid.*
[11] Jikei Yokoi, "Nōkai ni tsuite" [In regard to the agricultural association] *Teikoku nōkai hō*, IV, 4 (April 1914), pp. 1-10.
[12] *Ibid.*, p. 5.

can be proud of. In this fashion, the reported harvests have gradually increased.[13]

The inference that may be drawn from the above statement, substantiated by later comments, is that the reported production was increasing at a faster rate than the actual production. The reliability of Yokoi's statement—which, if not true, is slanderous—cannot be seriously questioned because it was carried in the official organ of the Imperial Agricultural Association. An English observer of rural Japan, J. W. Robertson Scott, noted in 1915-16 that rice production was underreported. He states,[14] ". . . The statistics show a production 15 per cent less than the actual harvest. Formerly the underestimation was 20 per cent. The practice has its origin in the old taxation system." Because precise yields are not necessary if records are to be falsified, the percentages quoted are probably very crude. It is reasonable to infer from the statement, however, that underreporting of yield per *tan* of paddy rice persisted well into the twentieth century.

Table 4-1 is interesting and enlightening in view of the Finance Ministry message to the Cabinet and what Yokoi and Robertson Scott reported. The 11.2 and 10.1 per cent increases in the first two five-year periods show the more accurate reporting of yield that occurred in the second half of the 1880's which raised reported yields sharply.[15] The decline in yield from 1888-92 to 1893-97 may be at least partially a response to an expectation that a major interprefectural land value adjustment would occur soon, as indeed it did in 1898-99. This expectation would tend to motivate prefectures to lower prefectural yield data or to maintain them at low levels. With assurance that land re-

---

[13] It is clear that the survey mentioned refers to the cadastral survey of the 1870's. The implication of the statement about why harvest reports were reduced is that since other villages can be expected to underreport their harvests, failure to underreport would invite excessive taxes. "Several tenths" is my translation of *nan wari*.

[14] J. W. Robertson Scott, *The Foundations of Japan* (London, 1922), p. 87.

[15] For reasons why statistical reporting became more accurate see pp. 80-82.

valuation would not occur again, yield reports rose around the turn of the century. The rise from 1893-97 to 1898-1902 is about equivalent to the increase in the first two periods. But the 10.6 per cent rise in this five-year period should be adjusted for the 4.0 per cent decline that occurred in the previous period. Then we find that the ten-year change from 1888-1892 to 1898-1902 was 6.2 per cent; this makes the average five-year change 3.1 per cent which is lower than any of the other positive five-year changes. In the next five-year period, the increase jumps to 7.2 per cent; in each succeeding period a small relative decline takes place. An interesting feature of the changes in the five-year periods from 1898-1902 to 1913-1917 is that the absolute increases are successively 0.110, 0.108, and 0.109 *koku*, which may be a coincidence, but which may also have been the result of an attempt to raise average yields by about the same absolute amounts. The percentage decline in yields occurred despite greater proportional increases in fertilizer use in the later periods.[16] The greater absolute and relative decline in yield from 1913-17 to 1918-22 may mean that the reported yield had finally caught up with the actual yield by the latter five-year period. We cannot prove by irrefutable logic that tax incentive for underreporting of yield had disappeared by this time, but the evidence presented and those to be presented below indicate that underreporting had become negligible by the end of World War I.

Government Concessions on Yield Reports

The above accounts seem to show that the villages in most cases successfully thwarted government attempts to obtain accurate harvest reports during the cadastral survey of the 1870's. In reality the government seems not to have resisted a downward adjustment of the yield. The adjustment resulted from a global revenue target established by the government for the nation as a whole. The total burden was apportioned to the prefectures which in turn apportioned their shares to the cities and villages.[17] The global target appears to have been

[16] For the trend in fertilizer consumption see Table 4-2, p. 83.

[17] Ario, *op.cit.*, pp. 52-53, 78-100. Also see Takeo Ono, *Meiji zenki tochi seido shiron* [Treatise on early Meiji land system] (Tokyo, 1948),

a fixed money revenue.[18] For paddy fields the government anticipated an average per *tan*[19] value of around 40.80 yen or a per *tan* revenue of 1.22 yen. This was based on an expected average paddy rice yield of 1.6 *koku* of rice per *tan*, an average rice price of 3 yen per *koku*, an interest rate of 6 per cent and certain other conditions.[20] For land valuation purposes the interest rate did average around 6 per cent[21] because the government established this figure as the norm. The price of rice, however, averaged 4.185 yen[22] which is nearly 40 per cent greater than 3 yen. With this change, if the yield averaged 1.6 *koku*, the land value would have risen to about 57 yen per *tan*; or if the land value was maintained at 40.80 yen, the yield would have had to drop to 1.14 *koku* per *tan*.[23] It is probable that the government would have preferred to raise the money revenue target as prices rose, but it may have found a full adjustment politically infeasible at the time. What occurred in reality was that the assessed value ended higher and the yield lower than expected. In 1881 the value averaged 46.37 yen per *tan*,[24] which was 14 per cent more than the original per *tan* value target of 40.80 yen. It follows that the yield per *tan* had

p. 95. To obtain brief descriptions of how different prefectures determined the average yield of a village, see *ibid.*, pp. 86-95.

[18] Ario, *op.cit.*, p. 52. The anticipated revenue shown in one document is 33.5 million yen against a pre-revision revenue of 37.4 million. (*MZZKSS*, Vol. 7, p. 346). The pre-revision revenue was primarily a tax in kind, in which case, the money value is a conversion at the prevailing price of rice. By pre-revision revenue is meant Meiji government revenue before the tax revision.

[19] I work with per *tan* values rather than totals because totals are dependent on land area which was not a reliable figure.

[20] Ario, *op.cit.*, p. 53. For details on how to compute the land values see Appendix A, pp. 187-91.

[21] The rates for the various prefectures and districts within prefectures varied closely around 6% with many prefectures reporting a flat 6% rate. (*MZZKSS*, Vol. 7, Appendices 7, 8, pp. 442ff.)

[22] *MZS*, Vol. 5, p. 373.

[23] The relationship between the three variables can be expressed by the following equation: $V = kQP$ where V = land value; Q = yield; P = price; and k = constant coefficient when the interest rate and other relevant values are given. (*Ibid.*, pp. 345-46.)

[24] Computed from *Tōkei nenkan*, Vol. 2, p. 13.

to be about 19 per cent less than the expected yield, or about 1.3 *koku* per *tan* assuming a constant interest rate. The land valuation yield appears to have averaged 1.32 *koku* per *tan*.[25] It probably was no accident that the per *tan* value of paddy fields after the four revaluations was 40.01 yen, which is close to the original land value target of 40.80 yen per *tan* for paddy fields.

One indirect evidence that farmers reacted to the legal stipulation that land would be revalued each quinquennium is the reported yields for the six-year period from 1879 to 1884. It has been noted that the land valuation yield was around 1.3 *koku* per *tan*, which we argued was an understatement of the actual yield. In the above six-year period, the yield in each year was less than 1.25 *koku* per *tan*, and from 1880 and 1884, the yield in each case was less than 1.2 *koku*. In fact the range in the six-year period was 1.249 in 1879 to 1.047 in 1884, a difference of 0.202 *koku*. In the five-year period from 1880 to 1884, the difference between the highest and lowest figures was 0.176 *koku*.[26] These figures are remarkable because on the face they indicate six persisting years of poor crops and an unusual stability in yield. However, the reported yields are not consistent with the historical evidence assembled by Benjiro Nakazawa from various sources. The reported paddy rice yields and descriptions of harvest conditions for a period of ten years are shown below.[27]

Since the historical descriptions are necessarily subjective, translations of the terminology used cannot be precise. However, my translations representing the best to the poorest crops

[25] Hideichi Horie, "The Agricultural Structure of Japan in Meiji Restoration," *Kyoto University Economic Review*, XXXI, 2 (October 1961), 15.

[26] The yield data are from Statistical Appendix: Table 5.

[27] The reported yields are from Statistical Appendix: Table 5. The harvest descriptions are taken from Benjiro Nakazawa, *Nihon beika hendō shi* [History of fluctuations in Japan's rice price] (Tokyo, 1933), pp. 301, 305, 309, 313, 317, 321, 325, 329, 333, 337. The yield for 1878 according to one source (*NRTHI*, p. 182) is 1.015 *koku* per *tan* and it is reported by Nakazawa as a poor crop. Since this yield is based on incomplete crop reports, it was not included in the above list.

Year	Reported yield	Harvest description
1879	1.249	Bumper crop; best in 30 years
1880	1.223	Bumper crop
1881	1.169	Normal to poor crop
1882	1.173	Good crop
1883	1.177	Normal crop (?)
1884	1.047	Seriously bad crop; rare in recent times
1885	1.312	Good crop
1886	1.426	Bumper crop
1887	1.526	Normal crop
1888	1.444	Good crop

can be ranked in the following order: bumper, good, normal, poor, bad. We have two extreme cases in the ten-year period—the bumper crop in 1879, and the bad crop in 1884. It is a remarkable fact that the bumper crop reported to be the best in 30 years is less than the land valuation yield of 1.32 *koku* per *tan*, which it is being argued is also an understatement. The total yield difference between the bumper and bad crop is 0.202 *koku* per *tan* as we have seen. Then interestingly, a normal crop in 1887 is 0.277 *koku* greater than an extremely unusual bumper crop of nine years previously. Furthermore, the normal crop of 1887 is exactly 0.1 *koku* greater than the bumper crop of 1886. Nakazawa reports the 1887 crop to have been 10 per cent less than the 1886 crop, which supports the qualitative description.[28] An examination of Figure 4-1 (p. 81) shows that the yields during the six years from 1879 to 1884 were unusually stable compared to later dates. Since seed improvements, fertilizer use, and improved farming techniques have tended to cause fluctuations in yield to decline over time, the existence of a high degree of stability at this time is suspect. The inconsistencies that have been pointed out are only explicable if it is assumed that the villages were underreporting yield at this time, and it was felt that they could not very well reduce the yields to ridiculously low levels as would have been required if the yields in poor crop years were reduced in proportion to the actual decline in production.

The evidence presented above indicates that the government

[28] Nakazawa, *op.cit.*, p. 337.

did not obtain accurate yield estimates during the cadastral survey because it had little basis to refute low village estimates except the available Tokugawa period yields which may have averaged around 1.3 *koku* per *tan*. Furthermore, the establishment of a global money revenue target by the government coupled with the advent of inflation probably helped the government to accept more gracefully a lower land valuation yield, since the revenue target could be met despite a reduced yield estimate.[29] The fact that the land valuation yield was revised downward during the interprefectural land value adjustment of 1898-99[30] is further evidence that the government regarded the land valuation yield as a nominal figure rather than one that revealed the actual yield.

The yield continued to be underreported by the villages after the cadastral survey for fear that accurate reporting would cause an upward revaluation of village land. The expectation of revaluation persisted until 1898. From around that time, however, the underreporting apparently declined; that is, the ratio of reported yield to actual yield increased.

For convenience, government policy on land valuation has been discussed in terms of paddy field valuation. However, the same general statements can be made about upland fields as about paddy fields with one qualification: upland field valuation was regarded as relatively less important than paddy field valuation and even less precision was demanded in determining the yield. For example, despite the widespread practice of multiple cropping, the yield of upland fields was taken to be that of one principal crop.[31]

Evaluation of Yield Reports

Another approach to the question of whether the reported yields were an understatement is to obtain actual yield reports that are independent of officially reported yields. This is true

[29] Kunio Niwa strongly argues that the farmers and the government adjusted the yield for land valuation purpose to the revenue target of the government. (*Op.cit.*, pp. 427-29.) See also Ono, *Meiji zenki tochi seido shiron, op.cit.*, pp. 95-98.

[30] See pp. 194-95. See also *MZS*, Vol. 5, pp. 663-64.

[31] *MZZKSS*, Vol. 7, p. 340.

for the Tokugawa period as well as for the Meiji era, as underreporting appears to have been practiced successfully in that
time also. The following three sets of data are relevant: (1)
yield in early Meiji; (2) yield in late Tokugawa; and (3) yield
in earlier periods if yield tended to increase over time, or the
trend in yield was known.

A number of studies are available that have attempted to
obtain actual yields. For early Meiji the best of these may be
the cost-of-production surveys conducted during the Matsukata
deflation of the 1880's which severely depressed the agricultural sector. For example, average paddy rice yields of 1.619,
2.546, and 2.5 *koku* per *tan* were reported, respectively, in
villages in Niigata (1884-89) and Tokyo (1890) Prefectures
and in the Kofu valley of Yamanashi Prefecture.[32] Over the
same years the officially reported yields in the above prefectures were 1.256, 1.633, and 1.364 *koku* per *tan*, respectively.[33]
A study of rent burdens in 48 communities in various parts of
Japan showed an average yield on medium grade paddy fields
of 1.871 *koku* per *tan* toward the end of the Tokugawa period.[34]
The above are a small sampling of the kind of data that may be

[32] Takeo Ono, *Nōson shi* [History of rural Japan] (Tokyo, 1941), pp.
116, 119, 121.
[33] *NRTHI*, relevant pages.
[34] Moritarō Yamada, *Nihon shihon shugi bunseki* [An analysis of
Japanese capitalism] (7th edn., Tokyo, 1955), p. 187.

Underreporting of cultivated land area and yield is also shown for the
Tokugawa period in an admirable study of Chiaraijima Village, Musashi
Province (present Aichi Prefecture) by William J. Chambliss, *Chiaraijima
Village: Land Tenure, Taxation, Local Trade, 1818-1884* (Tucson, Ariz.,
1965).
Some apparent points of inconsistency exist between Chambliss' study
and mine. Only one of these points will be noted here. Whereas I argue
that underreporting of yield persisted in the nation until around 1900,
Chambliss argues that in Chiaraijima Village yields may have been accurately reported during the cadastral survey (pp. 83-86). The two
views are, of course, not necessarily inconsistent, since my argument
applies to the national average reported yield and his to a specific village. Moreover, from the author's description, it is clear that the village
was not representative of most villages in the nation in that the level of
taxation was unusually low in the Tokugawa period (pp. 80-82) and
opportunities to obtain income from other sources were more plentiful
(pp. 15-25).

found. They are, of course, scattered data and cannot be regarded as conclusive. They are, nonetheless, suggestive.

Earlier records of paddy rice yields also exist. Curiously, the reported yield in each of three widely separated periods in Japan—Kamakura period (1191-1333), Bunroku era (1592-1596), and Jōkyō era (1684-1688)—was the same; 1.3 *koku* per *tan* for medium grade paddy fields,[35] which can be assumed to be the average for all fields. This unanimity seems to indicate that land productivity had remained constant for around 400 years. However, the yield per *tan* remained constant only because the defined area of the *tan* had decreased over time—the Kamakura *tan* was 20 per cent greater and the Bunroku *tan* 10.25 per cent greater than the Jōkyō *tan* which is equal to the modern *tan*. The capacity of the *koku* has remained almost constant after a change in the Kamakura period.[36]

The meaning of the nominal constancy of yield per *tan* apparently is that Japan, like any traditional society almost entirely dependent on agriculture for her basic needs, has maintained policies which have allowed the average family unit to have sufficient land to pay taxes and feed itself. The area so determined can be assumed to have been known as one *chō* consisting roughly of equal shares of paddy and upland fields, and it was believed necessary that paddy fields average 1.3 *koku* of rice per *tan* for the family to carry out its obligations. As land productivity rose, the actual area of the *chō* decreased in the years noted.[37]

It is probable that the yields in all three periods were those determined by cadastral surveys. This was the case in the Bunroku era.[38] The establishment of yields of 1.3 *koku* per

[35] *DNSS*, Vol. 2, pp. 248, 267, 283.

[36] Actually the dimensions of the *tan* and the capacity of the *koku* often differed in different prefectures. The Kamakura period *koku* appears to have varied from 49.32 to 98.63% of the modern *koku*. Keigo Hōgetsu, *Chūsei ryōseishi no kenkyū* [A study of the feudal weight system] (Tokyo, 1961), p. 103. It is certain that the Kamakura *koku* used in establishing the 1.3 *koku* yield per *tan* as the average for medium grade fields was very close in capacity to the modern *koku*.

[37] The Malthusian process appears to have been operating to decrease the real size of family holdings as the productivity of land increased.

[38] See p. 78.

nominal *tan* in each of the three periods suggests that wide-spread cadastral surveys had occurred to establish new bases for land taxation. Instead of keeping the *tan* constant as would be usual, the authorities kept the yield constant and changed the defined area of the *tan*.[39]

Using modern *tan* units, the average yield of all grades of paddy fields in each period are shown below.[40] There are no national per *tan* yield records to show what the increase was after the 1680's. However, according to recent studies in this field, a gradual but very substantial increase occurred in paddy field output per *tan* in the 200 years following the Jōkyō era. Thomas C. Smith has summed up this view as follows:[41]

> . . . Japanese agriculture . . . underwent notable technological (though not mechanical) changes long before the modern period. Between 1600 and 1850 a complex of such changes greatly increased the productivity of land. . .
>
> . . . Most resulted from the spread of known techniques from the localities in which they had been developed to areas where they were previously unknown or unused.

He states that the increasing publication of technical treatises had led to the exchange and diffusion of agricultural innova-

[39] Another possible reason for the Meiji land valuation yield of about 1.3 *koku* may be noted. Could it have been that the villages and the government, lacking a firm basis for agreeing on a particular yield, compromised on time-honored Tokugawa yields in most villages thus deriving the above average for the nation?

[40] It is assumed that the defined capacity of the *koku* was identical in all three periods, but that the Kamakura *tan* was 20% greater and the Bunroku *tan* 10% greater than the modern *tan*.

Period	Yield per modern tan
Kamakura period (1191-1333)	1.08 *koku*
Bunroku era (1592-1596)	1.18 *koku*
Jōkyō era (1684-1688)	1.30 *koku*

[41] Thomas C. Smith, *Agrarian Origins of Modern Japan, op.cit.*, p. 87. The outstanding authority on Tokugawa agricultural developments, Toshio Furushima, has done some of the most important studies on technical change and agricultural productivity. See, for example, his *Kinsei nihon nōgyō no tenkai, op.cit.*, which collects a number of studies under one cover.

tions.[42] For example, commercial fertilizers, which were probably the most important of all innovations in raising yields, had become supplements to natural fertilizers almost everywhere by the nineteenth century. There had also occurred an enormous increase in rice plant varieties and a widespread awareness of their existence.

There are other evidences of growing agricultural land productivity including the following: increased production of industrial crops; accelerated development of rural industries;[43] growth of urban centers and castle towns;[44] the development of an extensive network of trade; and an amazingly high level of literacy.[45] Because Japan's population and arable land area remained roughly constant from around the beginning of the eighteenth century to the middle of the nineteenth century, the above trends imply that rural workers were being released from the production of food and that per capita income was rising in Japan.

If yield per *tan* continued to rise as argued and if the Bunroku and Jōkyō yields are accurate, the official yield of 1878-82 of 1.166 *koku* per *tan* must be an understatement, since this is somewhat less than the Bunroku yield of almost 300 years previously. On the other hand, if the Meiji yields are accurate, then the earlier yields overstate productivity. There appear to be good grounds for the belief that the pre-Meiji yields are accurate.

One basis for belief that the reported pre-Meiji yields approximated the actual yield is that the reports were based on actual sampling of fields. The sampling took place under the surveillance of a highly skilled specialist—a tax official who was trained from childhood for his function of appraising harvests and the productivity of fields.[46] He was also responsible

[42] Smith, *Agrarian Origins of Modern Japan, op.cit.*, pp. 87ff.

[43] E. S. Crawcour, "Changes in Japanese Commerce in the Tokugawa Period," *Journal of Asian Studies*, XXII, 4 (August 1963), 397.

[44] John W. Hall, "The Castle Town and Japan's Modern Urbanization," *Far Eastern Quarterly*, XV, 1 (November 1955), 47.

[45] Herbert Passin, *Society and Education in Japan* (New York, 1965), p. 47, places male literacy at 40-50% by the end of the Tokugawa period.

[46] *MZS*, Vol. 5, pp. 394-95.

to the shogunate, not to the village. The standard sampling procedure[47] was to obtain the harvest in brown rice measure from sampling lots one *tsubo* in area which is equal to one part in 3,000 parts of the *chō*.

There are reasons for particular confidence in the Bunroku yield. It was published in 1595,[48] well toward the end of the cadastral survey which began in 1583 and ended in 1598,[49] which indicates that most of the surveying had been completed before the yield was determined. Moreover, special attention was directed to obtaining accurate returns, and it is reported that the threat of crucifixion and other forms of capital punishment hung over those who falsified returns.[50] On the other hand, the government probably would not have dared to be less than fair in setting yield schedules to grade land owing to strong peasant resentment of the survey. The last observation applies equally to the Kamakura and Jōkyō yields.

In the century following the Bunroku era surveys, the peace and order imposed by the Tokugawa shogunate could have been expected to raise yields. The very rapid building up of the major population centers, particularly Edo (Tokyo), and of the castle towns indicates that agricultural productivity had to rise very substantially by the Genroku period (1688-1703) when the Tokugawa period may have reached its highest cultural level. Without such a rise in productivity, rural labor could not have been released for employment in the cities and towns.

Scattered yields are available for the period after the Jōkyō era. A document written in the Meiwa era (1764-1772) records paddy rice yields in villages of average productivity in Chikuzen Province (part of the present Fukuoka Prefecture). For superior grade fields, the average yield is recorded as 1.818 *koku* per *tan*; for medium grade, 1.515; for inferior grade, 1.212; and for very inferior grade, 0.909.[51] Averaging the four

[47] Andō, *op.cit.*, pp. 212-25.   [48] *DNSS*, Vol. 1, p. 235.

[49] George Sansom, *A History of Japan, 1334-1615* (Stanford, 1961), p. 316.

[50] *Ibid.*, pp. 316-19.

[51] Takeo Ono, ed., *Kinsei jikata keizai shiryō* [Provincial economic

gives a yield of 1.363 *koku*. Whether this is the true average depends on the relative areas of the various grade fields, which are not given. It is possible that the yield of the medium grade field—because medium suggests average—is a better approximation of the average for the province. Given a probable rise in yield in the next 100 years, whether the actual Meiwa yields were 1.363 *koku*, 1.515, or any intermediate figure, the actual Chikuzen average in 1878-82 would have been considerably greater than the national average of 1.166 in 1878-82 or the Fukuoka Prefecture average of 1.287 in 1881-85. Furthermore, because the Meiwa data are taken from official records, it is possible that they understate yield.[52]

Studies of family records (which are more likely to be accurate than official records) by Toshio Furushima show yields much in excess of 1.166 *koku*. The journal of the Imanishi family of Kawachi Province (the present Osaka Prefecture) shows paddy rice yields averaging 2.31 *koku* in the 15-year period from 1798 to 1812.[53] The average officially reported yield per *tan* in Osaka Prefecture in 1881-85 was 1.496 *koku*.[54] This family also rented 31.721 *tan* of paddy fields, all of which pro-

---

materials of the Tokugawa period] (10 vols., Tokyo, 1932), Vol. 1, p. 174.

Arable land was divided into more than three grades of land depending on the province and the period.

[52] Understatement of area and yield in the leased holdings of one landlord in Kawachi Province (part of the present Osaka Prefecture) is revealed by a comparison of official village records and data in the family journal. The time is around 1850. The officially recorded leased area was 37.464 *tan*. The area from which rent was collected as revealed in the journal was 52.731 *tan* which can be taken as the probable true area. The undermeasurement index is 1.41. The *kokudaka*—the officially recorded yield for tax purposes—was 60.862 *koku*, making the official yield per *tan* 1.625 *koku*. Although the total production of the leased area is not given, the rent expressed as *koku* of rice is given. This was 86.141 *koku*, 42% higher than the official yield. Dividing this by the probable true area gives a per *tan* rent of 1.634 *koku*, which is more than the official yield per *tan*. The true yield per *tan* must obviously be considerably greater than the rent; a possible minimum may be 2.5 *koku*. (Basic data taken from Furushima, p. 535, Table 35.)

[53] *Ibid.*, p. 345, Table 2.

[54] Computed from *NRTHI*, p. 58.

duced one crop per year. The annual production is not given but the rent was 39.715 *koku*,[55] which on a per *tan* basis is 1.25 *koku*. The yield per *tan* probably was about the same as for fields farmed by the family; that is, about 2.31 *koku*. Furushima also estimates (with extreme reservation because of limited data) that the rent on one-crop paddy fields in the northeastern part of Honshu was 0.8 to 0.9 *koku* in the Tokugawa period.[56] If this is correct, the average actual yield in that area could hardly have been less than 1.5 *koku* per *tan*.

Since government statistics are being questioned, it is necessary to examine them to see whether the reported yield changes are consistent with our hypothesis. The annual yield[57] and a five-year moving average are shown in Figure 4-1. In the early 1880's, the average yield was less than 1.2 *koku* per *tan*; in fact, the annual yield tends to decline from 1879 to 1884. A sharp rise occurs in the late 1880's, and then the average yield remains roughly constant until about the turn of the century from which time the yield climbs fairly steeply until another plateau is reached about 20 years later.

Without other evidence the observed plateaus and rises in reported yield can perhaps be regarded as typical of the kind of changes that occur in agricultural production. It has been observed, however, that the incentive to underreport weakened around the turn of the century when the 20-year rise in yield commences. It is also known that Yokoi stated that the villages tended to inflate the increases from around the time of the Russo-Japanese War (1904-1905).

One probable reason for the sharp rise in the reported paddy rice production per *tan* of about 20 per cent that occurred in the late 1880's is the establishment of new statistical regulations, procedures, forms, and detailed instructions by the

[55] Furushima, *op.cit.*, p. 352, Table 7.

[56] *Ibid.*, p. 522.

[57] The annual national yield was computed by dividing the reported total harvest by the reported area planted to the crop. The village harvest is the product of the estimated village yield per unit area and the estimated area planted to the crop in the village; the sum of the village harvests is the national harvest.

FIGURE 4-1

REPORTED PADDY RICE YIELD, 1878-1942, FIVE-YEAR MOVING AVERAGE,
AND REVISED PADDY RICE YIELD

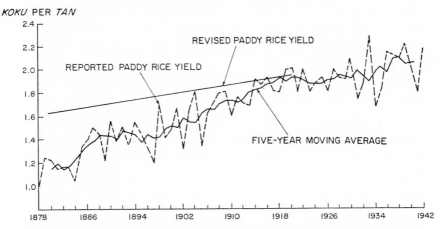

SOURCES: Reported paddy rice yield from Ministry of Agriculture and
Forestry Economics Bureau, Statistics Section, *Nōsakumotsu
ruinen tōkeihyō: ine, 1881-1956* [Agricultural crop statistics:
rice, 1881-1956] (Tokyo, 1957), p. 182, for 1878 yield. All
others from Statistical Appendix: Table 5.
Revised paddy rice yield from Table 4-3, p. 92.

Ministry of Agriculture and Commerce from 1883 to 1886,[58]
following the creation of the Ministry in 1881. In 1884, statistical forms were standardized, much more detailed instructions
were issued on the collection of statistics, and more comprehensive surveys of the most important crops were directed.
For example, information sought on rice included the area
planted, production, planting and harvesting dates, and area
of damaged crops. In 1886, instructions were issued for pre-
harvest reports on growing conditions (including the effects of
the weather and pests), expected harvest, and expected devia-
tion from the normal harvest of rice, wheat, barley, naked
barley, tea, cotton, and rapeseed. A second reason for the sharp
rise probably was the greater importance placed on reliable
statistics at this time, as is evident from the care put into their

[58] The basic authority was given in the *Nōshōmushō tasshi 21* (December 28, 1883) whose descriptive designation is *Nōshōmushō tsūshin kisoku*
[Statistical regulations of the Ministry of Agriculture and Commerce].

collection. This view of statistics was at least partially related to the depression of the 1880's when the suffering of farmers and other segments of the population drew much attention. A final reason that may be mentioned is the abandonment in 1884 of the policy to revalue land every five years, which may have caused a temporary weakening of the incentive to under-report.

In 1889 the instructions for pre-harvest reports were abolished. That was also the year when the first interprefectural revaluation occurred and about the time the farm sector had emerged from the depression. Probably due to these reasons the need for reliable statistics appears to have faded around that time, and for the next decade the yield is observed to remain almost constant. In the 1890's Japan became a food-importing nation, and once again she became conscious of the need for reliable statistical reports. The second and final interprefectural arable land revaluation occurred in 1898-99. It was also about this time that the yield per *tan* started the 20-year rise.

Doubt is cast upon the argument being developed here by two articles[59] which explain the rapid growth of agricultural production in the Meiji era by reference to three technical factors: the more intensive use of fertilizers, particularly commercial fertilizers; the improvement of seeds; and the diffusion of farming techniques through experienced farmers. Of these, the intensive use of fertilizers is regarded as by far the most important cause of increased per *tan* yield of rice. It will be argued here that the above factors could not have been as effective as previously believed.

Gains from fertilizers are both observable and calculable to the cultivator. A direct relationship may usually be noted between the quantity of fertilizers used and the yield per unit area. If the relationship held true in Japan—and it did as a

[59] Bruce F. Johnston, "Agricultural Development and Economic Transformation: A Comparative Study of the Japanese Experience," *Food Research Institute Studies*, III, 3 (November 1962), 223-276; and R. P. Dore, "Agricultural Improvement in Japan, 1870-1900," *Economic Development and Cultural Change*, IX, 1 (October 1960), 69-91.

rule—fertilizers could hardly have been a significant factor in the reported production increases before 1905. Table 4-2 shows average five-year changes in fertilizer consumption.

TABLE 4-2

TREND OF FERTILIZER CONSUMPTION, FIVE-YEAR AVERAGES,
1883-1932

Period	Value in 1934-36 prices million yen	Index 1883-87=100	% change from previous period
	(1)	(2)	(3)
1883-1887	212.0	100.0	–
1888-1892	218.8	103.2	3.2
1893-1897	231.9	109.4	6.0
1898-1902	248.2	117.1	7.0
1903-1907	270.5	127.6	9.0
1908-1912	322.6	152.2	19.3
1913-1917	362.2	170.8	12.3
1918-1922	410.4	193.6	13.3
1923-1927	451.9	213.2	10.1
1928-1932	516.0	243.4	14.2

SOURCE: Yūjirō Hayami, "Hiryō tōka ryō no suikei" [Fertilizer consumption estimates], Nōgyō Sōgō Kenkyū, XVII, 1 (January 1963), 253.

Commercial fertilizers constituted less than 15 per cent of total fertilizers used in the nineteenth century,[60] and self-supplied fertilizers, therefore, constituted more than 85 per cent. The fact that the latter made up the bulk of all fertilizers requires caution in the use of Table 4-2 because rather risky assumptions necessarily had to be made in estimating their value.

Column (3) of Table 4-2 reveals that the percentage increase in the use of fertilizers climbed steadily from 3 per cent to 9 per cent from period to period through 1903-07. Then a very sharp increase to 19 per cent occurs after which increases drop to 12 and 13 per cent. What is clear is that increases in fertilizer use were greater after 1903-07 than before. In contrast to this, Column (2) of Table 4-1 (p. 66) shows percentage increases

[60] Computed from Yūjirō Hayami, "Hiryō tōka ryō no suikei" [Fertilizer consumption estimates], Nōgyō Sōgō Kenkyū, XVII, 1 (January 1963), 253.

in paddy rice yield to be substantially higher prior to 1903-07. Greater increases could have been expected after this period on the basis of the trend in fertilizer consumption, yet Table 4-1 shows an almost unbroken decline in the percentage increase of paddy rice yield from 1878-82 to 1918-22. Furthermore, most of the increase in fertilizer use was applied to specialty crops such as mulberries instead of to rice and other staple foods.

It is possible that small initial applications of a particular fertilizer could have caused high percentage increases of production if a severe deficiency of a particular plant nutrient had existed. The highly efficient use of fertilizer implied by such a response could not have been possible in Meiji Japan. Such a response assumes widespread and severe deficiencies of particular fertilizers, modern methods of soil analysis, and almost exclusive application of the deficient fertilizer. Since Japan had a long history of fertilizer use and almost all that was used in early Meiji was organic fertilizer, a deficiency of a particular plant nutrient was most unlikely. Even if such a deficiency had existed, since modern soil analysis methods were unknown, the deficiency could hardly have been pinpointed so that the most efficient use of fertilizer could be achieved.

Benefits from seed improvement are much more difficult to determine than gains from fertilizers. Seed improvement can mean any of a number of changes, the two most important of which are increase in yield per unit area and betterment of quality. The latter is an intangible, and even the former is difficult to gauge. Although a new seed may be shown to yield a given per cent more rice per *tan* than another under experimental conditions, its performance in the field can be quite different. Even if it lives up to expectations, it may in time succumb to a new disease or a mutant form of an old one. Or again, it may flourish in a given locality only until diseases that attack it become prevalent there.

Although seed improvement is difficult to measure, it is now a commonplace that application of scientific principles and methods has tended to accelerate the development of desired varieties. During the Tokugawa period when the search for more and better seeds went on widely,[61] the principles of genetics were unknown and the appearance of a new variety was the result of a fortuitous variation of a plant that an observant cultivator set aside for seed. Mendelian principles were applied to plant breeding in the government experimental stations around 1910, about a decade after their introduction in Japan.[62] Intensive experimental work on seed improvement did not start until the Taishō era (1912-1926). By that time prefectural experimental stations had also matured and much of the selective breeding, which was the most important accomplishment of the era, was undertaken by them.[63] Beginning about 1925, the stress shifted to crossbreeding. This led to the development of many superior varieties of rice; most of these being notable for their heavy yield.[64]

It is hardly necessary to discuss the role of experienced farmers in raising land productivity. Their role in raising yield per *tan* had to be almost entirely through bringing to the attention of other farmers the benefits of fertilizers and new, improved seeds. Since fertilizer use and seed improvement have already been discussed, it is not necessary to repeat the discussion here. One observation may be made, however. The use of experienced farmers to educate other farmers was a continuation of a Tokugawa practice of diffusing techniques used by farmers who obtained superior results.[65] These results were obtained usually by exceptional circumstances of soil, location, or sheer diligence by the farmer, or some combination of the three. Applied under different circumstances and with less care and effort, the results could have been detrimental. One of the critics of indiscriminate use of experienced farmers

[61] Smith, *Agrarian Origins of Modern Japan, op.cit.*, pp. 94-95. Because a given seed tends to become less productive in a locality over time, it is desirable to have a continual stream of new improved seeds being developed.

[62] *NNHS*, Vol. 2, p. 438. Agricultural experimental stations as we know of them today were established in 1893. However, embryonic experimental stations did exist earlier in various prefectures. Their contribution is believed to have been negligible. (*NNHS*, Vol. 3, p. 256.)

[63] *Ibid.*, Vol. 9, pp. 85-103.

[64] *Ibid.*, pp. 109-11.   [65] Ono, *Nōson shi, op.cit.*, p. 201.

was Finance Minister Matsukata (later Prime Minister) who deplored the absence of theory in their instructions.[66]

Another technical reason to believe that agricultural production tended to increase slowly is that Japan was primarily an innovator in respect to improvement in the agricultural sector. This contrasts strongly with the modern manufacturing sector where Japan was an avid imitator in adopting Western industrial techniques imported from abroad and which made possible a high rate of growth in that sector. Japan did not find most Western agricultural techniques suitable to her needs because they were adapted to dryland or large-scale farming. She needed techniques suited to her type of small-scale farming where particular interest has always been placed on increasing the productivity of paddy fields. Lacking models to follow, Japan could have been expected to go through a relatively slow and labored growth which is the usual lot of innovators in production.[67]

Some conclusions can be drawn about the impact of technical factors on agricultural production. The analysis of trends in paddy rice yield and fertilizer consumption not only does not negate the hypothesis that yield was understated, but strongly supports our argument that there was a progressive decline in the degree of underreporting over time. The examination of progress in experimental stations also indicates that increases in yield could have been expected toward the end of the period under study and particularly in the Taishō era (1912-26) and later. Both the fertilizer consumption and seed improvement factors point to a more rapid increase in yield in the latter half of the period from 1878-82 to 1918-22. The fertilizer consumption trends, in particular, support a rapid increase beginning around 1908-12.

[66] Toshihiro Kojima, "Meijiki nōgyō tōkei no mondai ishiki" [Meiji problems as revealed in agricultural statistics] *Nōgyō Sōgō Kenkyū*, XII, 4 (October 1958), 93.

[67] Although most specific Western agricultural techniques were found unsuitable, it is a notable fact that those innovations which effectively raised production were largely Western; *e.g.*, seed improvement, increased use of commercial fertilizer, pest control, and the like.

In the discussion of underreporting up to this point, such matters as incentive and opportunity, statements by scholars, government policy,[68] empirical investigations of yield, and a study of technical factors that affect yield have been covered. Two conclusions can be reasonably drawn on the basis of the evidence thus far presented. The first is that a substantial understatement of yield per unit area exists in government statistics of the Meiji era. The second is that underreporting tended to decline over time.

Construction of Paddy Rice Yield Index

Since a major objective of this study is to revise the estimates of agricultural production and growth rate, our next problem is to construct an index of the change in yield. Revision can be based either on the assumption that an operationally useful regularity exists in the underestimation, or that it does not. Because we have argued that arbitrary changes in production statistics occurred at different times and for different reasons, the assumption that an operationally useful regularity exists would not be warranted. Therefore, our strategy will be to estimate absolute yields for two periods centering on 1880 and 1920.

The problem is basically that of picking numbers out of a possible range of yields per *tan* and testing each against relevant historical evidence. Ultimately, then, we must select those yields which meet the greatest number of tests and which cannot be rejected by established evidence.

The average government yield in 1918-22 was around 1.9 *koku* per *tan*. Can this be accepted as a reasonable approximation of the actual yield? There are at least five grounds for believing so. (1) Statements by Yokoi and J. W. Robertson Scott indicate that the degree of underreporting had been declining. (2) Incentive to underreport had probably disappeared around 1900 and was probably replaced by an incentive

[68] It is further argued in Appendix B (pp. 209-18) that government policy as reflected through the enactment and administration of the Arable Land Adjustment Law and other laws also tended to increase yield after the turn of the century, and particularly after World War I.

to inflate yield gains as Yokoi indicated in his statement. (3)
Examination of Figure 4-1 shows that yield climbed sharply
to around 1920 and then leveled off, suggesting that the period
of inflated increases of yield had come to an end around that
time. (4) A study of daily per capita calorie consumption also
suggests that underreporting of yield might have ended around
1920. According to Table 4-3,[69] which is based on government
statistics, Japanese consumed 1,351 calories from grain, potato,
pulse, meat, and dairy product sources in 1878-82. This consumption had climbed to 2,114 calories[70] in 1915-25, and then
fell to around 1,900 in the next decade.[71] The calorie supply in
1915-25 might have been around 2,300 if omitted sources (fish,
vegetables, fruit, sugar, and other unenumerated sources) are
added. Consumption of 1,351 calories from the sources mentioned above is clearly an understatement of the actual consumption since the people of the least developed of present
underdeveloped countries probably consume about 50 per cent
more than this amount. On the other hand, 2,100 to 2,300
calories may roughly be what is consumed in the economically
backward nations today and what Japan may have consumed
then. For example, Helen Farnsworth of Stanford University's
Food Research Institute has stated that actual food consumption in India may have been about 2,200 calories instead of
the officially reported 1,850 calories.[72] Although most economically backward nations report a calorie consumption of 1,900

[69] See p. 92.

[70] Adjustment is not made for undermeasurement. If the undermeasurement adjustment is made, the supply would have been less than 100
calories higher in 1878-82.

[71] I believe that underreporting of yield commenced again on a limited
scale in the 1920's as farmers sought government aid on grounds that
their income levels were low. Underreporting became particularly conspicuous during World War II and several years thereafter owing to the
introduction of a compulsory delivery system. (Jerome B. Cohen, *Japan's
Economy in War and Reconstruction* [Minneapolis, 1949], pp. 461-63.)

[72] Helen Farnsworth, "The Role of Wheat in Improving Nutritional
Status and Labor Productivity in Lesser Developed Countries," *Inter-
national Wheat Surplus Utilization Conference Proceedings* (Brookings,
South Dakota, 1958), p. 57.

calories, both Farnsworth and M. K. Bennett[73] believe the figures seriously understate actual consumption. In view of the above considerations it is likely that yield was accurately reported around 1920. (5) Accurate reporting was also made easier when, in 1914, statistical forms and procedures for estimating the harvest of rice, wheat, barley, and naked barley were revised.[74] The survey procedure was made much more detailed in the effort to obtain accuracy. Among other things, the village was divided into a number of survey districts which made possible a better appraisal of village yield. Moreover, the village yield was to be estimated by three or more appraisers who were scientific experts or men of experience, or, alternatively, by taking sample harvests from fields determined to be the village average. This survey procedure became effective in 1915. Because it takes a few years to adjust to changes of this kind, underreporting may not have been immediately eliminated, even if the villages were inclined to make accurate crop reports, as they appear to have been at this time.

However, a nagging question remains about underreporting of yield around 1920. Robertson Scott's statement made on information obtained around 1915 that rice production was understated by 15 per cent seems to suggest that production around 1920 may also have been substantially understated. Actually paddy field undermeasurement probably accounts for about 7 per cent of the understatement, seemingly leaving 8 per cent attributable to the underreporting of yield per *tan*. It is possible that the 8 per cent figure actually applies to an earlier period because a lag may be expected between practice and knowledge of its quantitative impact when the practice itself is changing. If this is so, since the practice was that of reducing the degree of underreporting, the underreporting of yield could have

[73] Bennett, *op.cit.*, pp. 189-212, states that underreporting of production and consumption may be attributed to the imperfections in statistical reporting machinery and techniques and to ulterior motives on the part of reporting units or governments. These reasons apply equally for early Meiji statistics in Japan.

[74] *Nōshōmushō kunrei 13 bessatsu: nōshōmu tōkei yōshiki* (November 21, 1914), notes to Forms 1 and 2.

been eliminated by around 1920. Aside from this lag factor it must also be borne in mind that Robertson Scott's figure must necessarily have been a very crude estimate as accurate yield estimates would scarcely have been made when it was intended to falsify the reported figures. If underreporting continued to remain in yield statistics, the above evidence would suggest that it had become an unimportant factor by around 1920.

In addition to the two possibilities that the 1.9 yield may be correct or be an understatement, there is a third possibility— that the yield was overstated. Since a desire to inflate yield reports apparently existed up to around 1920, mention of the third possibility is not merely an attempt to touch all bases. Neither Yokoi's statement nor the movement of government yields around 1920 is inconsistent with this possibility. However, it will be conservatively assumed that yield was not overstated at this time.

The average paddy rice yield of 1.166 for the period around 1880 has been discarded. There are no national data on which new estimates can be based (since government yield statistics are not acceptable). There remain only less certain and less direct methods of estimation.

The probable range of values within which the new estimate would lie can be obtained. The minimum cannot be less than 1.3 koku which is the estimated average yield in the Jōkyō era (1684-88), given our conclusion that yield increased during the Tokugawa period. The maximum value cannot be more than 1.9 koku which is within the probable range of yield around 1920. There is one figure between 1.3 and 1.9 koku for which a better case can be made than for any other figure. It is 1.6 koku, which, fortuitously, is the average of 1.3 and 1.9. According to Ario, the tax official who participated in the two Meiji land surveys, the government expected an average paddy rice yield of 1.6 koku per tan to emerge from the survey.[75] The fact that the government used the 1.6 koku yield in its instructions[76] for computing the paddy field value during the survey

[75] Ario, op.cit., p. 53.

[76] Dajōkan fukoku 272 bessatsu: chihōkan kokoroesho (July 1873), Article 12.

appears to confirm the official's statement. Where did the government obtain this figure, for it had not even started the survey when the instructions were published? There is no record of how this was done, but it may have been obtained by consulting Tokugawa period tax officials in various parts of the country. As stated previously these officials were highly skilled specialists who were trained from childhood for their function of appraising harvests and the productivity of fields. If the Meiji government did obtain the yield figure as described above, it was probably a good approximation of the actual average yield.

None of the factors examined thus far appears to be inconsistent with the 1.6 *koku* hypothesis—with the exception of Tokugawa and early Meiji yield data. The latter suggest that the yield was greater than 1.6 *koku* during the cadastral survey. However, the yield data consist of scattered samples of limited areas, and it is possible that the yields are all taken from superior fields with the exception of the Chikuzen Province yield which is said to be the average for the province. Nevertheless, the possibility that the actual yield during the 1870's was higher than 1.6 *koku* does remain, inasmuch as the 1.6 *koku* yield expected by the government may have been a conservative figure.

It has been argued that there are bases for accepting a 1.6 *koku* per *tan* yield during the cadastral survey, and a 1.9 *koku* per *tan* yield around 1920. However, because of the uncertainties attached to yield estimation even under the best of circumstances, a range of yields will be selected for each period instead of a single figure.[77] For the 1918-22 period the range will be 1.9 to 2.0 *koku* on the ground that underreporting might have existed at the time but that if it did it probably was by a small percentage. The range selected for the 1873-77 period is 1.5 to 1.7 *koku*. Given estimated yields of 1.3 *koku* in the 1680's and 1.9 to 2.0 in 1918-22 and considering agricultural

[77] Originally, I was disposed to take the single most reasonable figure for each period. I am much indebted to Professor Harry T. Oshima for persuading me of the wisdom of selecting a range of values. Professor Tsutomu Ouchi of Tokyo University offered criticism along similar lines.

developments from the 1680's to the 1920's, the yield could scarcely have been greater than 1.7 or less than 1.5 *koku* in the 1870's. If the yield ranged from 1.5 to 1.7 *koku* in 1873-77 and from 1.9 to 2.0 in 1918-22, the yield increased by 11.8 per cent at the least and 33.3 per cent at the most in the 45-year period. If median yields of 1.6 and 1.95 *koku* are assumed, the increase is 21.9 per cent. In Table 4-3, quinquennial yields are estimated on the assumption that yield increased at a constant rate.[78]

TABLE 4-3

INDICES OF CORRECTED ESTIMATES OF PADDY RICE YIELDS IN KOKU
PER TAN UNDER VARYING ASSUMPTIONS OF YIELD,[a]
FIVE-YEAR AVERAGES, 1873-1922

Assumed paddy rice yield (*koku*)	1.7 and 1.9		1.6 and 1.95		1.5 and 2.0	
	Yield *koku*	Index 1873-77 = 100	Yield *koku*	Index 1873-77 = 100	Yield *koku*	Index 1873-77 = 100
	(1)	(2)	(3)	(4)	(5)	(6)
1873-1877	1.700	100.0	1.600	100.0	1.500	100.0
1878-1882	1.721	101.2	1.636	102.2	1.549	103.3
1883-1887	1.743	102.5	1.672	104.5	1.599	106.6
1888-1892	1.764	103.8	1.709	106.8	1.651	110.1
1893-1897	1.786	105.1	1.747	109.2	1.705	113.7
1898-1902	1.808	106.4	1.786	111.6	1.760	117.3
1903-1907	1.831	107.7	1.826	114.1	1.817	121.1
1908-1912	1.854	109.0	1.867	116.7	1.876	125.1
1913-1917	1.877	110.4	1.908	119.3	1.937	129.2
1918-1922	1.900	111.8	1.950	121.9	2.000	133.3

NOTE: [a] Constant growth rate is assumed in all cases. The assumed paddy rice yields in the order given apply respectively to 1873-77 and 1918-22.

Construction of Dryland Crop Yield Index

The argument that the increase in paddy rice yield was partially fictitious applies equally to dryland crops. A case can be

[78] It is probable that yield per *tan* increased at a faster rate in the latter half of the period under study. The constant rate assumption is made because no reliable basis exists for adopting any other rate.

made that the gain in yield per *tan* of dryland crops was slower than that of rice with the possible exception of cocoons, wheat, and barley. In general, much greater attention was given to the care and fertilization of paddy fields than to that of upland fields with the major exception of mulberries. In respect to seed improvement, dryland crops have received much less attention than rice[79] with the exception of those associated with sericulture. A more important reason that may lead one to believe that dryland crop yields were understated more proportionally in the early Meiji era than paddy rice yield is that tax officials paid relatively little attention to the valuation of upland fields, thus probably providing landowners with greater opportunity for understatement. The cursory attention that upland field valuation received may be inferred from the almost total absence of communications and instructions relating to upland field valuation in Volume 7 of *Collection of financial and economic materials of early Meiji* (MZZKSS). If dryland crop yield understatement is proportionally greater than paddy rice yield, a more rapid rate of increase of the former might be expected in government statistics.

However, there are offsetting factors. The importation of foreign seeds in the case of barley and wheat which were widely grown in economically developed countries might have increased yields in Japan. But they were not an unqualified success. Despite their superiority in respect to yield, it was reported by the Kinai region experimental station in 1908 that imported barley and wheat seeds were almost worthless for use in Japan because they matured late.[80] Two other reasons have been given for their failure to be adopted: susceptibility to wind and rain damage and incompatibility with the practice of growing crops between rows owing to their height.[81] Limited planting of foreign varieties of barley and wheat seeds did occur in Hokkaidō and the Tohoku region[82] where weather conditions and farming practices were more suitable.

[79] *NNHS*, Vol. 5, pp. 678ff.
[80] *NNHS*, Vol. 3, p. 40.
[81] *Ibid.*, p. 197.
[82] *Ibid.*, p. 24.

Serious attention was also paid to the improvement of sericulture by the government and by private individuals. Early in
the Meiji era disease control, improvement of quality, mulberry
culture, and other aspects of sericulture became a major concern of the national government, and particularly the prefectural government of Nagano.[83] The fact that improvement
could occur at more stages in cocoon than in rice production
suggests that cocoon yield per *tan* of mulberries rose more
rapidly than rice yield per *tan*. The reported increase in cocoon
production per *tan* of mulberry planted cannot be determined
because the area planted to mulberries is most uncertain before 1889. However, something like a doubling of the yield
appears to have occurred. Assuming that it had increased considerably more, the change in dryland crop yield would have
been one-fifth as much since the total area planted to mulberries in 1920 was only 18 per cent of the upland field area.
Even if the cocoon production had increased by another 50
per cent, the growth rate of agricultural production would have
been affected by less than 0.02 percentage points.

Government statistics show that dryland crop yield per *tan*
generally rose more rapidly than paddy rice yield. Statistics are
available for a number of important dryland crops prior to
1885 when the change in policy in statistical reporting occurred. Although the yield series for many of these crops are
broken between 1885 and 1894, sufficient information is available to make a few observations. The increase in the yield per
tan of seven of ten dryland crops over the period from 1879-84
to 1915-25 is greater than that of rice.[84] A weighted average
of ten crops reveals an 86 per cent rise[85] in the period against
an increase of 64 per cent for rice.

Is the higher value for dryland crops a result of a greater
understatement in 1879-84? Did the understatement of yield
decline as rapidly as for paddy rice? These are questions that

[83] *Ibid.*, Vol. 5, pp. 547-48, 562-75.
[84] Statistical Appendix: Table 6. The ten crops are wheat, barley,
naked barley, sweet potatoes, white potatoes, soy beans, foxtail millet,
barnyard millet, buckwheat, and cocoons.
[85] *Ibid.*

cannot be answered on the basis of available information and for this reason a direct estimate of dryland crop yield cannot be made. The only alternative is to base it on the estimated paddy rice yield. In establishing a relationship between the two there are perhaps three considerations that may serve as guides. First, according to government statistics the dryland crop yield in 1915-25 is 186.3 per cent of the yield in 1879-84, and for paddy rice yield the 1915-25 yield is 164.0 per cent of that in 1879-84. The former is 13.6 per cent greater than the latter. Second, the government put more money and effort into improving paddy rice yield than into improving dryland crop yield except for cocoons. Third, foreign seed imports may have increased the yield of wheat, barley, and possibly other crops. If the second factor is given the greatest weight, it might be assumed that the dryland crop yields would have increased by less than our corrected paddy rice yield increases of 11.8 to 33.3 per cent. But if the first and third factors are given greater weight then it might be assumed that the dryland crop yield increases were greater than the paddy rice yield increases.

In the absence of firmer evidence it will be assumed that the average yield of all dryland crops increased at a rate 13.6 per cent greater than that of paddy rice yield. This assumes that the estimated increases in the corrected yield indices of paddy rice and dryland crops are proportional to the increases in their respective reported yield indices. Under this assumption the indices of dryland crop yields in 1918-22 were 127.0, 138.5, and 151.4 (1873-77 = 100) when the indices of paddy rice yields were 111.8, 121.9, and 133.3, respectively. The indices are shown in Table 4-4.

Tests for Plausibility of New Yield Estimates

One check for plausibility of the 1.6 hypothesis is to estimate the yield per *tan* required to meet the food needs of the Japanese population in 1878-82. This approach is particularly applicable to Japan since almost all of her calorie requirements came from plant sources.[86] Estimates of calories available for

[86] Bruce F. Johnston, *Japanese Food Management in World War II* (Stanford, 1953), p. 70.

TABLE 4-4

INDICES OF CORRECTED ESTIMATES OF DRYLAND CROP YIELDS
IN KOKU PER TAN[a] UNDER VARYING ASSUMPTIONS OF
PADDY RICE YIELD, FIVE-YEAR AVERAGES, 1873-1922

Assumed paddy rice yield[b] (koku)	1.7 and 1.9	1.6 and 1.95	1.5 and 2.0
	(1)	(2)	(3)
1873-1877	100.0	100.0	100.0
1878-1882	102.7	103.7	104.7
1883-1887	105.5	107.5	109.7
1888-1892	108.3	111.5	114.9
1893-1897	111.2	115.6	120.3
1898-1902	114.2	119.9	125.9
1903-1907	117.3	124.3	131.8
1908-1912	120.5	128.8	138.1
1913-1917	123.7	133.7	144.6
1918-1922	127.0	138.5	151.4

NOTES: [a] It is assumed that the dryland crop yield index is 13.6
per cent higher than that of paddy rice in 1918-22.
[b] The assumed paddy rice yields apply respectively to
1873-77 and 1918-22. Constant growth rate is assumed
in all three cases.

consumption made by Seiki Nakayama[87] using government statistics will be employed in our analysis. Table 4-5 shows
calories supplied per day per capita from grains, pulses, potatoes, meat, dairy products, and eggs from 1878-82 to 1923-27.
The supply in 1878-82 was 1,351 calories from above sources,
a totally inadequate supply. In 1918-22 it had increased to
2,201 calories. If a more conservative 15-year period from
1913-17 to 1923-27 is taken as the base, the supply was 2,114
calories, an increase of 56 per cent from the 1878-82 supply.
In Nakayama's computations, some sources of calorie supply
(principally sugar, fish, vegetables, fruits) were omitted but
they probably accounted for less than 10 per cent of the total.[88]

[87] Seiki Nakayama, "Shokuryō shōhi suijun no chōki henka ni tsuite"
[Long run trend of food consumption in Japan, 1878-1955], Nōgyō Sōgō Kenkyū, XII, 4 (October 1958), pp. 13-37.
[88] In 1930-34 the three sources—fish, fruits, vegetables—accounted
for about 7% in a food balance sheet prepared for the U.S. State Department. (U.S., Dept. of State, Office of International Research, Japan's

TABLE 4-5

CALORIES AVAILABLE FOR CONSUMPTION[a] PER DAY
PER CAPITA FROM SELECTED FOODS, FIVE-YEAR
AVERAGES, 1878-1927

Period	Grains,[b] pulses,[b] potatoes	Meat, milk, eggs	Total
1878-1882	1,349	1.7	1,351
1883-1887	1,520	2.5	1,523
1888-1892	1,830	2.8	1,833
1893-1897	1,876	6.6	1,883
1898-1902	1,941	7.4	1,948
1903-1907	2,006	7.6	2,014
1908-1912	2,119	8.9	2,128
1913-1917	2,084	10.3	2,094
1918-1922	2,189	12.1	2,201
1923-1927	2,031	14.9	2,046

SOURCE: Seiki Nakayama, "Shokuryō shōhi suijun no chōki henka ni tsuite" [Long term trend of food consumption in Japan, 1878-1955], *Nōgyō Sōgō Kenkyū*, xii, 4 (October 1958), 25.

NOTES: [a] Calories available for consumption are computed by deducting food used as fodder, loss in processing, and seed requirements and allowing for changes in stock and for exports and imports.

[b] By grains is meant rice, wheat, barley, naked barley, corn, foxtail millet, barnyard millet, proso millet, and buckwheat. Pulses include only soy beans and *azuki*, a small red bean.

The omitted part, however, became proportionally more important over time; therefore, if it were possible to include all sources of calorie supply, the percentage change in supply would probably have been greater than 56 per cent.

Let us assume that the actual calorie supply per day per capita in 1878-82 was 2,114. The undermeasurement factor will be disregarded since it can be assumed to affect both periods equally. The 1878-82 calorie supply must be corrected for con-

Food, Beverage, and Tobacco Position, 1928-36 [OIR Report No. 4126, 1948], p. 88, Table 42.) Since these sources tended to account for a greater proportion of calorie intake as the national income rose, it is probable that they accounted for less than 7% in earlier years. Sugar accounted for 2 to 3% of the total calorie supply in early Meiji according to Seiki Nakayama in an interview in Tokyo in the summer of 1964.

cealment since there was no concealment in 1913-27. This adjustment requires an upward revision of the 1,351 calories by about 10 per cent,[89] which makes the calorie supply 1,486. The remaining difference of 628 calories is assumed to have been a result of the understatement of yield per *tan*. The adjusted total of 1,486 calories must be raised by 42 per cent to obtain 2,114 calories.[90] If the recorded yield of 1.166 *koku* per *tan* is increased by 42 per cent, the result is 1.656 *koku*. This is somewhat more than the yield that Ario said the government expected from the cadastral survey. To look at it from another perspective, if the 1.166 *koku* per *tan* yield is raised to 1.6 *koku*, then the calorie supply becomes 2,036, and if raised to 1.5 *koku*, the supply would be 1,912. The latter figure is roughly the calorie consumption of many present economically backward nations according to their official statistics; it is also a figure that Helen Farnsworth and M. K. Bennett believe understates the actual consumption.

The above analysis confirms the hypothesis that the yield per *tan* was about 1.6 *koku* in early Meiji, if the area adjustments and the assumption of constant calorie consumption are correct, or are reasonably close to being so, or have offsetting biases. Moreover, the assumption of a constant calorie consumption can probably be relaxed somewhat because waste and losses in transit and storage were greater in early Meiji than later. This means that the actual calorie consumption out of a given output of food was less in the earlier period.

The area adjustment can be regarded as tolerably accurate on the basis of the analysis in Chapters II and III.

The assumption of a constant calorie consumption is probably tenable also. To be sure there are circumstances that seem to indicate that calorie consumption increased during the Meiji

[89] The increase in Taxed Arable Land Area was about 11%. But a part of this increase can be attributed to the inclusion of land given to shifting agriculture, some of which was previously not counted. It is not possible to determine how much of such land was newly included. This accounts for the selection of the round 10%.

[90] It is assumed that the yields per *tan* of other sources of calories are raised by the same proportion as the paddy rice yield.

era. An increase in physical size, other things being equal, increases calorie requirements for the obvious reason that carrying more weight requires a greater energy use. Japanese have grown in stature over the years although the change up to around 1920 was relatively small. Another factor usually associated with increased food consumption is a rise in per capita income. One of the principal contentions of this study is that per capita income rose relatively slowly and little, and for the masses of low-income farmers and workers, the real wage rose very little to about the time of the Russo-Japanese War. It is a fact, however, that the average real income did rise and food consumption may have risen somewhat.[91] But this increase need not necessarily be an increase in calorie consumption except in countries where the initial staple food supply did not adequately feed the population. In these countries most of the increase in food expenditures would probably go toward the purchase of calorie-rich foods. In other countries, increases in income have been accompanied by a change in the composition of foods consumed. The shift is typically from the grains and potatoes to the meats, dairy products, vegetables, and fruits. The contention in this book that the general level of income in Japan was much higher than previous estimates indicate is also consistent with the argument that staple food supply was adequate in the 1870's and 1880's. A shift away from carbohydrates in Japan, though not necessarily a significant one, is suggested by Table 4-5 which shows that the consumption of meat, eggs, and dairy products increased at an extremely rapid rate. The data presented above does permit

[91] Since farmers appear to have been dissaving judging from the increase in the proportion of tenant land during all of the Meiji era—37% in 1883, 40% in 1892, 46% in 1914 (E. Herbert Norman, *Japan's Emergence as a Modern State* [New York, 1940], p. 148n.)—and farm income was rising except during the Matsukata deflation, it may be reasonably inferred that farm consumption level was rising. Another reason for belief that it was rising is that the average farm family was increasing in size during the Meiji era. However, since many farmers were losing land and many others were probably mortgaging land, per capita food consumption could have been declining for cash revenue and food consumption are substitutes on the farm.

some increase in calorie consumption while maintaining the assumption that yield per *tan* in 1878-82 was 1.6 *koku*.

There are other considerations that indicate the need for a higher per capita calorie supply in the earlier period. As the early Meiji population was much more dominantly a farming population, and as both men and women tend to be more active on the farms than in most occupations, the calorie consumption would also tend to be higher. A higher consumption would also be required in the earlier period owing to poorer clothing, housing, and heating facilities because the human body would then require more energy to keep itself warm.

The principal reason for the belief that early Meiji food supply per capita was equal to or higher than in later years is that the food policy of the Tokugawa period—producing a more than adequate supply of food in normal crop years so that a tolerable supply would be available even in relatively poor crop years—almost certainly carried over into the Meiji era. This food policy was maintained as a buffer against crop failures since storage techniques and facilities were inadequate to carry sufficient emergency stocks. To enforce it, provincial governments kept resources in agriculture at a high level by tying peasants to the land, restricting certain classes of arable land to food crops, and establishing other impediments to resource mobility. The policy was not completely successful as evidenced by the severe famines of the 1730's, 1780's, and the 1830's. In fact the food consumption picture of the Tokugawa period (and earlier) is that of periodic food shortages and famine owing to the high incidence of natural calamities. In view of this, it is even possible that Japanese ate more regularly but consumed less food on the average in the later Meiji era than they did in late Tokugawa before food imports became available to relieve shortages.[92]

There were other reasons for this food policy. The provincial lords who enforced the policy were after all feudal lords who

[92] This point is made in respect to consumers in industrial societies in contrast to those in pre-industrial societies in E. J. Hobsbaum, "The British Standard of Living, 1790-1850," *Economic History Review,* Second Series, X, 1 (April 1957), 46.

wished to maintain self-sufficiency in food for defense purposes. Furthermore, the fact that transportation was prohibitively expensive except along the main transportation routes made such a policy highly advisable for economic reasons.

In addition to the need to maintain an adequate food supply, the need for cash income also dictated a policy of keeping resources in agriculture at a high level. The cash expenditures required in meeting the obligation of the alternative attendance system[93] could best be met by most feudal lords by enforcing the production of agricultural crops which could be sold for cash in markets outside the province.[94]

Support for the Tokugawa food policy could have been expected from the peasants for the most part since they were almost completely self-sufficient and famine was the principal threat to their well being. Resistance to this policy from landowners existed in areas near large population centers where agriculture had become commercialized to a large extent.[95]

Following the Meiji Restoration, self-sufficiency in food for security reasons ceased to be a local problem. However, the threat of hunger and social disorder still confronted the government and the people since storage, transportation, and communications facilities were still poorly developed. Moreover, the rice surplus probably tended to persist for the additional reason that the farmers needed more cash income than in the past in order to pay taxes in cash (previously mostly paid in kind), and to buy fertilizers and other goods and services which were becoming increasingly available. For most farmers, rice remained the most important and certain source of cash income.

As time passed, however, certain food-saving effects operated which made it possible to feed an increasing number of people with a given supply of food until these effects were fully realized. Soon after the Meiji Restoration all commercial barriers between provinces were abolished. Although this did not immediately cause an increased flow of food between the

[93] For a description of the alternate attendance system see p. 157.
[94] Craig, *op.cit.*, p. 28.
[95] Furushima, *op.cit.*, pp. 175ff.

provinces, since trade requires the build-up of service industries, it paved the way for an improved flow in the future. The commencement of foreign trade in the 1850's eased the threat of severe famine and reduced somewhat the need to maintain a policy which would produce a food surplus in normal crop years. However, the food-saving effects could only be fully realized with the improvement of storage[96] and national transportation facilities and the institution of a more efficient national (as opposed to provincial) administration of emergency food measures. These required time to become fully effective— particularly the all-important construction of transportation facilities which lowered the prohibitively high costs of transporting food over most of the country.[97]

For the reasons given above, although Japan did not have a long-run comparative advantage in food production, she continued to be a rice exporter until the 1890's, when a rough balance in rice supply and consumption was reached.

An examination of yields since the Kamakura period also suggests that our paddy rice yield assumptions may not be far off the mark. Considering that peace and order became established and communications improved as time passed, an increase in the growth rate of yield per *tan* could have been expected. Indeed this seems to have occurred according to the data in Table 4-6. Under the assumptions that paddy rice yields were 1.6 *koku* per *tan* in 1873-77 and 1.95 *koku* per *tan* in 1918-22, the annual growth rates were 0.44 per cent for the period from 1873-77 to 1918-22 and 0.66 per cent for the period from 1918-22 to 1955-61. These rates are compatible with the earlier discussion of yield-increasing factors. If the average yield per *tan* in 1918-22 is assumed to be 1.9 *koku* the growth rates are 0.38 and 0.75 per cent in the two respective periods. With a yield of 2.00 *koku* in 1918-22 the rates are 0.50 and 0.59 per cent, which would mean that the

[96] Lockwood, *op.cit.*, p. 247n., states, "Losses from storage can easily run up to 5 to 10 per cent, even in normal years."

[97] *Ibid.*, pp. 105-09. See also Thomas C. Smith, *Political Change and Industrial Development in Japan: Government Enterprise, 1868-80* (Stanford, 1951), p. 38.

TABLE 4-6

GROWTH RATE OF YIELD IN KOKU PER TAN,
SELECTED PERIODS

Period	Yield (koku)	Annual growth rate of yield from previous period %
Kamakura period (1191-1333)	1.08	–
Bunroku era (1592-1596)	1.18	0.03
Jōkyō era (1684-1688)	1.30	0.11
1873-1877	1.60	0.11
1915-1925	1.95	0.44
1955-1961[a]	2.50	0.66

SOURCES: Kamakura, Bunroku, and Jōkyō data from p. 76n. The
1915-25 data are computed from Ministry of Agriculture and Forestry, Agriculture and Forestry Economic Bureau, Statistical Section, Nōrinsho ruinen tōkeihyō, 1868-1953 [Historical statistics of
the Ministry of Agriculture and Forestry, 1868-1953], p. 24. The
1955-61 yield is computed from Tōkei nenkan, 1960, p. 86, and
Jiji Tsūshinsha, Jiji Almanac 1963 (Tokyo, 1962), p. 873.
NOTE: [a] The 1955-61 yield was selected to represent the postwar period because yields in these years were obtained by carefully
planned random sampling and as such are regarded as reliable.

yield-increasing factors were of roughly equivalent force in
the two periods. Since our argument has been that these factors
were generally more powerful in the later period, a yield of 2.00
koku in 1918-22 appears somewhat on the high side.

Summary

The opportunity and incentive to underreport yield was
high in the Meiji era until about the turn of the century. One
opportunity provided by the government came during the cadastral survey (1870's) when it made concessions on land valuation yields. During the survey the paddy rice yield averaged
1.32 koku per tan, which is about equal to the average yield
reported two centuries previously. In the five-year period of
1878-82, the average reported yield dipped to 1.166 koku per
tan. This decline can be attributed to village policy of reporting yields considerably lower than the actual yield as a means
of preventing revaluation of village land at a higher level or of
obtaining a lower land valuation since the law stipulated that

revaluation would take place every five years. The incentive to underreport continued to persist to around the turn of the century, although a very substantial increase occurred in the mid-1880's largely due to a strong government effort to obtain accurate statistics during the Matsukata deflation. It is argued that the increase in the 1880's did not fully correct the understatement of yield, and that around the turn of the century a substantial understatement still persisted. But at about this time a period began in which greater increases than actually occurred were reported. Thus, reported yield increased from 1.37 in 1893-97 to 1.93 in 1918-22.

It is concluded here that the reported yield had about reached the level of actual yield by 1918-22. For the purposes of this book it is assumed that the yield at this time ranged from 1.9 to 2.0 *koku* per *tan*. For 1873-77, the yield was estimated to range from 1.5 to 1.7 *koku*.

The corrected yields were tested for plausibility by use of independent data, the most important of which was a test of calorie consumption. It was determined that calorie consumption in Japan given a yield of 1.166 *koku* per *tan* had to be raised by about 50 per cent in 1878-82 to bring it to the levels existing in present underdeveloped countries. When the yield was increased to 1.6 *koku*, calorie consumption rose to levels equivalent to these nations.

CHAPTER 5

Corrected Value and Growth Rate of Agricultural Production

THE PRINCIPAL OBJECTIVE of this chapter is to estimate the average five-year values of agricultural production in constant (1913-17) yen, corrected for understatement of production, for the 50-year period under study.[1] The value that is to be obtained will not be the actual value of production since the particular level of the latter value is determined by such factors as weather and short-term changes in the amount of fertilizers used—factors for which allowances cannot be made with the techniques of estimation used here. The value that is obtained here will be referred to as the corrected (or revised) value. It assumes normal weather conditions and a stable improvement or increase in yield-increasing factors other than weather. It is a constant yen value unless specifically noted otherwise. Deviations of this value from the actual value (in constant yen), if the latter were known, would largely be a result of weather conditions. The corrected value, therefore, is less useful in obtaining precise changes in levels of agricultural production than in determining the rates of growth, because, like the latter, it reflects trends, not short-term fluctuations. Nevertheless, it is believed that this value is a better approximation of the actual constant yen value of agricultural production than existing estimates.[2]

[1] The basic mathematical formula used to obtain the corrected value series is given in Chapter 1, p. 11.

[2] Extreme caution must be exercised in the use of the corrected value. In addition to the qualifications noted in the text, another characteristic of the corrected value can be indicated. Corrected value estimates for the middle of the period from 1873 to 1922 are likely to be significantly understated since it is assumed that yield per unit area grew at a constant rate despite indications that yield grew at a faster rate in the latter half

*Computation of Corrected Estimate of Agricultural
Production*

To obtain the corrected value series, indices of the volume
of production of paddy rice and of all other agricultural production and the base year values of the two classes of agricultural production must be computed. The 1913-17 period will
be taken as the base period rather than 1918-22 to avoid war
and postwar price and production distortions.[3] The indices of
the volume of corrected paddy rice production are the product
of the revised indices of yield and area planted to paddy rice.
The indices for the ten five-year periods are given in Table 5-1.
It is assumed that paddy rice yields per *tan* ranged from 1.5
to 1.7 *koku* in 1873-77 and from 1.9 to 2.0 *koku* in 1918-22. The
increases in production in the 45-year period (between the
middle years of the extreme five-year periods) are found to
range from 28 to 52 per cent. If one assumes median yields of
1.6 *koku* in 1873-77 and 1.95 *koku* in 1918-22, the increase in
production is 39 per cent.

The indices of the volume of corrected agricultural production less paddy rice, which are the product of the area and yield
indices, are given in Table 5-2. These indices were constructed
with the assumption that the dryland crop yield index rose by
13.6 per cent more than the paddy rice yield index. The increases in production under the varying assumptions about
paddy rice yield range from 67 to 99 per cent. The increase
when paddy rice yields are assumed to be 1.6 and 1.95 *koku*,
respectively, in the two terminal periods is 82 per cent. These
increases are more than double those of paddy rice production.
A major part of these differences is accounted for by the
greater expansion in area planted to dryland crops than in that
planted to paddy rice.

The base period (1913-17) corrected values of total agricultural production, including values of paddy rice production and

---

of the period and since weather conditions appeared to depress yields
around the turn of the century.

[3] Severe wartime price and production effects were not felt in Japan
until 1917.

TABLE 5-1

CORRECTED INDEX[a] OF PADDY RICE PRODUCTION UNDER VARYING PADDY RICE
YIELD ASSUMPTIONS, FIVE-YEAR AVERAGES, 1873-1922
(1873-77=100)

Assumed paddy rice yields[b] (koku)	1.7 and 1.9		1.6 and 1.95		1.5 and 2.0	
	Area index	Yield index	Quantity index	Yield index	Quantity index	Yield index	Quantity index
	(1)	(2)	(3)	(4)	(5)	(6)	(7)
1873-1877	100.0	100.0	100.0	100.0	100.0	100.0	100.0
1878-1882	101.1	101.2	102.3	102.2	103.3	103.3	104.4
1883-1887	102.3	102.5	104.9	104.5	106.9	106.6	109.1
1888-1892	103.8	103.8	107.7	106.8	110.9	110.1	114.3
1893-1897	104.3	105.1	109.6	109.2	113.9	113.7	118.6
1898-1902	105.9	106.4	112.7	111.6	118.2	117.3	124.2
1903-1907	107.5	107.7	115.8	114.1	122.7	121.1	130.2
1908-1912	109.7	109.0	119.6	116.7	128.0	125.1	137.2
1913-1917	112.2	110.4	123.9	119.3	133.9	129.2	145.0
1918-1922	114.2	111.8	127.7	121.9	139.2	133.3	152.2

SOURCES: Column (1): Table 2-8.
Columns (2), (4), (6): Table 4-3.
NOTES: [a] Corrected index refers to the index corrected for understatement of production.
[b] The assumed paddy rice yields apply respectively to 1873-77 and 1918-22.

of agricultural production less paddy rice, will be estimated
from data in Kazushi Ohkawa, et al., The Growth Rate of the
Japanese Economy Since 1878. (Values taken from this source
or computed from this source without correction for understatement of production will be referred to for convenience as
the Ohkawa values.) The annual rate of Ohkawa value of total
agricultural production in the base period is shown to be 1806.4
million yen in Table 5-3. The Ohkawa value of rice production
including paddy and upland rice is 911.3 million yen in the
1913-17 period shown in the same Table. The value of upland
rice production must be deducted from the above figure. This
value is not known for the 1913-17 period, as neither the total
value nor the price of this variant of rice is available. However,
the value of upland field production is known for the 1923-27
period. From this data it was determined that the average price

of upland rice was 91 per cent of all rice during the five-year period.[4] It is assumed here that the two prices were identically related in the 1913-17 period. Since the volume of upland rice production in the 1913-17 period is known, the average upland rice value may be computed to be 18.5 million yen.[5] Deducting the latter from the value of total rice production leaves the average paddy rice value of 892.7 million yen. Then, since the Ohkawa value of total agricultural production is 1806.4 million yen, the Ohkawa value of agricultural production less paddy rice is 913.7 million yen.

Two adjustments are made to change the Ohkawa base year values to corrected base year values. They are an adjustment for undermeasurement of area planted to crops, and another for underreporting of yield.[6] The adjustments for undermeasurement of areas planted to paddy rice and dryland crops are

[4] Computed from Ministry of Agriculture and Forestry, Secretariat, Statistical Section, *Meiji rokunen naishi Shōwa yonen nōrinshō ruinen tōkeihyō* [Historical statistics of the Ministry of Agriculture and Forestry, 1873-1929] (Tokyo, 1932), p. 9.

[5] The volume and estimated prices and value of upland rice production from 1913 to 1917 are:

Year	Production (1000 *koku*)	Price yen	Value million yen
1913	1100	19.02	20.9
1914	1130	14.07	15.9
1915	1333	11.29	15.0
1916	1557	12.87	20.0
1917	1136	18.41	20.9

Average of 1913-17   18.5

(Production volume from *NRT*, p. 24. The price is computed from data in Ministry of Agriculture and Forestry, Secretariat, Statistics Section, *op.cit.*, p. 9.)

[6] Adjustment for concealment is believed unnecessary, since it was probably negligible at this time. The undermeasurement index of 1.049 is for upland fields. Strictly the double-cropped paddy field area planted to dryland crops should be inflated by the paddy field undermeasurement index. This procedure does not significantly affect the value of dryland crop production. Moreover, in view of the probable upward bias that the area of land planted to dryland crops has, the use of the lower index is preferred.

TABLE 5-2

CORRECTED INDEX[a] OF AGRICULTURAL PRODUCTION LESS PADDY RICE
UNDER VARYING PADDY RICE YIELD ASSUMPTIONS,
FIVE-YEAR AVERAGES, 1873-1922
(1873-77=100)

Assumed paddy rice yields[b] (*koku*)		1.7 and 1.9		1.6 and 1.95		1.5 and 2.0	
	Area index	Yield index	Quantity index	Yield index	Quantity index	Yield index	Quantity index
	(1)	(2)	(3)	(4)	(5)	(6)	(7)
1873-1877	100.0	100.0	100.0	100.0	100.0	100.0	100.0
1878-1882	100.6	102.7	103.3	103.7	104.3	104.7	105.3
1883-1887	101.3	105.5	106.9	107.5	108.9	109.7	111.1
1888-1892	103.5	108.3	112.1	111.5	115.4	114.9	118.9
1893-1897	105.5	111.2	117.3	115.6	122.0	120.3	126.9
1898-1902	110.2	114.2	125.8	119.9	132.1	125.9	138.7
1903-1907	115.0	117.3	134.9	124.3	142.9	131.8	151.6
1908-1912	121.5	120.5	146.4	128.8	156.5	138.1	167.8
1913-1917	126.1	123.7	156.0	133.7	168.6	144.6	182.3
1918-1922	131.6	127.0	167.1	138.5	182.3	151.4	199.2

SOURCES: Column (1): Table 2-10.
Columns (2), (4), (6): Table 4-4.
NOTES: [a] Corrected index refers to the index corrected for understatement of production.
[b] The assumed paddy rice yields apply respectively to 1873-77 and 1918-22. It is assumed that dryland crop yield increased by 13.6% more than paddy rice yield.

made by inflating with their respective 1956 undermeasurement indices of 1.069 and 1.049,[7] which are assumed to have remained constant. The yield adjustments are less simple. The reported average paddy rice yield in 1913-17 is 1.843 *koku* per *tan*.[8] The assumed yields in the 1913-17 period are 1.877, 1.908, and 1.937 *koku* depending on the specific assumptions made about yields in 1873-77 and 1918-22. The yield inflators for each of these assumed yields are 1.018, 1.035, and 1.051, respectively. It is assumed that other agricultural production was underreported by the same proportions and is properly inflated by the same set of yield inflators. The corrected base year values of

[7] Statistical Appendix: Table 6.
[8] Table 4-1, p. 66.

TABLE 5-3

Ohkawa Base Year (1913-17) Values of Total Agricultural
Production, Paddy Rice Production, and Agricultural
Production Less Paddy Rice
(unit = 1,000 yen)

Year	Total value of agricultural production	Value of rice production	Value of upland rice production	Value of paddy rice production	Value of agricultural production less paddy rice
	(1)	(2)	(3)	(2)-(3) (4)	(1)-(4) (5)
1913	1974.6	1050.5	20.9	1029.6	945.0
1914	1658.5	881.2	15.9	865.3	793.2
1915	1378.6	694.1	15.0	679.1	699.5
1916	1704.4	826.6	20.0	806.6	897.8
1917	2316.0	1103.9	20.9	1083.0	1233.0
1913-17 average	1806.4	911.3	18.5	892.7	913.7

Sources: Columns (1) and (2) computed from Kazushi Ohkawa, et al., The
Growth Rate of the Japanese Economy Since 1878 (Tokyo, 1957),
p. 56. Column (3): Footnote 5, p. 108.

paddy rice production, agricultural production less paddy rice,
and total agricultural production are given in Table 5-4 where
appropriate area and yield adjustments that were made are
shown.

Having obtained the corrected indices of the volumes of
paddy rice and other agricultural production and the corrected
base year values, we may now compute the corrected value
series. The new values of paddy rice production under various
yield assumptions are given in Table 5-5; those of agricultural
production less paddy rice in Table 5-6; and those of total agricultural production in Table 5-7. The percentage increases in the
latter under the three yield assumptions are 45.1, 58.4, and 73.1.

The annual growth rates of the corrected value of agricultural production range from 0.8 to 1.2 per cent, as shown in
Line 9, Table 5-8. The rate, when the paddy rice yield assumptions are 1.6 and 1.95 koku per tan is 1.0 per cent which also is
the average of the two extreme rates. As might be expected
from the increased expansion of arable land area after the turn

TABLE 5-4

BASE YEAR (1913-17) VALUES OF AGRICULTURAL PRODUCTION
CORRECTED FOR UNDERMEASUREMENT OF AREA AND
UNDERREPORTING OF YIELD UNDER VARYING
PADDY RICE YIELD ASSUMPTIONS

		Assumed paddy rice yields in 1873-77 and 1918-22	Paddy rice production	Other agricultural production	Total agricultural production
		(1)	(2)	(3)	(4)
Ohkawa value (million yen)	(1)		892.7	913.7	1806.4
Undermeasurement index	(2)		1.069	1.049	
Yield inflator[a]	(3)	1.7 and 1.9	1.018	1.018	
Corrected value[b] (million yen)	(4)	1.7 and 1.9	971.5	975.8	1947.3
Yield inflator[a]	(5)	1.6 and 1.95	1.035	1.035	
Corrected value[b] (million yen)	(6)	1.6 and 1.95	987.7	992.0	1979.7
Yield inflator[a]	(7)	1.5 and 2.0	1.051	1.051	
Corrected value[b] (million yen)	(8)	1.5 and 2.0	1003.0	1007.4	2010.4

SOURCES: Line (1): Table 5-3.
Line (2): Chapter 3, p. 62.
Lines (3), (5), (7): Yield inflators computed by dividing reported 1913-17 paddy rice yield of 1.843 into assumed 1913-17 yields given in Table 4-3.
NOTES: [a] Yield inflation required for other agricultural production is assumed to be the same as for paddy rice production.
[b] The corrected value is the product of the Ohkawa value, the undermeasurement inflator, and the yield inflator.

of the century, the growth rates after the 1898-1902 period (Line 8) are higher than those to this period (Line 7)—the increase averaging around 40 per cent. This trend revealed in the growth rates of all agricultural production applies as well to its components—paddy rice production and other agricultural production.[9] The interesting contrast between the latter two is that the growth rates of agricultural production less rice are about twice that of paddy rice production.

Summary

This chapter is the culmination of the agricultural income estimation phase of this book. Here we apply the correction factors developed in Chapters 2, 3, and 4 for the following

[9] Nevertheless, as stated in footnote 2, pp. 105-106, the difference in the growth rate between the two periods may be understated.

TABLE 5-5

CORRECTED VALUE OF PADDY RICE PRODUCTION IN 1913-17 PRICES
UNDER VARYING PADDY RICE YIELD ASSUMPTIONS,
FIVE-YEAR AVERAGES, 1873-1922

Assumed paddy rice yields[a] (koku)	1.7 and 1.9		1.6 and 1.95		1.5 and 2.0	
	Production index	Value[b]	Production index	Value[b]	Production index	Value[b]
	1873-77 =100	million yen	1873-77 =100	million yen	1873-77 =100	million yen
	(1)	(2)	(3)	(4)	(5)	(6)
1873-1877	100.0	784	100.0	738	100.0	692
1878-1882	102.3	802	103.3	762	104.4	722
1883-1887	104.9	822	106.9	789	109.1	755
1888-1892	107.7	844	110.9	818	114.3	791
1893-1897	109.6	859	113.9	840	118.6	820
1898-1902	112.7	883	118.2	872	124.2	859
1903-1907	115.8	908	122.7	905	130.2	901
1908-1912	119.6	937	128.0	944	137.2	949
1913-1917	123.9	971	133.9	988	145.0	1003
1918-1922	127.7	1001	139.2	1027	152.2	1053

SOURCES: Columns (1), (3), (5): Table 5-1.
NOTES: [a] Assumed paddy rice yields are respectively for 1873-77 and 1918-22.
  [b] Columns (2), (4), and (6) were computed by converting base year values with the production indices. The base year values used were 971.5, 987.7, and 1003.0 million yen taken from Table 5-4.

two purposes: (1) to obtain the value and index of total agricultural production from 1873-77 to 1918-22 by estimating the indices and the base year values of paddy rice production and all other agricultural production; and (2) to determine the growth rates of paddy rice output, all other agricultural production, and total agricultural production.

The index of agricultural production obtained is conceptually an indicator of the trend of growth of production rather than an estimate of actual production for each five-year period.

The growth rate of total agricultural production is found to range from 0.8 to 1.2 per cent. About 43 per cent of the increase in production over the period of the study can be attributed to

TABLE 5-6

CORRECTED VALUE OF AGRICULTURAL PRODUCTION LESS PADDY RICE IN
1913-17 PRICES UNDER VARYING PADDY RICE YIELD ASSUMPTIONS,
FIVE-YEAR AVERAGES, 1873-1922

Assumed paddy rice yields[a] (*koku*)	1.7 and 1.9		1.6 and 1.95		1.5 and 2.0	
	Production index	Value[b]	Production index	Value[b]	Production index	Value[b]
	1873-77 =100	million yen	1873-77 =100	million yen	1873-77 =100	million yen
	(1)	(2)	(3)	(4)	(5)	(6)
1873-1877	100.0	626	100.0	588	100.0	552
1878-1882	103.3	646	104.3	614	105.3	582
1883-1887	106.9	669	108.9	641	111.1	614
1888-1892	112.1	701	115.4	679	118.9	657
1893-1897	117.3	734	122.0	718	126.9	701
1898-1902	125.8	787	132.1	777	138.7	766
1903-1907	134.9	844	142.9	841	151.6	837
1908-1912	146.4	916	156.5	921	167.8	927
1913-1917	156.0	976	168.6	992	182.3	1007
1918-1922	167.1	1045	182.3	1073	199.2	1100

SOURCES: Columns (1), (3), and (5): Table 5-2, Columns (3), (5), (7).
NOTES: [a] Assumed paddy rice yields are respectively for 1873-77 and 1918-22.
   [b] Columns (2), (4), and (6) were computed by converting base year values
   with the production indices. The base year values used were 975.8, 992.0,
   and 1007.4 million yen taken from Table 5-4.

the expansion in land area as corrected here and about 57 per
cent to increases in yield also as corrected here. The growth rate
of agricultural production less paddy rice is found to average
about 80 per cent more than that of paddy rice production.

TABLE 5-7

CORRECTED VALUE AND INDEX OF TOTAL AGRICULTURAL PRODUCTION IN
1913-17 PRICES UNDER VARYING PADDY RICE YIELD ASSUMPTIONS,
FIVE-YEAR AVERAGES, 1873-1922

Assumed paddy rice yields[a] (*koku*)	1.7 and 1.9		1.6 and 1.95		1.5 and 2.0	
	Value	Production index	Value	Production index	Value	Production index
	million yen	1873-77 =100	million yen	1873-77 =100	million yen	1873-77 =100
	(1)	(2)	(3)	(4)	(5)	(6)
1873-1877	1410	100.0	1326	100.0	1244	100.0
1878-1882	1448	102.7	1376	103.8	1304	104.8
1883-1887	1491	105.7	1430	107.8	1369	110.0
1888-1892	1545	109.6	1497	112.9	1448	116.4
1893-1897	1593	113.0	1558	117.5	1521	122.3
1898-1902	1670	118.4	1649	124.4	1625	130.6
1903-1907	1752	124.3	1746	131.7	1738	139.7
1908-1912	1853	131.4	1865	140.6	1876	150.8
1913-1917	1947	138.1	1980	149.3	2010	161.6
1918-1922	2046	145.1	2100	158.4	2153	173.1

SOURCES: Column (1): Sum of Column (2), Table 5-5, and Column (2), Table 5-6.
Column (3): Sum of Column (4), Table 5-5, and Column (4), Table 5-6.
Column (5): Sum of Column (6), Table 5-5, and Column (6), Table 5-6.
NOTE: [a] Assumed paddy rice yields are respectively for 1873-77 and 1918-22.

TABLE 5-8

ANNUAL GROWTH RATES OF CORRECTED VALUE OF AGRICULTURAL
PRODUCTION UNDER VARYING PADDY RICE YIELD ASSUMPTIONS
(unit=per cent)

Assumed paddy rice yields[a] (*koku* per *tan*)		1.7 and 1.9	1.6 and 1.95	1.5 and 2.0
		(1)	(2)	(3)
Paddy rice production				
1873-1877 to 1898-1902	(1)	.48	.67	.87
1898-1902 to 1918-1922	(2)	.63	.82	1.02
1873-1877 to 1918-1922	(3)	.55	.74	.94
Other agricultural production				
1873-1877 to 1898-1902	(4)	.92	1.12	1.32
1898-1902 to 1918-1922	(5)	1.43	1.62	1.83
1873-1877 to 1918-1922	(6)	1.15	1.34	1.54
Total agricultural production				
1873-1877 to 1898-1902	(7)	.68	.88	1.07
1898-1902 to 1918-1922	(8)	1.02	1.21	1.42
1873-1877 to 1918-1922	(9)	.83	1.03	1.23

SOURCES: 1. Paddy rice production growth rates computed from Table 5-5.
2. Other agricultural production growth rates computed from Table 5-6.
3. Total agricultural production growth rates computed from Table 5-7.
NOTE: [a] Assumed paddy rice yields are respectively for 1873-77 and 1918-22.

CHAPTER 6

Comparison of Corrected Estimates with Previous Estimates of Agricultural Production

ALTHOUGH estimates of the value and the growth rate of agricultural production have been revised, an evaluation of the new figures requires comparisons with previous estimates. The first section of this chapter will be given to a numerical comparison with three other estimates of agricultural production, and with a fourth estimate made by the author and not corrected for understatement of production. The second section of this chapter presents further evidence to substantiate the contention that the new estimates are more consistent with other historical data and relationships than previous estimates. The third section will discuss the effect of the new estimates of agricultural production on the growth rate of the economy as a whole.

Comparison with Other Estimates of
Agricultural Production

The three published estimates selected for comparison are those of Bruce F. Johnston,[1] Ohkawa and associates,[2] and Saburo Yamada.[3] They will be referred to as the Johnston, Ohkawa, and Yamada estimates. Both the Johnston and Ohkawa estimates are based on official statistics, and neither has been corrected for understatement of area planted to crops or for underreporting of yield per unit area. The Yamada estimates

[1] Johnston, "Agricultural Productivity and Economic Development of Japan," *op.cit.*, pp. 498-513.

[2] Ohkawa *et al.*, *op.cit.*, pp. 49-77.

[3] Saburo Yamada, "Nōgyō sanshutsu gaku no suikei" [Estimation of the value of agricultural production], *Keizai Kenkyu*, XV, 1 (January 1964), 71-76.

while using government statistics do in effect make minor adjustments for understatement of production as we shall see. None of the three estimates are strictly comparable to the corrected estimates. For this reason comparison is also made with an uncorrected estimate that I made which is comparable to the corrected estimates in respect to technique of estimation, the time period covered, and the number of crops included. Furthermore, this estimate provides a check on the biases inherent in the method of aggregation used to obtain the corrected estimates. This estimate will be referred to as "my uncorrected estimate."

The Johnston estimates show a 77 per cent increase in agricultural production in a period of 30 years[4] from which an annual growth rate of 1.9 per cent can be computed. This contrasts with the corrected growth rate range of 0.8 to 1.2 per cent. For two reasons, Johnston's figure may actually understate the growth rate of officially recorded agricultural production. Because Johnston's production index is based only on the production of six staple food crops and omits cocoon production, in which productivity rose more rapidly than that of the average of the six food crops,[5] it probably understates the rate of increase implicit in government statistics. The use of a longer and later base period of 1881-90 (in contrast to the 1878-82 base of corrected production) also causes the increase to be somewhat lower than if an earlier base had been chosen, because a spurt in reported production occurred in the middle of the 1880's, as stated in Chapter 4. The 1.9 per cent Johnston growth rate is almost twice that of the average growth rate of 1.0 per cent of corrected estimates, and more than 50 per cent greater than the maximum rate of 1.2 per cent.

[4] Johnston, "Agricultural Productivity and Economic Development of Japan," *op.cit.*, p. 499. Johnston took decennial averages from 1881-90 to 1911-20 in obtaining his figure. His decennial production indices are:

Period	Index	Period	Index
1881-1890	100	1901-1910	146
1891-1900	127	1911-1920	177

[5] Many new crops were introduced into Japan in early Meiji; therefore, it is probable that reported land productivity in their cases also grew more rapidly than the average of the six crops.

Even more startling is the growth rate found in the Ohkawa estimates. The increase in the value of agricultural production in 1913-17 prices in the 35-year period from 1878-82 to 1913-17 is 136 per cent as shown in Table 6-1. This increase is equivalent to an annual growth rate of 2.4 per cent which is twice the maximum growth rate of the corrected value of agricultural production. The Ohkawa growth rate probably overstates the rate implicit in the official statistics. This conclusion is drawn from the unusually steep increase of 127 per cent in the constant yen value of that component of agricultural production which excludes paddy rice and cocoon in the 20-year period from 1878-82 to 1898-1902. This contrasts with an increase in the value of paddy rice of 42 per cent and an increase of 73 per cent in the value of cocoon production.[6] Since historical evidence indicates that the increases in the values of cocoon and rice production overshadowed that of other crops, it can only be inferred that biases were introduced in the estimation that overstated the growth of agricultural production, at least until the turn of the century.

In one respect it is not surprising that the Ohkawa index should show a higher growth rate than the Johnston and the corrected estimates. The Ohkawa index is a value index, whereas the other two are volume indices. Owing to quality changes, introduction of new crops, and changes in the composition of crops, value tends to rise more rapidly than volume quite apart from inflationary price changes. The volume index, however, avoids a major difficulty of the value index: the problem of pricing of crops which is a particularly difficult one where markets are still poorly developed.

In agriculture quality changes tend to be of lesser importance

[6] The Ohkawa value of all agricultural production increased by 71 per cent from 766 million yen in 1878-82 to 1,309 million yen in 1898-1902 in 1913-17 prices according to Table 6-1. The value of paddy rice production in 1913-17 price rose from 463 to 658 million yen; that of cocoon production rose from 64 to 111 million; and that of all other agricultural production from 239 to 543 million yen. (Current values of paddy rice and cocoon production computed from Ohkawa *et al.*, *op.cit.*, pp. 55-57; and deflators computed from *ibid.*, pp. 126-27.)

than in other sectors of the economy. In the Japanese case the differentiation into volume and value indices is not likely to have caused a major difference in growth rates for two reasons. One is that over 80 per cent of the area planted to crops continued to be planted to the principal food crops—the grains, pulses and potatoes—and this ratio remained almost constant. Quality changes in such crops do not significantly affect value added per *koku* except in the very short run. The second reason is that despite improvement in quality the price of cocoons relative to those of other crops declined. For example, from 1878-82 to 1913-17 the average price of rice rose by 81 per cent and that of cocoons by 27 per cent. Cocoons were by far the most important of the non-food products, requiring the use of about 9 per cent of the cultivated land area. The downward bias of the price change, however, was partially offset by increases in the area planted to this valuable crop. What the precise change in area was is not known.

Yamada's estimates[7] reveal an 84 per cent increase in production from 1878-82 to 1913-17 (see Table 6-2). His estimated growth rate of 1.8 per cent per annum (1874-78 to 1918-22) is very close to that of Johnston, but in other respects his is the most interesting of the three studies from the perspective of this book.

Yamada's estimates are noteworthy for three reasons. First, they are adjusted for the acute upward shift in the mid-1880's in the production of the principal grains (rice, wheat, barley, naked barley) and for other unspecified items. Since this adjustment is for total production what Yamada does without so specifying is to adjust for what I have claimed is the understatement of yield per unit area and of area planted to crops. Although the point is not very clear, the adjustment apparently was not consistently carried out for all crops. Furthermore, there is no correction for undermeasurement of arable land. Yamada saw no need for adjustment of data after the 1880's, and explanations are not given for the adjustments that he does

[7] Yamada, *op.cit.*, pp. 71-76.

TABLE 6-1

OHKAWA VALUE AND INDEX OF AGRICULTURAL PRODUCTION IN
1913-17 PRICES, FIVE-YEAR AVERAGES, 1878-1917

Period	Value in current prices million yen	Price index 1913-17=100	Value in 1913-17 prices million yen	Index of (3) 1878-82=100
	(1)	(2)	(3)	(4)
1878-1882	431.2	56.3	766	100
1883-1887	333.1	37.4	891	116
1888-1892	460.2	42.8	1075	140
1893-1897	632.1	56.3	1123	147
1898-1902	958.5	73.2	1309	171
1903-1907	1230.6	85.9	1433	187
1908-1912	1501.3	92.9	1616	211
1913-1917	1806.4	100.0	1806	236

SOURCES: Column (1) computed from Kazushi Ohkawa *et al., The Growth Rate of the Japanese Economy Since 1878* (Tokyo, 1957), pp. 55-57. Column (2) computed from price indices in *ibid.*, pp. 126-27, and weights, *ibid.*, p. 123.

TABLE 6-2

YAMADA VALUE AND INDEX OF AGRICULTURAL PRODUCTION AT
1913-17 PRICE LEVEL, FIVE-YEAR AVERAGES, 1878-1917

Period	Value in 1955 prices billion yen	Value at 1913-17 price level[a] million yen	Index of value
	(1)	(2)	(3)
1878-1882	565	966	100.0
1883-1887	628	1073	111.1
1888-1892	695	1188	123.0
1893-1897	714	1220	126.3
1898-1902	778	1330	137.7
1903-1907	841	1437	148.8
1908-1912	934	1596	165.2
1913-1917	1038	1774	183.6

SOURCE: Column (1): Saburo Yamada, "Nōgyō sanshutsu-gaku no suikei" [Estimation of the value of agricultural production], *Keizai Kenkyū*, XV, 1 (January 1964), 75.

NOTES: [a] The values at the 1913-17 price level are the product of Column (1) and the coefficient, 0.001709. The coefficient is the quotient of the dividend 1,774 million yen and the divisor 1,038 billion yen. The 1913-17 value of 1,774 million yen is from *ibid.*

make. A second interesting feature of his study is that his data carry back to 1874,[8] thus utilizing statistical data not previously used in estimation of agricultural production. A third notable point is that he bases his estimates on 95 commodities for which he has constructed continuous series by extrapolation or interpolation wherever data were deficient (and, of course, made upward adjustments whenever he thought understatement was indicated). The 95 include almost all of agricultural production. Since he does not adjust his estimate to include all agricultural production, his figures are admittedly an understatement of the actual production, albeit a small one.[9]

It is Yamada's belief that correction of understatement should take place by appropriate adjustments of the original government statistics. This procedure assumes that there are certain discernible regularities in the understatement. The fact that he sees no understatement after the 1880's makes his assumption more tenable. I argue, of course, that the understatement extended over a much longer period and that village incentive to underreport production and government concern over accurate statistics tended to fluctuate. In these circumstances the assumption of a discernible regularity in the understatement does not appear tenable, and a better procedure would be to make as few assumptions as possible with investigation in depth of the tenability of those few assumptions.

A comparison between Ohkawa, Yamada, and the corrected values of agricultural production at 1913-17 prices[10] is instructive (see also Figure 1-1):

	Value 1878-82	Value 1918-22	Growth rates
Corrected estimates	1376 million yen	1980 million yen	1.0 per cent
Ohkawa estimates	766	1806	2.4
Yamada estimates	966	1774	1.8

[8] He uses data from the cadastral survey of the 1870's as one basis for his correction. I have argued that they understate area and yield per *tan.*

[9] My estimates probably also understate production since it is based on Ohkawa data in the base year. Ohkawa estimates probably fail to take full account of multiple cropping.

[10] The Johnston estimates, if put in value terms with the 1913-17

A remarkable difference exists in the values of production in the first five-year period between the corrected value and the Ohkawa value. The former is 80 per cent greater than the latter.

My uncorrected production index was obtained by computing uncorrected indices of area planted and the yield per *tan* of paddy rice and dryland crop production for the same set of crops used in estimating the corrected values. Indices of production were obtained only for the two terminal periods 1878-82 and 1918-22, since the objective was to obtain the increase in production over the 40-year period and to compute the growth rate over the same period.

If by this procedure a growth rate higher than that of Johnston and lower than that of Ohkawa *et al.*, were obtained, the technique of estimation could be construed as an effective one tending to obtain a truer estimate of the growth rate implicit in the official statistics than either of the other two estimates.

The production index for reported paddy rice production in 1918-22 is 193 when 1878-82 is the base period.[11] The same index for all other agricultural production is 283.[12] The uncorrected values in the 1918-22 period will be taken to equal the corrected values without the undermeasurement adjustment but with the assumption that paddy rice yield was 1.95 *koku* per *tan* in 1918-22. Under the above assumptions the uncorrected value of paddy rice production at 1913-17 prices is 962

---

value equal to the Ohkawa value, would show approximately the same relative change as the Yamada values.

[11] The increase in reported production of paddy rice was from an average of 29,744 thousand *koku* in 1878-82 to an average of 57,426 thousand *koku* in 1918-22. (Computed from *NRT*, p. 24.)

[12] The increase in area planted to dryland crops is estimated to be 52%. The average area in 1878-82 is assumed to be represented by the 1880 Taxed Upland Field Area of 1,847 thousand *cho* (Statistical Appendix: Table 1B) plus 767 thousand *cho* which is 30% of the paddy rice area in 1880 of 2,558 thousand *cho* (Statistical Appendix: Table 3A), a total of 2,614 thousand *cho*. The area in 1918-22 was 3,980 thousand *cho*. (See Table 2-10, p. 48.) The increase in yield per *tan* was 86% from 1879-84 to 1915-25. (Statistical Appendix: Table 6.) This increase will be taken to represent the increase from the 1878-82 period to 1918-22. The total change from reported area and yield changes is, then, 183%.

million yen[13] for 1918-22, and it is 498 million yen for 1878-82 as shown in Table 6-3. The uncorrected values for other agricultural production with the same assumptions are 1,023 million yen[14] in 1918-22 and 361 million yen in 1878-82. The uncorrected values of total agricultural production are 1,984 million yen in 1918-22 and 859 million yen in 1878-82. The relative increase from the earlier period to 1918-22 is 131 per cent. The annual growth rate of the uncorrected value of agricultural production is 2.1 per cent.

My uncorrected estimate indicates that the growth rate inherent in government statistics are about twice the corrected

[13] The figure is obtained by dividing the corrected 1918-22 value of 1,027 million yen by 1.069, the undermeasurement index for paddy fields.

[14] The figure is obtained by dividing the corrected 1918-22 value of 1,073 million yen by 1.049, the undermeasurement index for upland fields.

TABLE 6-3

COMPARISON OF CORRECTED AND UNCORRECTED VALUES OF
AGRICULTURAL PRODUCTION FOR 1878-82 AND 1918-22
IN 1913-17 PRICES

	1878-82 value million yen	1918-22 value million yen	Per cent increase %	Growth rate %
	(1)	(2)	(3)	(4)
Paddy fields				
Corrected value	762	1027	35	0.8
Uncorrected value	498	961	93	1.7
Other agricultural production				
Corrected value	614	1073	75	1.4
Uncorrected value	361	1023	183	2.6
Total agricultural production				
Corrected value	1376	2100	53	1.0
Uncorrected value	859	1984	131	2.1

SOURCES: Corrected values are from Tables 5-5, 5-6, and 5-7. The growth rates of corrected values are from Table 5-8. It is assumed that the paddy rice yields per *tan* were 1.6 and 1.95 *koku* in 1873-77 and 1918-22, respectively.
Uncorrected values were computed by the same technique of estimation employed to compute the corrected values, except that adjustments were not made for understatement of area planted to crops and the yields per *tan*.

growth rate. It is more than those of Yamada and Johnston, and less than that of Ohkawa *et al.* It may be concluded that the method of aggregation used in computing the corrected growth rate of agricultural production is probably no worse than the method used in the Ohkawa and Johnston estimates, and, in fact, may be superior to it.

The various values associated with the corrected and uncorrected values reveal interesting contrasts. Table 6-3 shows that the growth rates of uncorrected values are roughly double those of corrected values for the three categories of agricultural production. (It must be borne in mind that the corrected values apply to the assumption of median paddy rice yields per *tan* of 1.6 and 1.95 *koku* in 1873-77 and 1918-22, respectively.) Another noteworthy difference is that the corrected value for 1878-82 is 60 per cent greater than the uncorrected value, which is to say that the corrected value of agricultural production in 1878-82 was 60 per cent greater than the official statistics indicate.

Evaluation of the Corrected Estimates of Agricultural Production

Whether we consider the values of production in early Meiji, the increases over a comparable period, or the growth rates, the estimates corrected for understatement of production in the Meiji era are a conspicuous and disturbing change from previous estimates. For this reason, it is important to present all available evidence to establish that the new estimates are not a statistical sleight-of-hand. Most of the evidence thus far presented is substantive and indicates that a real understatement did exist. Ultimately, in controversies of this type, however, judgment must be based on whether the new data are consistent with other historical evidence and relationships which have been accepted. Many of the arguments presented in support of our area and yield adjustments have been of this nature. In the rest of this section evidence of this character related to total agricultural production will be presented.

It has already been demonstrated that the reported food production in the 1878-82 period was wholly inadequate to sustain a healthy productive population. Yet history attests to the vigor and the energy of the Japanese during the Meiji era which could hardly have been true if the food supply had not been adequate. Although the early Meiji agricultural production was underreported, this does not in itself prove that the Ohkawa and the Johnston growth rates overstate the actual increase that occurred. The two growth rates would be consistent with an adequate food supply in 1878-82 if the understatement of agricultural production (food constituted over 80 per cent of the value of agricultural production through the entire period under consideration) of approximately the same degree persisted through to 1918-22. In this event, however, Japan should have had such an abundance of food that she would have been a major food exporter instead of a food importer.[15] Furthermore, it has been shown that production in 1918-22 was only very slightly underreported if at all. It can be concluded that the two growth rates were out of line with the food supply conditions of the period under study.

Historically, the farmers of a traditional economy have been observed to respond very slowly to stimuli. The centuries-old deeply rooted values, rhythms of work and play, and patterns of thought take a long time to change. The agricultural sector of the Japanese economy in the period under study was typically traditional in most respects. Moreover, despite the rapid expansion of arable land in Hokkaidō, it is probably fair to state that Japan was producing under the condition of a limited land supply. Given the above conditions, very rapid rates of growth can hardly have been expected. Yet the growth rate of agricultural net product per worker in Japan was said to be among the highest of any nation,[16] including those devoted largely to commercial farming under virtually unlimited land supply conditions. The rate of growth of corrected agricultural production, which is not at all exceptional, is more consistent with what could have been expected in Japan.

The growth rates of agricultural production of 0.8 to 1.2 per

[15] Net rice imports were more than 10% of domestic production in 1915-25. (Computed from *NRT*, pp. 160-61.)

[16] Ohkawa and Rosovsky, *op.cit.*, pp. 65-66, 44.

cent are more consistent with the population growth rate and foreign trade in rice than previous estimates. The Japanese population rose from 35.6 million in 1875 to 56.0 million in 1920, an annual growth rate of 1.0 per cent which is equal to the average growth rate of corrected agricultural production of 1.0 per cent. The finding that corrected paddy rice production under median yield assumptions rose by an average annual rate of 0.7 per cent per annum (see Table 5-8, Column (2), p. 115) suggests that food consumption per capita declined from 1873-77 to 1918-22. But owing to increased rice imports and the production of upland rice, the total corrected rice supply grew at a 1.0 per cent rate in the 40-year period from 1878-82 to 1918-22.[17] In addition, very substantial amounts of other food products were imported including wheat, soy beans, sugar, and animal products. Furthermore, food distribution improved during the period owing to a continuing betterment of the transportation and communication systems. Therefore, it would appear that the calorie intake of food would have remained at least constant in the 40-year period if the growth rate of agricultural production is taken to be 1.0 per cent per year. The fact that Japan had become heavily dependent on food imports by around 1920, after having been a net food exporter until around 1895, is more compatible with this growth rate than those of Johnston and Ohkawa.

The Effect on the Growth Rate of the Economy as a Whole

The downward revision of the agricultural growth rate also downgrades the growth rate of the economy as a whole. The Ohkawa estimate of the growth of the Japanese economy from 1878-82 to 1913-17 is 4 per cent per year. By simply substituting the corrected net value of agricultural production[18] for

[17] I estimate that average rice supply in 1878-82 was 43.7 million *koku* and that in 1918-22 it was 64.7 million *koku*. The population growth rate during the same period was 0.9% per year.

[18] The corrected net value of agricultural production is the value of final goods produced in the agricultural sector minus purchases of intermediate products from other sectors. The net value was obtained by using the Ohkawa net income ratio which is the ratio of net value of agricultural production to the gross value. (Ohkawa *et al., op.cit.,* p. 64.)

the Ohkawa value of agricultural production and using the Ohkawa estimates for all other production[19] the growth rate of the economy is reduced to 2.8 per cent per year in the 35-year period.[20] But even this lower rate is an overestimation of the actual growth rate since the government statistics of secondary and tertiary production, on which the Ohkawa estimates are based, overstate their growth rate for the reasons given below.

Two reasons may be given for the overstatement in the secondary sector.[21] One reason derives from the Ohkawa definition of national income. The Ohkawa estimates do not include as social product a good or a service produced for home consumption by a household that is not engaged in the production of that good or service for the market.[22] Therefore, goods that are normally classified as products of the secondary industry that were produced in the household for home consumption were not counted. Only goods that were produced by "factory production and domestic manufacture (household industry)" are counted.[23] During the Meiji era and until relatively recent times, the rural household produced almost all of its own cloth, clothes, footgear, housing, many farm implements, and most processed foods and beverages, such as soy sauce, bean paste sauce (*miso*), pickles, rice wine (*sake*), and the like. The urban

[19] All other production includes those normally classified under secondary and tertiary sectors plus those from the forestry and fishery industries.

[20] Over the 40-year period from 1878-82 to 1918-22 the growth rate of the economy is 3.0%, which is 0.2% greater than for the 35-year period from 1878-82 to 1913-17. The 35-year period is used above because it is believed to be a more normal period than that which includes the five-year period from 1918-1922 which was heavily affected by World War I.

Harry T. Oshima primarily relying on labor force data estimated that the national income of Japan in 1881 was 10 to 25% greater than those of Y. Yamada (*op.cit.*) and Ohkawa *et al.* (*op.cit.*). ("Notes on an Alternative Method of Estimating the National Income and Expenditure of Japan, 1881", *op.cit.*, p. 251) His estimates make the growth rate 3.3 to 3.7%.

[21] The Ohkawa secondary sector consists of mining, manufacturing, and public utilities, whereas the sector is usually regarded as consisting of mining, manufacturing and construction.

[22] Ohkawa *et al.*, *op.cit.*, pp. 8-9.

[23] *Ibid.*, p. 78. Not included is the output of government enterprises which were counted in the tertiary sector.

household also produced some of the things it consumed such as clothes. The increase in output per worker for this type of production was probably very low. Since the proportion of such goods to total secondary sector production was surely greater in early Meiji than later, this practice gives an upward bias to the rate of increase in the production of goods normally classified as produced in the secondary sector.

The above concept of national income with some modification is suitable for estimating the national product of economically developed nations. Since production in such nations is highly specialized and almost all of the production is counted in practice (except the services rendered by housewives, and a few minor items), national income obtained by using the concept serves as a fair measure of the change in real output. But for economically less developed nations this concept provides a hybrid national income that is a measure of real output insofar as agricultural production is concerned, but only a measure of industrialization (or specialization) in regard to other forms of production; that is, even when actual secondary sector production remains constant, production as defined increases when a shift from production for home consumption to production for the market takes place. The above concept of the national income is not suitable for the less developed nations. It gives an unduly bright picture of the change actually taking place which may discourage developing nations in the longer run. Moreover, since this concept provides only a partial view of the economy, it tends to give less than satisfactory data for analysts and model-makers. For example a flow of labor from the agricultural household to urban industrial employment reduces not only the production of agricultural crops, but a host of other goods and services provided by the household. Use of the narrow concept of national income will fail to provide quantitative data from which accurate parameters for analytical and planning models can be obtained.

The second reason for the overstatement of the growth rate is that the enumeration of secondary sector production became more complete over time. The Ohkawa estimates use the series compiled at the Nagoya Commercial College (the present Nagoya University) without adjustment.[24] Examination of the Nagoya series for factory production as used in *The Growth Rate of the Japanese Economy Since 1878* reveals that the value of production for any year is simply the sum of the values of the various classes of production for which data were compiled in that year. As data for new classes of goods became available they were added to the total. For example, ceramics, chemicals, and miscellaneous are counted from 1868; food and beverage from 1872; textiles and metals from 1879; gas and electricity from 1880; and printing and bookbinding from 1886. Within each of the classes, it is evident from the data that new sub-classes or previously uncounted firms (and their production) were included as time passed. Between 1885 and 1886 a sharp increase in factory production is shown. The gross value of production in current prices was estimated to be 89 million yen in 1885 and 128 million yen a year later.[25] The increase in real terms was even greater. The price level of nonagricultural products fell about 7 per cent in the one-year period[26] making the estimated value of production in 1886, 139 million yen in 1885 prices. The increase in real terms for the one-year period is then 56 per cent. A one-year increase in factory production of this magnitude can be regarded as an impossibility.[27]

Since procedures and forms used in statistical reporting of factories and production were revised in March 1886, it may be inferred that the above increase resulted from a fuller coverage of industries and plants. It is noteworthy that in the same period a marked increase in reported agricultural production also took place which can be attributed to the same cause. In Chapter 4 (pp. 81f) it was noted that owing to the depression

[24] *Ibid.*, pp. 78-83. The series will henceforth be referred to as the Nagoya series.

[25] *Ibid.*, p. 81.

[26] *Ibid.*, p. 130.

[27] Historical descriptions of the 1885-86 year indicate a stagnant economy.

the government placed great importance in the collection of reliable statistics.

From the evidence presented above it may be inferred that there was a greater tendency for a stronger upward bias in the growth rate of the first half of the period under study than of the latter half. The fact that the growth rate in reported production was 8.8 per cent per year from 1878-82 to 1898-1902 and 4.2 per cent from 1898-1902 to 1913-17 supports the inference.

Just before this book went to press a new index of industrial production for a somewhat later period was brought to my attention, which tends to support my argument. This was prepared by Y. Yasuba for a conference sponsored by the Tokyo Economic Research Center in January 1965.[28] This work shows that industrial production increased by four times from 1905-10 to 1931-35, as against an increase of seven times for the Nagoya index in the same period. The Yasuba index, like the Nagoya index, does not include in industrial production secondary sector products produced for household consumption.

A number of factors account for the difference in the growth of industrial production. Two points, however, are relevant to our argument:[29] (1) Yasuba states that a tendency to falsify production reports existed for business and tax reasons; (2) noting that production rose sharply in the first few years after reporting of production began for a given commodity, he states that the increase owed more to fuller coverage in time than to an actual rise in production. It has been argued above that the same factors caused an understatement of industrial production before 1905 as well.

Shown below are the Nagoya and Yasuba indices of industrial production (1906-10=100) and the growth rates from previous five-year period:[30]

[28] Y. Yasuba, *Nihon no kōgyō seisan shisū* [Japan's industrial production index] (mimeograph; Tokyo, January 1965).

[29] *Ibid.*, pp. 16-17.

[30] Computed from *ibid.*, pp. 57-60.

| Period | Nagoya estimates | | Yasuba estimates | |
	Index	Growth rate (per cent)	Index	Growth rate (per cent)
1906-10	100	–	100	–
1911-15	158	9.5	126	4.7
1916-20	261	10.6	191	8.6
1921-25	362	6.2	238	4.6
1926-30	535	8.1	323	6.4
1931-35	705	5.7	416	5.2

The Nagoya growth rates appear to have a generally downward trend, whereas the Yasuba rates appear to show a contrary trend if the wartime boom in industrial production is discounted. The growth rates for the 25-year period are 8.1 per cent for the Nagoya index and 5.9 per cent for the Yasuba index. The Yasuba estimates indicate that the growth rate of the Japanese economy in the interwar period was probably significantly less than previously believed.

We turn now to understatement of production in the tertiary sector. The Ohkawa tertiary sector, owing to limitations imposed by the then available data, consists of communication, transportation, construction, commerce, and government, with the latter including government manufacturing enterprises. Ohkawa *et al.*, state that construction and government enterprises belong rightfully in the secondary sector and that they intend to put them in that sector when data permits.[31]

The question of what the social product consists of is also applicable to the tertiary sector. Clearly when services were not available in the market place, they had to be self supplied. Therefore, the household transported its own rice, carried its own messages, kept its own strongbox for storing money and valuables, and the like. If we assume that these self-supplied services are part of the national product, then not counting them causes tertiary production in the early years to be understated.

The value of production in this sector was determined on a different basis from that in the other sectors for the period from

[31] *Op.cit.*, p. 100.

1878 to 1918. A method was used which made the value to 1918 a function of the wage rates in the primary and secondary sectors, the per capita incomes in the same two sectors, and the gainfully occupied population in the tertiary sector. To the extent that the value of production in the tertiary sector is dependent on per capita incomes in the primary and secondary sectors, the growth rate of the value of production in the tertiary sector will have an upward bias because the growth rates in the latter two sectors have this bias. However, inasmuch as the wage rates used in the estimation tended to rise much more slowly than per capita income, this upward bias will tend to be modified to some extent.

The dependency on the estimated gainfully occupied population probably gives the growth rate an upward bias. The gainfully occupied population figures for the tertiary sector are of questionable reliability as Ohkawa et al., point out.[32] In the first place the concept is a loose one. It was basically an administrative convenience for labeling an individual by his occupation. If a man works at a given employment for one hour a week and has no other employment, then in his administrative district he could be classified as gainfully occupied at that employment. Even if an individual were unemployed at the time the census was taken, he would be classified as gainfully employed in the occupation from which he had been laid off. It is clear then that the gainfully occupied population cannot be equated with the employed population. This, however, is the figure that is used in estimating the income of the tertiary sector. An upward bias is likely because the estimated gainfully occupied population increased by 23 per cent in the 15-year period between 1878 and 1893[33] while the population of those in the 15-64 year age bracket increased by only 5.4 per cent.[34] If this highly questionable 23 per cent increase held true for

[32] *Ibid.*, pp. 146-49.

[33] Computed from *ibid.*, pp. 140, 145.

[34] Computed from Yoichi Okazaki, *Meiji shonen ikō Taisho kunen ni itaru danjo nenreibetsu jinko suikei ni tsuite* [Population estimates by sex and age from 1870's to 1920] (Institute of Population Problems Research Series No. 145, February 1, 1962, Tokyo, 1962), pp. 38-39.

the tertiary sector also, it could have given the increase in the estimated value of production a further upward bias. The actual increase in the estimated gainfully occupied population of the tertiary sector during this same 15-year period was 65 per cent as against an increase of 11 per cent in that of the combined primary and secondary sectors.[35]

The evidence presented suggests that the growth rate of the tertiary sector computed by the Ohkawa method would tend to be higher in early Meiji than in the latter half. The growth figures bear this out. The growth rate in the 1878-82 to 1898-1902 period is 6.0 per cent; in the following 15-year period it is 4.1 per cent.

From the evidence presented it is probable that the increase in production in the secondary and tertiary sectors was substantially overstated. But this evidence does not provide us with a basis for estimating the growth rate of the economy as a whole. We can, however, state with assurance that the growth rate of the economy was considerably less than 2.8 per cent in the 35-year period from 1878-82 to 1913-17.

A number of economists have observed a "spurt" in production during an early period in the economic development of economically advanced nations. Kazushi Ohkawa and Henry Rosovsky have observed and identified such an accelerated growth in early Meiji in the Ohkawa income estimates[36] (therefore, in official statistics). The estimates show that the growth rate of the economy was 4.9 per cent from 1878-82 to 1898-1902 and 2.8 per cent from 1898-1902 to 1913-17.[37] A notable spurt is indicated in the earlier of the two periods.

The new estimates of total production reduce the rates of growth to 3.0 per cent in the 20-year period to 1900 and to 2.6 per cent in the following 15-year period. Furthermore, the critique of production estimates for the secondary and tertiary industries suggests that the actual production rose at a substantially lower rate than 3.0 per cent in the first 20-year period.

[35] Computed from Ohkawa *et al., op.cit.,* p. 145.
[36] "A Century of Japanese Economic Growth," *The State and Economic Enterprise in Japan,* ed., William W. Lockwood (Princeton, 1965), p. 68.
[37] Computed from Ohkawa *et al., op.cit.,* p. 18.

If this is correct, the apparent spurt of the Japanese economy observable in growth rates derived from official statistics was not as great as previously believed, if indeed a spurt did occur. If a spurt actually did occur, it would have been due to increases in the secondary and tertiary industries. According to previous growth figures a sudden increase in agricultural production was a quantitatively important element in the spurt.

It is likely that growth was stimulated in the nonagricultural sector when economic restrictions were lifted at the beginning of the Meiji era owing to the existence of the reserves of productivity in agriculture that could be and were mobilized for use elsewhere. (See Chapter 7, pp. 151ff.) However, what occurred in the early Meiji years was primarily a redirection of demand which involved a transfer of resources from industries catering to the needs of a privileged class (Tokugawa ruling class) to industries fulfilling the needs of a broader segment of the population in which the production of capital goods was becoming increasingly important.[38] Therefore, the increase in the tempo of economic activity was probably less spectacular than the term "spurt" seems to imply. Moreover, if a growth spurt took place, it need not have been followed by a deceleration in growth except those associated with business cycles.

Summary

The growth rate of the corrected index of agricultural production (cost of intermediate products purchased from other sectors is not deducted) is compared with that of other estimates of gross agricultural production. These include estimates by Bruce F. Johnston, Kazushi Ohkawa and associates, and Saburo Yamada. As a check on the biases inherent in my method of aggregating the value of agricultural production, this method was used to obtain an estimate not corrected for underreporting of yield and area planted to crops. The growth rates of various estimates of agricultural production given in ascending order follow:

[38] For a further discussion of why labor transfer probably did not greatly increase labor productivity, see Chapter 7, pp. 153-54.

Corrected estimate	0.8—1.2%
Yamada estimate	1.8%
Johnston estimate	1.9%
My uncorrected estimate	2.1%
Ohkawa estimate	2.4%

The corrected estimate presents a startling change from previous estimates.

The Yamada estimate is the closest to the corrected estimate as it should be since he made some corrections for understatement of production. The Johnston estimate probably understates and the Ohkawa estimate probably overstates the growth inherent in government statistics. My uncorrected estimate seems to indicate that the method of aggregation used does not by itself significantly bias the index.

By adding the corrected net value of agricultural production (net of intermediate goods purchased from other sectors) to the net value of all other production as estimated by Ohkawa *et al.*, the growth rate of the economy is reduced to 2.8 per cent per year in the 35-year period from 1878-82 to 1913-17. This is a decline from 4.0 per cent estimated by Ohkawa *et al.* Since it is probable that secondary and tertiary sector production are also understated, the actual rate of growth of the economy is probably substantially less than 2.8 per cent. The partially corrected growth rate in the first 20 years of the 35-year period was 3.0 per cent and in the final 15 years, 2.6 per cent. Since it seems likely that the understatement of production was much greater in the earlier period than in the latter, some doubt is cast upon the "spurt" thesis advanced by Ohkawa and Rosovsky.

CHAPTER 7

Agriculture in the Economic Development of Japan

A CHANGE in the data on agricultural production of the magnitude made here has significance far beyond the direct change in agricultural income and growth rate that is immediately apparent. Economic change is an extremely complex phenomenon even when only the so-called economic variables are considered. Changes in the growth rate and the income level of agriculture not only affect the growth rate and income of the entire economy, but they cannot take place independently of changes in the same variables in other sectors. To disaggregate somewhat, it is also apparent that changes in the level of income in the agricultural sector are related to changes in labor force, land area, the level of saving and consumption, and the level of investment; and it is clear that these changes are related to changes in the same variables in the nonagricultural sector.

In this chapter I will attempt to indicate the significance of the findings of this study for the economic development of Japan, particularly in respect to resource transfer, redistribution of income, and transfer of saving from the agricultural to the nonagricultural sector. Since growth does not take place in a vacuum, attention will first be given to Tokugawa conditions, especially to resource transfer.

The discussions in this chapter arise from problems raised by the conclusion that the value of production in the Meiji era and particularly in early Meiji, was seriously understated. The validity of much previous thinking on Japanese economic development of this period is put into question.

136

Resource Transfer from Agriculture in the Tokugawa Period

One of the interesting aspects of the growth process involves the transfer of resources, particularly labor, from the traditional sector of a developing economy to the modern sector. Usually the traditional sector is taken to be synonymous with the agricultural sector, a simplification that is justifiable for many purposes and which is also employed here.[1]

In discussions of Japan's modern economic growth Meiji resource transfer has deservedly received much attention. The Meiji transfer, however, was not a new development. It was a continuation of a trend that began in the Tokugawa period owing to economic changes of that period.

Although at one time it was fashionable to refer to Japan of the latter half of the Tokugawa period as a stationary state,[2] research discussed in Chapter 4 indicates that product per capita rose substantially in that time. From around the beginning of the eighteenth century to the middle of the nineteenth century the population remained about constant. During this period, since total production almost certainly increased, per capita product must also have increased. In agriculture, we have shown that from the 1680's to the 1870's, paddy rice yield per *tan* probably rose from about 1.3 to 1.6 *koku*, an increase in land productivity of about 23 per cent.[3] A greater diversification of crops also took place during this time. Recent research indicates that industrial and commercial activity likewise increased during the Tokugawa period, particularly in the rural areas.[4] Beginning about 1800, rural industrial and com-

---

[1] Although much has been made of Japan's traditional small-scale industries in the secondary and tertiary sectors, for the purposes intended here the simplification seems appropriate.

[2] According to Professor Kenzō Hemmi of Tokyo University the first published mention of the latter half of Tokugawa Japan as a "stationary state" was made by F. Y. Edgeworth. ("Stationary State in Japan," *Economic Journal*, V [September 1895], 480-81.)

[3] A decline in cultivated land area could have offset the increase in yield per *tan*, but the area appears to have remained about constant.

[4] Smith, *Agrarian Origins of Modern Japan, op.cit.*, pp. 83, 118, 130, 134. See also Charles D. Sheldon, *The Rise of the Merchant Class in Japan* (Locust Valley, New York, 1958), pp. 144-64.

mercial activity assumed national importance.[5] Most of the increase in rural industrial activity—almost entirely financed and operated by rural landlord-merchants—was induced by the existence of surplus (underemployed) labor and capital, by the development of the national market (including a rural market since peasant real income also rose), and by the availability of a wide range of raw materials.

The significance of the changing structure of rural production is that a continuous transfer of rural labor and capital from agricultural production to rural nonagricultural production must have taken place, particularly after 1800.

Since this change presaged the breakdown of the feudal system and posed a threat to agricultural production,[6] the ruling class took drastic measures in the attempt to stem the transfer. These included attempts "to stop immigration to Edo and even to return recent immigrants to their villages; to prohibit the migration of labor from one lord's jurisdiction to another; to prevent labor in the village from following occupations other than farming; to stimulate the birth rate, to fix wages, and much else."[7]

[5] Crawcour, "Change in Japanese Commerce in the Tokugawa Period," *op.cit.*, pp. 397-99.

[6] It was Tokugawa period policy to produce a food surplus in normal crop years in order to have a tolerable supply in poor crop years. (See Chapter 4, p. 100.) The excessive transfer of labor from agriculture to other sectors would have threatened this policy.

[7] Smith, *Agrarian Origins of Modern Japan*, *op.cit.*, pp. 111-12.

As a consequence of the food surplus policy, in most years the prices of agricultural products—particularly food products—were probably depressed relative to nonagricultural products. This effect would tend to be unfavorable to the agricultural sector and to the ruling class vis-à-vis the merchant class. This policy may have been one of the causes of the rising economic power of the Tokugawa merchant class.

It has been said that highly productive *honden* (main, as opposed to added or new, fields) were often abandoned in favor of less productive *shinden* (newly reclaimed fields) owing to the excessive tax burden on the former. It is probable that the abandonment was in part a response to the low prices of staple foods to whose cultivation *honden* were restricted. On *shinden* free cropping was permitted. Toshio Furushima shows that returns to non-food crops such as cotton and tobacco were substantially higher in the Tokugawa period. (*Op.cit.*, pp. 186, 443-51, 602.)

The policy was only partially successful. The existence of a great many regulations to terminate the flow is in itself evidence that the flow existed and that it was regarded as detrimental to the interests of the ruling class. The increase in rural nonagricultural production is also evidence of resource transfer. The growth of rural industry and commerce may have been due in part to the success of the measures to prevent the outflow of labor from the villages to the cities. To the provincial ruling class the retention of labor in the villages was desirable since such labor would still be available to agriculture in peak labor demand periods and would also increase the total income of the rural provinces.

In the developments discussed above the alternate attendance (*sankin kōtai*) system[8] played a pervasive role. As a consequence of its institution, the transportation and communications systems improved, production techniques were diffused, commodity and labor market information became widely available, and demand expanded for new goods and services to the remotest provinces. These in turn promoted establishment of rural industries and commerce, formation of a national market, movement of capital and labor resources, development of a national consciousness, and diffusion of other urban influences. It is possible that the urbanizing influence of the alternate attendance system was an important factor in the development of what appears to have been the widespread practice of population control (in the form of abortion, infanticide, and contraception) without which the rise in per capita income in the Tokugawa period might not have occurred.

Despite the development of rural industry and commerce, the nearly total self-sufficiency of the average peasant household indicates that at least seasonal underemployment continued to exist in agriculture. The economic reason for household production of nonagricultural goods was that sufficient labor time remained after agricultural labor had been performed for the household to produce at very little marginal labor cost almost everything it needed, including cloth and clothing, housing,

[8] For a description of the system, see p. 139.

soy sauce, bean paste sauce, liquor, and fertilizers. Further-more, the existence of free time prompted many families to produce for the market a wide variety of consumer goods, the most important of which were cloth and straw products. Most of the underemployed labor time in the agricultural household was undoubtedly seasonal because the increasing incidence of double cropping in the Tokugawa period required that the farm household have available sufficient labor to meet successfully the heavy labor needs of the spring and fall seasons.[9]

There is little doubt, however, that the trend during the Tokugawa period was a net transfer of labor and capital from agricultural to nonagricultural production as labor and land productivity in agriculture rose.

Resource Transfer from Agriculture in the Meiji Era

Almost universal acceptance[10] has been accorded to the general proposition that Japan's industrialization during the Meiji era was heavily dependent on the rapid growth of agri-cultural production. The argument is summarized below.

Agricultural production and real income are said to have risen at more than 2 per cent per year which is somewhat more than twice the 0.9 per cent growth rate of population. Since the agricultural labor force declined somewhat during this period, it is claimed that the speed of growth is attributable to agricul-tural developments which caused labor productivity to increase at about 2.6 per cent per year.[11] A proposition of major impor-tance is therefore advanced that this remarkable increase in agricultural labor productivity released a cheap and "unlimited" supply of labor to other sectors since most of the population growth was taking place in farm families. Meanwhile, it is said, a large part of agricultural income was appropriated by the government through various taxes that weighed heavily on the agricultural sector. It is also said that agricultural saving

[9] Double cropping requires that within a short span of time one crop be harvested and the ground be prepared and planted to the second crop.

[10] A conspicuous exception is W. W. Lockwood who is extremely cautious in using Meiji statistics. He questions land area data in *op.cit.*, p. 86, Table 2, and suspects underreporting of production in *ibid.*, p. 170.

[11] Ohkawa and Rosovsky, *op.cit.*, p. 44.

mounted, inasmuch as consumption in the agricultural sector rose slowly if at all, and the tax burden is believed to have declined owing to inflation. During this period net agricultural investment is believed to have remained at low levels. This led to a second important proposition; namely, that the speed of growth of agricultural production was responsible for a large transfer of savings to other sectors. Landlords are believed to be responsible for most of these savings, and they invested a large part of their savings in the nonagricultural sector as entrepreneurs in their own right.

Although this generalized presentation cannot do justice to the full arguments of Bruce F. Johnston, Kazushi Ohkawa, Gustav Ranis, Henry Rosovsky, and others, I believe it is a fair summary of the previous non-Marxist interpretation[12] of agriculture's role in Japan's economic development in the Meiji era.

The findings in this study, which deny that production and labor productivity increased as rapidly as claimed, put into question the relevance of the propositions on transfers of labor and capital funds to the nonagricultural sector. Later in this section alternative explanations of resource transfer will be offered. But before doing so, certain inconsistencies in the previous argument will be presented.

It is implied by the previous argument that the agricultural labor force increased sharply in the late 1880's. That is, since the argument accepts the government production statistics, it must perforce accept the sudden increase in the reported cultivated land area of the 1880's. In a short period of time during which substantial increases in labor productivity cannot be expected to take place, labor input tends to increase in proportion to the increase in land area. Since the reported arable land area increased by about 10 per cent between 1886 and 1888, acceptance of the increase (which is implicit in using

---

[12] I shall not attempt to go into the intricacies of Marxist interpretations which derived from a fundamentally different perspective from my own. Marxists were primarily concerned with the development of capitalism as a stage in economic development; I am concerned with growth in real output.

uncorrected government production statistics) would require the acceptance of a comparable increase in the agricultural labor force then or soon thereafter, or a decline in yield per unit area. We have already noted (Chapter 4) that reported yield increased during this period.

Were there, then, other factors operating at that time which tended to reduce labor requirements by a substantial amount in a very short period of time? Examination of other important agricultural developments of the time reveals that all of them would have caused an absolute increase in agricultural labor requirements. These include greater use of fertilizers, multiple cropping, and increased production of cocoons. Seed improvement would also tend to increase labor use since in most cases it would increase the harvest per unit area of land.

Until the late 1950's, agricultural labor force estimates made by Seibi Hijikata shown in Column 1, Table 7-1, were almost universally accepted. These estimates show an increase of about 7 per cent between 1878-82 and 1888-92 which approaches the reported increase of 10 per cent in arable land area in the 1880's.

In the 1960's, however, the Hijikata estimates have been almost universally discarded in favor of the Hemmi or the Ohkawa estimates.[13] Table 7-1 shows that the Hemmi agricultural labor force although declining somewhat remains almost constant over the 40-year period. The Ohkawa estimates show a somewhat greater decline.

The official agricultural production data including a sharp increase in arable land area, however, are far more compatible with the Hijikata estimates of agricultural labor force than the Hemmi or Ohkawa estimates. Therefore, the concurrent acceptance of official production data and the Hemmi or Ohkawa labor force estimates by previous investigators[14] is an incon-

[13] The Ohkawa agricultural labor force estimates in Table 7-1 are not the same as the labor force data that appear in Ohkawa et al., op.cit. In the latter Hijikata estimates are used, whereas the Ohkawa estimates used in Table 7-1 appeared in the work cited for that Table.

[14] In his 1951 article, "Agricultural Productivity and Economic Development of Japan," op.cit., Bruce F. Johnston, of course, uses the Hijikata estimates.

TABLE 7-1

HIJIKATA, HEMMI, AND OHKAWA ESTIMATES OF THE
AGRICULTURAL LABOR FORCE, FIVE-YEAR AVERAGES
(unit=1000)

Period	Hijikata estimates	Hemmi estimates	Ohkawa estimates
	(1)	(2)	(3)
1873-1877	14,744	14,770	–
1878-1882	15,649	14,742	15,573
1883-1887	16,307	14,802	15,511
1888-1892	16,728	14,755	15,466
1893-1897	16,901	14,580	15,397
1898-1902	16,830	14,405	15,303
1903-1907	16,516	14,356	15,184
1908-1912	15,959	14,318	14,490
1913-1917	15,160	14,310	14,613

SOURCES: Columns (1) and (2) from Mataji Umemura, *Chingin-koyō-nōgyō* [Wages, employment, agriculture] (Tokyo, 1961), p. 119.
    Column (3) from Kazushi Ohkawa and Henry Rosovsky, "The Role of Agriculture in Modern Japanese Economic Development," *Economic Development and Cultural Change*, IX, 1, Part 2 (October 1960), p. 46, Table 2.

sistency if our conclusion about the relation between arable land area and agricultural labor requirements is correct.

On the other hand, the corrected index of agricultural production which shows a slow and steady growth of agricultural production and a slow rise in arable land area to the turn of the century is clearly more compatible with the Hemmi and Ohkawa estimates as opposed to the Hijikata estimates. At the same time the general acceptance of the former two estimates helps to validate the contention in this paper that agricultural production did not rise as spectacularly as the government statistics indicate.

Between the Hemmi and Ohkawa estimates, the Hemmi estimates have gained wider acceptance because the estimation procedure for the Ohkawa estimates have not been divulged, whereas the basis for the Hemmi estimates[15] are the agricul-

[15] Kenzō Hemmi, "Nōgyō jinkō no koteisei" [Stability of agricultural

tural household statistics which are regarded as among the most reliable of Japanese statistics. Hemmi constructs his agricultural household and labor force estimates from prefectural data, assuming a constant relationship between the two series for each prefecture. In general he assumes that the average farm is a family farm utilizing only household labor. The benchmark years for all estimates are the census years of 1920, 1930, and 1940. In the case of Hijikata, who made his estimate in 1929, only the 1920 census data were available for use. The latter's agricultural labor force is derived from a quadratic least-squares equation based on incomplete agricultural labor force data for 34 prefectures anchored on the 1920 census data.[16]

Mataji Umemura, although clearly uneasy about the assumptions underlying the Hemmi data, finds the Hemmi estimate more acceptable than others in a careful analysis of direct and indirect evidence.[17]

A comparison of population[18] and Hijikata data gives further grounds for the abandonment of the latter. Table 7-2 shows that from 1875 to 1880 the labor force of the primary sector rose by 6.1 per cent, that of the secondary and tertiary sectors by 31.4, and that of the combined three sectors by 9.8. In contrast the population rose by only 2.6 per cent in the same period, and, more significantly, the population in the 15-59 age bracket rose by a miniscule 0.3 per cent. In the next five-year period, a similar pattern is revealed by the same set of variables. Just as inconsistent are the trends in population and labor force from

---

population], *Nihon no keizai to nōgyō*, Seiichi Tobata and Kazushi Ohkawa, eds. (Tokyo, 1956), pp. 124-41.

[16] Seibi Hijikata, "Shokugyōbetsu jinkō no hensen wo tsūjite mitaru shitsugyō mondai" [Unemployment problem viewed from the perspective of changing structure of industrial labor force] *Shakai Seisaku Jihō*, 108 (September 1929), 84.

[17] Mataji Umemura, *Chingin-koyō-nōgyō* [Wages, employment, agriculture] (Tokyo, 1961), Chapter 6.

[18] I use the estimate made by Yōichi Okazaki, the most recent and sophisticated available. (*Meiji shonen ikō Taishō kunen ni itaru danjo nenreibetsu jinkō suikei ni tsuite* [Population estimate by sex and age from the 1870's to 1920], Institute of Population Problems Research Series No. 145, Tokyo, February 1962).

TABLE 7-2

POPULATION AND HIJIKATA LABOR FORCE CHANGES, 1875-1915

	Total population (thousands)	% Change	Population 15-59 (thousands)	% Change	Labor force: primary industry (thousands)	% Change	Labor force: secondary tertiary industry (thousands)	% Change	Total labor force (thousands)	% Change	Labor force participation rate (9)/(1)	Labor force participation rate of 15-59 bracket (9)/(3)
	(1)	(2)	(3)	(4)	(5)	(6)	(7)	(8)	(9)	(10)	(11) %	(12) %
1875	37,198	–	22,012	–	15,155	–	2,637	–	17,792	–	47.8	80.8
1880	38,166	2.6	22,087	0.3	16,076	6.1	3,466	31.4	19,542	9.8	51.2	88.5
1885	39,245	2.8	22,312	1.0	16,758	4.2	4,406	27.1	21,164	8.3	53.9	94.9
1890	40,353	2.8	23,130	3.7	17,198	2.6	5,385	22.2	22,583	6.7	56.0	97.6
1895	41,789	3.6	24,366	5.3	17,385	1.1	6,384	18.6	23,769	5.3	56.9	97.5
1900	43,785	4.8	25,249	3.6	17,331	-0.3	7,437	16.5	24,768	4.2	56.6	98.1
1905	46,257	5.6	26,272	4.1	17,038	-1.7	8,560	15.1	25,598	3.4	55.3	97.4
1910	49,066	6.1	27,251	3.7	16,489	-3.2	9,680	13.1	26,169	2.2	53.3	96.0
1915	52,500	7.0	29,018	6.5	15,715	-4.7	10,811	11.6	26,526	1.4	50.5	91.4

SOURCES: Columns (1) and (2): Yōichi Okazaki, *Meiji shonen ikō Taishō kunen ni itaru danjo nenreibetsu jinkō suikei ni tsuite* [Population estimates by sex and age from 1870's to 1920] (Institute of Population Problems Research Series No. 145, Tokyo, February 1962), pp. 38-39.   Columns (5), (7), and (9): Seibi Hijikata, "Shokugyōbetsu jinkō no hensen wo tsujite mitaru shitsugyō mondai" [Unemployment problem viewed from the perspective of changing structure of industrial labor force], *Shakai Seisaku Jihō*, 108 (September 1929), pp. 78-80.

1875 to 1915. While the rate of increase of the total labor force is declining from 9.8 to 1.4 per cent for five-year periods and the other two labor force data show the same trend, the rate of increase of total population rises substantially in both cases. As can be expected the labor force participation rate of the population rises sharply from 47.8 to 56.9 per cent from 1875 to 1895 and then declines to 50.5 in 1915. Such changes in the participation rate are highly unlikely in relatively short periods of time since the rate is largely determined by social and institutional factors which cannot be expected to change rapidly.

When Hemmi agricultural labor data are substituted for Hijikata figures and added on to the Hijikata nonagricultural labor force data, the rate of increase of the total labor force remains fairly stable around an average of 4.7 per cent as Table 7-3 shows. Although the combined data are not entirely consistent with the total or the 15-59 age population movements, they are much more compatible with them than are the Hijikata labor force data used alone. The labor force participation rates of the Hemmi-Hijikata labor force are also more stable than those of the Hijikata data.

A study of the combined secondary and tertiary labor force (Table 7-2) reveals that its rate of increase in the earlier five-year periods appears to be implausibly high. Moreover, the rates of increase decline continuously from 31.4 per cent in the first five-year period to 11.6 per cent in the last.[19] At the beginning of modernization when traditional modes of behavior still remain deeply ingrained, can entrepreneurial skills, nonagricultural capital, and demand for commercial nonagricultural products have increased at these remarkable rates to accommodate the massive flow of labor? Furthermore, is it not more reasonable to expect the absorption of labor and other factors and the demand for nonagricultural goods and services to increase relatively rather than to decline relatively, or at least not decline so rapidly?

If the argument presented in this book is accepted—that there was understatement of production in all sectors of the

[19] All Hijikata labor force estimates are trends obtained from estimating equations fitted to scattered data based on the 1920 census data.

TABLE 7-3

Labor Force Participation Rates of the Hemmi-Hijikata
Labor Force Data, 1875-1915

	Hemmi agricultural labor force (thousands)	Hijikata nonagricul. labor force (thousands)	Total labor force (thousands)	% change of (3)	Labor force participation rate %	Labor force participation rate of 15-59 bracket %
	(1)	(2)	(3)	(4)	(5)	(6)
1875	14,770	3,042	17,812	–	47.9	80.9
1880	14,742	3,888	18,630	4.6	48.8	84.3
1885	14,802	4,846	19,648	5.5	50.1	88.1
1890	14,755	5,841	20,596	4.8	51.0	88.4
1895	14,580	6,857	21,437	4.1	51.3	88.0
1900	14,405	7,927	22,332	4.2	51.0	88.4
1905	14,356	9,068	23,424	4.9	50.6	89.2
1910	14,318	10,204	24,522	4.7	50.0	90.0
1915	14,310	11,352	25,662	4.6	48.9	88.4

Sources: Column (1): Mataji Umemura, *Chingin-koyō-nōgyō* [Wages, employment, agriculture] (Tokyo, 1961), p. 119.
      Column (2): Seibi Hijikata, "Shokugyōbetsu jinkō no hensen wo tsūjite mitaru shitsugyō mondai" [Unemployment problem viewed from the perspective of changing structure of industrial labor force] *Shakai Seisaku Jihō*, 108 (September 1929), pp. 78-80.
      Column (5): Ratio of Column (1), Table 7-2, to Column (3), this table.
      Column (6): Ratio of Column (3), Table 7-2, to Column (3), this table.

Japanese economy in the Meiji era and that the understatement was greater in the earlier years—then an answer is probably at hand. It is reasonable to conclude that as the number of firms and the amount of production were underenumerated by a greater percentage in the earlier years in the secondary and tertiary sectors, so the number of laborers must also have been similarly understated. The data in Table 7-2 also indicates an undercounting of labor in the earlier years since the rate of increase of labor was greater than that of the total population or, more significantly, of the population in the 15-59 age bracket.

It is due to the decline in the labor absorption rate of the combined secondary and tertiary sector (Table 7-2) that even the Hemmi-Hijikata labor force is hardly plausible. Moreover, the labor force participation rate of the 15-59 age bracket (the ratio of total labor force to the population in the 15-59 age bracket) changes from 80.9 to 90.0 per cent. Then can alternative labor force estimates be made? Two methods of deriving a nonagricultural labor force by the use of labor participation rates are available to us.

Let us assume that the labor force is a constant 53 per cent[20] of the population. In this event the rate of increase of the nonagricultural labor force (Estimate A), if we accept the Hemmi agricultural labor force data, is about 10 per cent per each five-year period in the first three periods and about 15 per cent in the next five periods (Table 7-4). If we assume that the labor

[20] The reason for the selection of the 53% figure is given in Table 7-4.

TABLE 7-4

ESTIMATION OF NONAGRICULTURAL LABOR FORCE BY USE OF
LABOR PARTICIPATION RATES, 1875-1915

	Total labor estimate A (thousands)	Nonagric. labor estimate A (thousands)	% change in (2)	Total labor estimate B (thousands)	Nonagric. labor estimate B (thousands)	% change in (5)
	(1)	(2)	(3)	(4)	(5)	(6)
1875	19,714	4,944	–	20,225	5,485	–
1880	20,228	5,486	11.3	20,320	5,578	1.7
1885	20,800	5,998	9.3	20,527	5,725	2.6
1890	21,387	6,632	10.6	21,280	6,525	14.0
1895	22,153	7,573	14.2	22,417	7,837	20.1
1900	23,206	8,801	16.2	23,229	8,824	12.7
1905	24,516	10,160	15.4	24,170	9,814	11.2
1910	26,005	11,687	15.0	25,071	10,753	9.6
1915	27,825	13,515	15.6	26,697	12,387	15.2

SOURCES: Column (1): 53% of Column (1), Table 7-2. Labor participation rate of 53% was selected because it is roughly midway between the low and high participation rates of Seibi Hijikata (Column 11, Table 7-2).
    Column (2): Column (1), this table, less Column (1), Table 7-3.
    Column (3): 92% of Column (3), Table 7-2. Labor participation rate of the 15-59 age bracket was assumed to be a constant 92% because at this rate the estimated labor force is roughly equivalent to that of Estimate A from 1880-1905.
NOTE: The percentage change in Column (1) is identical to Table 7-2, Column (2), and that in Column (4) to Table 7-2, Column (4).

force is 92 per cent[21] of the 15-59 age bracket, then the rate of increase of the nonagricultural labor force (Estimate B) climbs steeply from 1.7 to 20.1 per cent in the first four periods and then declines to an average of around 12 per cent in the next four periods (Table 7-4). These percentage changes in the nonagricultural labor force (Estimates A and B) are more plausible than is the steady decline shown by the rate of increase of the Hijikata labor force estimates. Estimates A and B, however, are only indicative of expected trends assuming constant participation rates, and they cannot be taken to be more than extremely crude approximations of the actual labor force.[22]

It was argued in Chapter 6 that the agricultural household put a substantial amount of its labor time into the production of nonagricultural goods and services. Conformity with this argument would require a transfer of a part of the agricultural labor force to the nonagricultural sector. If such a transfer is a constant proportion of the Hemmi agricultural labor force, the rate of increase of the nonagricultural labor force will be lower than indicated in the previous paragraph and particularly so for the earlier periods. If such a transfer becomes a progressively smaller proportion of the labor force as might be expected due to greater specialization of agricultural labor, the rate of increase of the nonagricultural labor force will become even lower in the earlier years.

Let us now return to the examination of previous views on labor transfer. The contention that industry had a cheap supply of labor from the 1880's up to around the Russo-Japanese War appears to have been empirically verified. In the 20-year period from 1883-87 to 1903-07 real wages in manufacturing apparently increased only 10 per cent.[23] During this same period real

---

[21] The reason for the selection of the 92% figure is given in Table 7-4.

[22] These estimates, moreover, are for two classes of labor, agricultural and nonagricultural. Hijikata has nine classes: agricultural (and forestry), fishery, mining, manufacturing, commercial, transportation and communication, government and professional, household servants, and others. (*Op.cit.*, p. 78.)

[23] Computed from Umemura, *Chingin-koyō-nōgyō, op.cit.*, p. 65. Although the wage data are not firm and are under continuous study and revision in Japan, they are probably sufficiently good to give rough

wages in agriculture rose by about 4 per cent for male workers.[24] If labor productivity in agriculture had risen 88 per cent from 1878-82 to 1903-07,[25] real wages in agriculture probably would have increased very substantially instead of remaining nearly constant since the terms of trade between agricultural and non-agricultural commodities remained about constant.[26] In this event, it is most unlikely that agriculture could have continued to supply labor to the nonagricultural sector at a nearly constant price. The increase in labor productivity implicit in this study—namely, about 25-30 per cent from 1878-82 to 1903-07— is far more compatible with the small increase in agricultural real wages than the 88 per cent rise in productivity given above.

The conclusion drawn by previous analysts that agriculture provided a cheap supply of labor for the nonagricultural sector is not being questioned. Table 7-3 reveals that the nonagricultural sector absorbed slightly more than the increase in the labor force in the period under study. Labor was cheap in two respects: first, because the real wage remained low and roughly constant and, second, because the cost of producing a major part of industrial labor was borne by the agricultural sector. The disagreement is over the way this transfer was effected and its timing.

According to previous explanations, two factors accounted for the labor transfers: increase in labor productivity and increase in agricultural population. The timing of labor transfer should then be primarily dependent on increases in labor

---

approximations of wage changes that occurred. My argument will hold up unless real manufacturing wage increases of more than 50% occurred from the early 1880's to around 1905.

[24] Agricultural money wages (five-year averages) for male workers were 73.1% of industrial money wages for male workers in 1883-87 and 69.2% in 1903-07. (*Ibid.*, p. 193.) Neither the manufacturing or agricultural money or real wage data are completely reliable. But they can be taken to represent the approximate magnitudes of the changes that occurred.

[25] Ohkawa and Rosovsky, *op.cit.*, p. 46.

[26] If anything it tended to turn somewhat in favor of agriculture as demand for agricultural products increased more rapidly than the supply.

productivity and agricultural population. That the transfer was partially dependent upon increases in agricultural population is not in question. However, the previous contention that agricultural labor productivity rose at 2.6 per cent per year is no longer tenable if the new production estimates are accepted. In addition, it has been argued that agricultural developments which could have been expected to increase agricultural production tended to increase labor requirements. In this event, a rapid increase in agricultural production should have caused a corresponding increase in labor use or a relative rise in agricultural wages. The conclusion in this paper that agricultural production rose much more slowly than previously estimated disposes of a need for a huge increase in the agricultural labor force. But since production did increase, albeit much less rapidly than previously believed, and the labor force apparently remained about constant, product per worker would appear to have increased.

The principal reason for the steady flow of labor from the agricultural to the nonagricultural sector was a change in the criteria for the allocation of labor that occurred after the Meiji Restoration. In Chapter 4 (pp. 100f) it was argued that during the Tokugawa period, almost all provinces attempted to retain agricultural labor on the farms by institutional and other restraints for two reasons. One was to achieve economic self-sufficiency as a defense measure insofar as this was possible because the provinces were after all feudal politico-economic units. The other was to assure a more than adequate supply of food in normal crop years, and to insure a tolerable supply even in relatively poor crop years to reduce the incidence of famines and social disorder. It was also argued that most peasants could be expected to support the policy. It has been further argued that the relative abundance of labor helped induce industrial production in the rural areas (Chapter 4).

Another probable reason exists for the abundance of labor in agricultural households. The breakdown of the alternate attendance system at the end of the Tokugawa period (a partial relaxation occurred in 1862) probably caused an increase in rural labor at the beginning of the Meiji era. The dissolution

of the system caused the departure from Tokyo of most feudal
lords and their households and the abandonment of regular
trips from the provinces to the capital. Under these circumstances, employment in Tokyo and on the five principal
roads leading to the city had to decline precipitously. It is
possible that some of the former service personnel had to go
into or return to agricultural employment. But of greater importance may have been the loss of employment outlets for a
time to the rural population which probably started to increase
at a faster pace toward the end of the Tokugawa period. Therefore, an increase in the agricultural population and labor force
could have been expected until new nonagricultural employment opportunities developed. Such opportunities may have
become sufficiently available to absorb the increase in the labor
force toward the end of the 1870's as the Hemmi and Ohkawa
estimates apparently show.

Although it has been assumed that the agricultural labor
force remained roughly constant, it is possible that an increase
in labor input occurred. Agriculture in Japan has been characterized by increasing long-run intensification of land use with
the possible exception of Hokkaidō. This indicates greater labor
input per unit area of cultivated land, other things being equal.
Other things, in fact, suggest an even greater labor input. The
most important of these "other things" is, of course, the effect
of innovations. I have argued above (pp. 141-42) that important innovations tended to increase labor use rather than
reduce it during the period of this study. In the period when
land use was intensifying, an increase in cultivated land area
also took place. Total cultivated land area reached a peak of
6,098 thousand *chō* in 1921, an increase of slightly over one
million *chō* since 1890. Although about 85 per cent of this increase occurred in Hokkaidō where labor use per *chō* of land
was less intensive than elsewhere, this factor also indicates an
increase in the agricultural labor force.

It is also possible that the labor force in agricultural households did remain constant while the labor input increased.
Agriculture did not take all the labor time of farm workers, as
has been argued above (p. 139). Therefore, a part of their time

was given to the production of goods and services that cannot properly be considered agricultural output. As a consequence of increasing specialization and exchange, these workers may have devoted an increasing proportion of their time to agriculture.

Conceptually it is desirable to measure the labor force in terms of man hours of labor input per year for most purposes. With this measure, if total labor input increased, the labor force would have increased. But the use of such a measure assumes the existence of adequate records. They do not exist for Meiji Japan.

When the restraints on labor mobility were lifted after the Meiji Restoration, a reallocation of labor to the nonagricultural sector probably occurred in accordance with market forces. But such movements require changes in the capital structure of the economy. Therefore, an overnight shift of labor is not possible, and a change could only be achieved over a period of time. Nevertheless, it appears that the movement occurred with sufficient speed to preclude the necessity of the agricultural sector to absorb additional labor.

This transfer probably did not increase labor productivity as much as might be expected by the description given above since this was not a transfer of wholly unproductive labor (labor of zero marginal product). Because the agricultural household was almost entirely self-sufficient, when labor time was not required for agricultural production, it could be diverted to the production of nonagricultural products for household use or for the market. It is also probable that agricultural household consumption rose which would increase the value of the marginal household product. A rise in consumption would follow any increase in the agricultural population. A gradual and long-term population increase occurred as a result of a rise in the population of farm children as the birth rate rose and the death rate of children declined. The possibility that farm population rose immediately after the Meiji Restoration has been noted above.

Two other reasons may be given why the labor transfer out of the agricultural household probably did not raise the productivity of the transferred workers as much as might otherwise have been expected. A transfer of labor out of agriculture usually meant a reduction in the area planted to second crops or inadequate preparation for their cultivation which, of course, would affect total output. Secondly, workers transferred out of agriculture, particularly in the earlier Meiji years, were probably suitable only for work of relatively low productivity, and even if the adaptability of such workers was high, they probably could not, as a rule, be placed in employment of high productivity owing to a shortage of complementary capital resources.

The overallocation of labor to the rural areas at the start of the Meiji era, the increase in agricultural population, and the slow rise in agricultural production which made it unnecessary for agriculture to increase its labor force were probably the most important reasons in the transfer to the nonagricultural sector of increments to the agricultural labor force during the early Meiji years. In later years factors that tended to decrease the labor/output ratio became increasingly important, particularly seed improvement, the use of animal and mechanical power, and land improvement. As agriculture continued to give up labor, however, the nation increased its food imports.

Since the restrictions on population and occupational mobility were lifted for all classes, the services of members of other classes also became available. The highly educated and disciplined sons of some samurai and landlords[27] became entrepreneurs and managers of new enterprises, as well as leaders in other spheres within the emergent nation far out of proportion to the number of samurai and landlords in the total population. Less qualified samurai offered their services in other capacities, and the addition of many thousands of samurai to the labor force was in itself an important contribution to the growth of the national product.[28] The abolition of the above restrictions

[27] Thomas C. Smith, "Landlord's Sons in the Business Elite," *Economic Development and Cultural Change*, IX, 1, Part 2 (October 1960), 93-107.

[28] Many, if not most, samurai households had occupational (nonstipendiary) sources of income in the latter part of the Tokugawa period.

per se may not have provided many samurai with sufficient motivation to offer their services in the job market; but the abolition, coupled with the fact that the Meiji economic reforms caused a severe decline in samurai income, left most of them no alternative but work.

If agriculture in early Meiji had more than enough resources to supply the nation's need for agricultural products, investment in agriculture could not have been sufficiently attractive to induce most agricultural savings to remain in it. At the very least, the conclusion in this study that arable land area remained almost constant in early Meiji and that agricultural production increased at a much slower pace than previously believed indicates that investment in agriculture had to be considerably less than implied by previous production data.

In respect to the relation between agricultural investment and production, previous analysts have argued that the Japanese experience demonstrates that production can increase rapidly without substantial investment. The findings in this study do not bear out this contention, since agricultural production did not increase rapidly.

Early Meiji Saving in the Agricultural Sector

In Japan's economic development almost all of the early saving came from domestic sources since Japan was able to achieve sustained growth without a substantial inflow of foreign capital in the first 30 years of the Meiji era.[29] It is generally accepted that a substantial part of the nation's saving had to be generated in the agricultural sector owing to its very great importance in the early Meiji economy.

Most previous analysts have either stated explicitly or have implied that the agricultural sector saved because they believed that agricultural production grew at an extraordinarily rapid rate during the Meiji era. An important inference which may

---

For these samurai, the abolition of restrictions on occupational mobility, enlarged the market for their services.

[29] Edwin P. Reubens, "Foreign Capital in Economic Development: The Japanese Experience, 1868-1913" (unpublished Ph.D. dissertation, Department of Economics, Columbia University), p. 15.

be drawn therefrom is that saving was much smaller prior to the purported spurt in agricultural production. The demonstration that the high growth rate of agricultural production was largely fictitious has seriously weakened the above hypothesis on saving.

If agricultural production grew at a much slower rate than previously believed, the question arises whether the agricultural sector saved significantly in the Meiji era. This section is an attempt to show that the sector did save, but our view as to how this took place differs from those of previous analysts.

A salient feature of Tokugawa period income distribution was the share appropriated by the ruling class (which is defined to include the samurai and daimyo).[30] This share has been variously reported to have ranged from 20 per cent[31] to over 90 per cent[32] depending on the time and province. The latter figure clearly allows for a very substantial understatement of production. Both of the above figures are for paddy fields. As for the tax on total agricultural production, W. G. Beasley shows that the Tokugawa land tax just before the Meiji Restoration ranged from 30 to 40 per cent of recorded provincial production in five major regions of Japan.[33] Since he points out that provincial records understated production owing to falsification of village returns,[34] it follows that the tax share had to be less than 30 to 40 per cent of output. Because it is known that production was substantially understated it is quite possible that the actual share was less than 30 per cent. One further piece of evidence suggests that the tax share of agricultural production was less than 30 per cent. In 1867, Sōjiro Ishikawa, a Shogunate official occupying a position similar to that of a present day budget director, submitted a

[30] Other members of the ruling class including nobles attached to the Imperial Court and men of religion whose income came from taxes levied on production are subsumed under the above two classes.

[31] *MZZKSS*, Vol. 7, p. 336.

[32] Hugh Borton, "Peasant Uprisings in Japan," *Transactions of the Asiatic Society of Japan*, 2nd series, Vol. 16, p. 18.

[33] W. G. Beasley, "Feudal Revenue in Japan at the Time of the Meiji Restoration," *Journal of Asian Studies*, XIX, 3 (May 1960), 257-58.

[34] *Ibid.*, p. 259.

budget in which the tax rate is recorded as averaging 25 per cent of total production instead of 40 per cent.[35] Although Ishikawa's budget was only for the Tokugawa family domains, it is being assumed here that the tax rate was roughly equivalent elsewhere since other domains generally tended to follow Tokugawa domain practices.

It may not be unreasonable to reduce the range of the ruling class share of agricultural income in the Tokugawa period to 20 to 30 per cent from 20 to 90 per cent. A part of this share went into administrative and capital construction expenditures (excluding the stipends of the ruling class members engaged in administrative work). But as the rate of growth of the Japanese economy remained at low levels and the population remained almost constant, it is unlikely that an appreciable part of the ruling class share went into new capital construction.[36] It may be assumed that nearly all of the ruling class share less depreciation became disposable income.

All or almost all of the disposable income of the ruling class was consumed. It is a matter of historical record that almost all daimyo were in grave financial trouble during the Tokugawa period and particularly during the latter part. Reports of their financial condition are virtually certain to be accurate inasmuch as it was a policy of the Tokugawa Shogunate to keep potential aspirants to national hegemony in poverty. The most effective of the Tokugawa measures to enforce this policy was the practice of alternate attendance (*sankin kōtai*) which required the daimyo to spend some part of his time in attendance at the shogun's court and to leave his wife and children at the court as permanent hostages.[37] The extraordinary expenditures associated with this practice may be called *forced consumption*. They included the costs of the trip to and from the court with a retinue appropriate to the daimyo's station, of maintaining

[35] Seiichi Takimoto, *Nihon hōken keizai shi* [History of Japan's feudal economy] (Tokyo, 1930), p. 124.

[36] The available historical record indicates that the major part of capital formation in the Tokugawa period came from the savings of commoners, mostly landlords and merchants. (See below, p. 166.)

[37] The practice of alternate attendance was relaxed in 1862 and totally abolished after the Restoration.

two households, and of keeping up appearances at the court where extravagance was the norm. In addition to these expenditures, the shogunate levied a surtax on the province revenues and exacted payments for such emergency needs as the construction of Tokugawa castles.

As for the samurai, their income tended to drop during the Tokugawa period despite a general rise in the level of income per capita. This occurred due to the increasing financial troubles of the daimyo who in desperation tried to increase their share at the expense of the commoners and the samurai. Under these circumstances, the behavior that can be expected from most people is disinvestment over time, and the samurai were probably no exception. The extent of samurai poverty may be judged from the great numbers of middle and lower class samurai who turned to farming or other occupations in order to subsist or pay off their debts, despite their abhorrence of employment which was associated with the commoners.[38] There is little doubt that the samurai, on the average, consumed all their income or more.

It was in this setting that the Meiji oligarchs following the Restoration brought about a socioeconomic revolution by introducing the land tax reform and associated measures. These measures, which came in rapid succession within a few years of the Meiji Restoration, changed, among other things, the agrarian and fiscal structure of the nation. The principle that the land belonged to the farmers was established. The daimyo relinquished or lost feudal rights over the land and the people of their provinces. The barriers between provinces were abolished. The people were given freedom to migrate and to choose their vocation irrespective of their family or class connections. The right of farmers to free cropping and alienation of land was established. The above changes accomplished the separation of the daimyo from his land and people and the establishment of a private property system.

The profound changes that occurred in income distribution were a result of the economic reforms associated with the land

[38] Hidezō Kikkawa, *Shizoku jusan no kenkyū* [Study of the economic rehabilitation of the samurai] (rev. edn., Tokyo, 1942), pp. 28-35.

reform of early Meiji. One phase of the redistribution was the reform and ultimate abolition of the hereditary stipendiary system, which successively led from reductions in stipends to a change to a pension system with the formal abolition of the feudal system and later to commutation of the pensions to bonds.[39] A second phase of the redistribution consisted of reforms more directly connected with the land system: the abolition of the feudal land rights, the institution of a private property system, and the enactment of a land tax that reduced the tax share of agricultural income.

A rough measure of the decline in ruling class income can be obtained from government surveys of the period. The stipends of the samurai and the disposable income of the feudal lords totaled about 13 million *koku* of rice at the end of the Tokugawa period. This declined to 9 million *koku* in 1869 and to 5 million *koku* in 1871.[40] Some compensation was given the ruling class for deprivation of their income rights from agriculture as noted above. Following the commutation, the interest income from the bonds came to 11.6 million yen.[41] At the land valuation price of rice of 4.185 yen per *koku* the total interest was worth just above 2.5 million *koku* of rice. With the onset of inflation the value in rice units declined further to less than 10 per cent of their level in the last years of the shogunate. In 1878-82 when the corrected value of agricultural production in current yen averaged 774 million yen, the interest income from bonds of the former ruling class was 1.5 per cent of agricultural income in contrast to the stipendiary income of 15 to 24 per cent during the Tokugawa period (see Table 7-6).

Following the expropriation, the claimants to agricultural income became the landowners, the cultivators, and the government.[42] The income distribution that is implicit in the tax reform of the 1870's places the share of the government at a

[39] *Ibid.*, pp. 29-70.

[40] *MZZKSS*, Vol. 8, introduction, p. 3.

[41] *Ibid.*, Vol. 4, p. 44.

[42] The ruling class still maintained an indirect claim on land in the sense that most of the government revenue, out of which the ruling class was paid, came out of the land tax.

high level. Its share was to be 34 per cent of gross harvest or 40 per cent of the net harvest.[43] This includes the national land tax or 3 per cent of land value and a surtax of one-third of the national tax. The national land tax rate was reduced to 2.5 per cent in 1877, a decline of 17 per cent which would make the land tax 28 and 33 per cent of gross and net harvest. All of these proportions are greater than the assumed effective tax rate of 20 to 30 per cent of harvest of the Tokugawa period. But, owing to understatement of production, none of these represents the actual burden in the Meiji era.

The burden of direct taxes—which included the land, income, and house taxes—on the agricultural sector after the Meiji Restoration as a proportion of gross value of agricultural production can be estimated. Using the tax data assembled by Seiji Tsunematsu, and the corrected value of agricultural production based on the paddy rice yield assumptions of 1.6 and 1.95 *koku* per *tan* for 1873-77 and 1918-22, the taxes are found to range from 7.5 to 11.9 per cent of the gross value (see Table 7-5). The rather exceptional 11.9 per cent rate occurred in the years when agricultural prices fell to very low levels owing to the deflation of the 1880's; in all other five-year periods the rate was 9.1 per cent or lower. The average rate for the entire period was 8.7 per cent, which makes the share retained by the agricultural sector about 91 per cent of the value of production. The relative importance of the land tax as a proportion of government revenues declined over time as the importance of the house and income taxes gained.[44] Interestingly, the total direct tax burden on the agricultural sector remained fairly

---

[43] Computed from the formula for the estimation of land value appearing in the Land Tax Revision Act of 1873. (Appendix A, p. 188.)

[44] In 1878-82 the land tax amounted to 88% of all direct taxes on the agricultural sector, and in 1913-17 to 52%. (Computed from Seiji Tsunematsu, "Nōgyō to zaisei no sayō" [Agriculture and public finance], *Nihon no keizai to nōgyō* [Japanese economy and agriculture], Seiichi Tōbata and Kazushi Ohkawa, eds. (Tokyo, 1956), pp. 374, 376, and 377.)

Although the land tax rate was lighter than previously estimated and was a tremendous boon to the landowners, the fact remains that the tax on other sectors was even lower. This was entirely consistent with the Meiji leaders views that protection and subsidization of the non-agricultural sector was needed for rapid industrialization.

TABLE 7-5

TAX SHARE AS PERCENTAGE OF CORRECTED VALUE OF
AGRICULTURAL PRODUCTION, FIVE-YEAR AVERAGES,
1878-1917

Period	Total direct taxes[a] million yen	Corrected value in current yen[b] of agric. prod. million yen	Tax share of corrected value %
	(1)	(2)	(3)
1878-1882	63.6	774	8.2
1883-1887	63.6	535	11.9
1888-1892	58.5	641	9.1
1893-1897	65.6	877	7.5
1898-1902	99.1	1207	8.2
1903-1907	113.6	1500	7.6
1908-1912	153.4	1733	8.9
1913-1917	167.7	1980	8.5

SOURCES: Column (1): Seiji Tsunematsu, "Nōgyō to zaisei no sayō" [Agriculture and public finance], *Nihon no keizai to nōgyō* [Japanese economy and agriculture], Seiichi Tōbata and Kazushi Ohkawa, eds. (Tokyo, 1956), p. 381.

NOTES: [a] The direct taxes included are land, income, and house taxes.

[b] The corrected value in 1913-17 prices (Table 5-7) are converted to current prices by use of a price index of agricultural production computed from Kazushi Ohkawa, *et al.*, *op.cit.*, pp. 123, 126-28. The price index is a wholesale price index. Since prices at the farm tended to rise more rapidly than wholesale prices, the corrected value in current prices may overstate the level of income somewhat in the earlier years.

stable during the entire period with the one exception noted above.

The agricultural sector's share of the value of agricultural production is a gross, not net, value. Out of its gross share of 91 per cent, the sector had to make payments for intermediate goods purchased from other sectors. Such payments were of the order of 15 to 20 per cent of the gross value of agricultural production, according to one estimate,[45] which would make

[45] Ohkawa, *et al.*, *op.cit.*, p. 64. The estimate may be an understatement because conceptually the payments to other sectors do not include fertilizers, tools, and other intermediate goods and services produced in the household.

agriculture's net share about 70 to 75 per cent. Logically, the sector's share should have been put in net terms since the net share is a better approximation and determinant of disposable income than the gross share. Moreover, the income redistribution resulting from the land reform caused a greater percentage increase in agriculture's net share than in the gross share. This conclusion derives from the fact that the income redistribution does not directly affect the cost of production and the government's absolute share is obviously independent of whether the accounting is in gross or net terms. Despite the advantages of using the net concept, the gross concept has been used for the following three reasons. First, the data on payments for intermediate products are unreliable. Second, it is difficult to ascertain the proportions paid to other sectors by tenants and landlords. Finally, the basic point that landowners' income increased very sharply as a result of the land tax reform can be adequately made with the gross value data; thus, there is no urgent reason to add further complications at this point.

Thus the direct tax burden on the agricultural sector, which was estimated to be between 20 and 30 per cent of the agricultural product in the Tokugawa period, was reduced in the Meiji era by more than 50 per cent even from the lower figure. In consequence, the agricultural sector appears to have gained from 11 to 21 per cent of the value of production in the period under study as a result of the Meiji land reform. These additions to the income of the agricultural sector being net of taxes, represented an immense transfer of income.[46]

[46] This immense transfer of income helps to account for the acquiescence of the Meiji landowners, probably the most powerful economic bloc of the period in Japan, to a land tax which appeared to place an undue burden on them.

If the nominal Tokugawa tax rates of 40 to 50% of harvest were accepted in this book, then the income transfer from the ruling class to the landowners would have been 31 to 41% instead of 11 to 21%. Certainly such an assumption in this book would have immeasurably strengthened the income transfer argument. On the other hand, it would not have been consistent with the contention in this book that agricultural production was understated in both the Tokugawa and Meiji periods. With two exceptions, to my knowledge, all standard Western studies of the Japanese economy continue to assume that the land tax

It can be said that inflation accounted for a part of the redistribution. But clearly redistribution was more than the accidental consequence of inflation. Without the transformation of the land tax from a proportional tax on harvest mostly payable in kind to a money tax on land value (which either remained fixed or decreased for almost all arable lands except those converted from upland fields to paddy fields), inflation could not have diluted the tax burden. Furthermore, it is clear that the Meiji leadership intended the tax burden to be substantially lower than the Tokugawa period level. The government, mindful of the heavy burden of taxation on agriculture relative to other industries, provided for successive reductions of the national land tax rate from 3 per cent to 1 per cent of land value. The rate was lowered to 2.5 per cent in 1877 in response to the low agricultural prices of 1876, but it never dropped below this figure as inflation decreased the real burden of the tax. Finally between the cadastral survey of the 1870's and 1899, a further 14 per cent reduction in the assessed value per *tan* of paddy fields took place. Considering the above, there is no room for doubt that the Meiji leadership intended a very great transfer of income to the agricultural sector.

The gain in the share retained by agriculture attributable to measures associated with the land tax reform probably increased only the landowner (property) share.[47] From the final

---

rate during the Tokugawa period was 40 to 50% of agricultural production. Among Western publications are those by G. C. Allen, *A Short Economic History of Modern Japan* (2nd rev. edn., London, 1962), p. 15; Lockwood, *op.cit.*, p. 4; Norman, *op.cit.*, p. 21. The exceptions are Smith, *Agrarian Origins of Modern Japan, op.cit.*, and Beasley, *op.cit.*

A secondary effect of the land reform was a further redistribution of income because of increasing concentration of land ownership in the hands of the wealthier landlords.

[47] The two classes in the nation that benefited from the land reform—the landowners and the daimyo—were the two that could have seriously impaired the effectiveness of the Meiji economic reforms if they had felt wronged. The landowners were potentially, if not in reality, the most powerful politico-economic bloc in the nation. They were hardly a unified bloc at this early date but a serious grievance could have united them against the government, a possibility that the Meiji oligarchs could not have been unaware of. The daimyo, if crossed, could have rallied the

years of the Tokugawa period to the early Meiji years, a significant change in tenant (labor) share of agricultural income
probably could not have been expected. Most available studies
seem to indicate that the tenant share remained roughly constant.[48] Furthermore, tenant incomes of the early Meiji era
probably were not under economic pressure to rise inasmuch
as agriculture apparently had a labor surplus in the Meiji years
except in the last few years.

The tenant share has been estimated to be about 50 per cent
of gross output during the Tokugawa years.[49] Given this, the
Tokugawa income distribution for the ruling class and the
landowner would have ranged between 20 and 30 per cent.
If the tenant share remained at 50 per cent in the Meiji era,
the share of the landlord would have increased to 41 per cent
and that of the government would have been about 9 per cent;
and, of course, the Tokugawa ruling class no longer had a direct
claim on agricultural income. As a result of the land reform,

---

vast numbers of dislocated and unhappy samurai around them. By
treating the daimyo and landowners generously the Meiji leadership not
only made the land reform politically feasible, but probably gained
powerful allies in the bargain and, at the least, neutralized most of the
elements in the two classes that were potentially dangerous.

The statement that the daimyo benefited from the land tax reform
appears to be inconsistent with the argument that the ruling class income
declined sharply. Actually, daimyo income dropped, but they were at
the same time relieved of the responsibility for paying samurai stipends
and other province expenditures and of alternate attendance at the
Tokugawa court, all of which had been severe drains on their financial
resources. This series of changes left most daimyo better off than they
had been during the Tokugawa period. (George Sansom, *The Western
World and Japan* [New York, 1951], p. 328).

[48] See, for example, Norman, *op.cit.*, p. 150n. Here the tenant's share
remained constant from the Tokugawa period into the early Meiji years
at 32%. The low figure results from failure to adjust for understatement
of yield and area.

[49] James I. Nakamura, "The Role of Meiji Land Reform in the
Economic Development of Japan" (Paper presented at the Conference
on Land and Land Tax Reform in the Less Developed Countries, Milwaukee, Wisconsin, August 26-28, 1963.).

It is not germane to the argument here to determine the exact value of
the tenant share. All we need do is to ascertain that it remained relatively
stable or that it declined so that the landowner was the chief beneficiary
of the income redistribution.

the share of property in agricultural income would have risen by from 33 to 100 per cent.[50] The tentative distributional share of agricultural income estimated above are tabulated in Table 7-6. Although the figures appearing in the table are not definitive (as none such are available), there can be little doubt that a revolutionary change in income distribution occurred even if a very heavy margin is allowed for error.

We must now ask whether the income transfer from the ruling class to the Meiji government and the landowners (since the tenant share apparently did not rise) had any effect on saving.[51]

It is probable that a part of the increment in landowner income was saved. A sharp rise in income within a short period is usually accompanied by at least a short term increase in saving. But there were factors that also tended to restrict consumption over a longer term. One such factor was the absence of something like durable consumer goods that could have raised consumption spending well above previous levels. Another strong inhibitor was the habit of thrift instilled in the peasantry during the Tokugawa period by the ruling class and nurtured during the Meiji era by the government. Peasant frugality was desired in the earlier period so that the share of the ruling class could be increased. In the Meiji era frugality and thrift were urged on all classes to assist in building up the nation's industrial and military strength. A third factor, and perhaps the most important, was that the recipients of the additional income were property owners who could be expected to save a higher proportion of incremental income.[52]

[50] This shows how very much landowners benefited from the land tax reform. In view of the strength of agricultural fundamentalism (*nōhonshugi*) in Japan during the Meiji era, it could hardly have been otherwise.

[51] A discussion of Meiji savings from various sources appears in Lockwood, *op.cit.*, pp. 268-88.

[52] One of the outlets for landowner savings was investment in arable land. Many reasons have been given for the tendency of landowners to invest in land during the Meiji era. I submit that the principal reason for the increase in tenant land is that people with investment funds found it profitable to invest in land, contrary to the views that have been held in the past. Investment in land was profitable because of the very great increase in income distribution to landowners. Clearly, investment in land

TABLE 7-6

ESTIMATED PERCENTAGE DISTRIBUTION OF AGRICULTURAL INCOME IN
LATE TOKUGAWA AND AFTER MEIJI LAND TAX REFORM

	Late Tokugawa	Early Meiji
	(1)	(2)
1. Landowners[a]	30-20%	41%
2. Tenants	50	50
3. Government	20-30	9
Ruling class	(15-24)[b]	(1.5)[c]
Other	(4-7)[b]	
4. Total	100	100

NOTES: [a] The landowners' share is defined to be the property share (rent
and interest) and that of the tenants, the labor share. The figures in this Table
represent only very crude orders of magnitude of the income transfer that
occurred. The reader is advised that their use is warranted only when a heavy
margin can be allowed for error.
[b] The figures are excluded from the total since they are already
included in Line 3. It is assumed that "other" expenditures constituted 20-25%
and the outlay for the ruling class was 75-80% of total government expenditures.
The "other" expenditures are a rough estimate of the capital, debt retirement,
and administrative expenditures of the Shogunate and provincial governments,
excluding samurai stipends and daimyo disposable income.
[c] This figure is excluded from the total because the former Tokugawa ruling class no longer had a direct share in sector income. It represents
the ratio of interest payments on pension bonds (11.6 million yen) to the
corrected current yen value of agricultural production in 1878-82 (776 million yen).

One observer has said of the Meiji landlord that he "presents
a sharp contrast to Ricardo's wastrel type . . . there is no evidence of any sizable diversion of the landlord's respectable
surplus to high living or speculation."[53]

It has been estimated that the net rent on land rose from 33
to 100 per cent over the Tokugawa rent. It has been argued
above that a part of this was saved. Unfortunately, no quantitative estimate can be hazarded on savings by landowners or
in the agricultural sector. However, there is evidence of savings taking place in the rural areas, most of which derived,
directly or indirectly, from agricultural sources.

Kōkichi Asakura, in his path-breaking study of Meiji era

cannot be added to net agricultural saving if the seller consumed the
proceeds from the sale.
[53] Ranis, *op.cit.*, p. 448.

banking institutions, demonstrates that rural landlord-merchants played a major role in early Meiji financing by providing savings and by establishing and operating banking institutions and industrial and commercial enterprises.[54] Their role was particularly important because most of the burgeoning commercial and other economic activities of this early period took place in the rural areas stimulated by foreign demand for tea and silk and increasing commercialization of rural activity. This commercialization was promoted by the government which sought payment of land taxes in money (in contrast with the normal Tokugawa payment in kind), and by the increasing demand for "store bought" goods on the part of the peasantry (induced by the increased peasant income).

Asakura also demonstrates that landlord-merchant capital

[54] Asakura, *op.cit.*, *passim*. For example, the early financing of the cotton textile industry, which was extremely important in the rapid development of the secondary sector, came almost entirely from landlord-merchants. (*Ibid.*, p. 74.)

TABLE 7-7

NUMBER AND CAPITALIZATION OF NATIONAL BANKS, PRIVATE BANKS, AND QUASI-BANKS, 1876-1885

	Private banks		Quasi-banks		National banks		All banks	
Year	Number	Capitalization (million yen)	Number	Capitalization (million yen)	Number	Capitalization (million yen)	Number	Capitalization (million yen)
	(1)	(2)	(3)	(4)	(5)	(6)	(7)	(8)
1876	1	2.0	?	?	6	2.5	7	4.5
1877	1	2.0	?	?	27	23.0	28	25.0
1878	1	2.0	?	?	95	33.4	96	35.4
1879	10	3.3	?	?	153	40.6	163	43.9
1880	39	6.3	120	1.2	153	43.0	312	50.5
1881	90	10.4	369	5.9	148	44.9	607	61.2
1882	176	17.2	438	8.0	143	44.2	757	69.4
1883	207	20.5	573	12.1	141	44.4	921	77.0
1884	214	19.4	741	15.1	140	44.5	1095	79.0
1885	218	18.8	744	15.4	139	44.5	1101	78.7

SOURCE: Kōkichi Asakura, *Meiji zenki nihon kinyū kōzō shi* [History of the structure of early Meiji financial institutions] (Tokyo, 1961), p. 187.

played an important role in the early Meiji capitalization of national banks, private banks, and quasi-banks.[55] Table 7-7 reveals the extremely rapid growth of these institutions. In respect to national banks it was generally accepted before World War II that daimyo and samurai wealth, primarily in the form of pension bonds and the resources of a few of the wealthiest merchant financiers such as the Mitsuis, were the source of capital. Since the War, however, it has become increasingly evident that a wide range of commoners provided a large share of national bank capital, with a host of landlord-merchants playing an important part. Over time, moreover, the participation of landlord-merchants increased in many banks.[56] For example, in Yamagata Prefecture, 268 of 280 original stockholders of the 81st National Bank established in 1877 were samurai.[57] By the end of 1883, total stockholders had declined to 16 and the number of samurai had declined to three during a period when total capitalization increased from 60,000 to 100,000 yen. The principal stockholder who was a landowner-merchant owned 1,340 of 4,000 shares of stock while the three samurai held a total of 26 shares.[58] This is an extreme case, but the detailed study by Asakura makes it quite clear that the view that national banks were financed primarily by capital from samurai, daimyo, and the wealthiest merchant financiers seriously overstated the case.

Landlord-merchant capital, however, played its greatest role in the financing of private banks and quasi-banks. A striking fact about these banks is that they start to increase at the time the new land tax became effective; that is, after the land reform caused landlord income to increase (see Table 7-5). They were generally established in largest numbers in those prefectures where agricultural cash crops—rice, cocoon, tea—were produced in quantity, and where landlord-merchants played a

[55] Quasi-banks (not organized under private bank regulations) were companies engaged in bill-broking, money-changing, holding of deposits, loan-making, trading in commodities, manufacturing, etc.

[56] Asakura, *op.cit.*, pp. 163, 165, 171.

[57] *Ibid.*, p. 83. The commoners, however, took the initiative in organizing the bank and held 20% of the stocks at the beginning. (*Ibid.*)

[58] *Ibid.*, p. 85.

particularly important part in the capitalization of quasi-banks.[59] An important part of the business of private banks and quasi-banks in early Meiji was financing the production, transportation, and marketing of cash crops. The quasi-banks whose activities extended far beyond banking, also invested funds directly in commodity trading and manufacturing.

Another scholar estimates[60] that about 20 per cent of the subscriptions to domestic long-term government bonds from 1868 to 1893 were made by large landlords, mostly absentee landlords living in large cities. Since the total long-term domestic debt outstanding increased from 40 to 264 million yen[61] from 1876 to 1893, the landlords' net purchases can be estimated to have been about 45 million yen in this period.

It is probable that a large part, if not most, of the funds of financial institutions and for security purchases came out of income transferred to landowners as a result of the land reform with an assist from inflation.

The conclusions of this section can be summarized in the following three propositions: (1) As a result of the measures associated with the land reform (including the reform of the hereditary stipendiary system) the share of agricultural income retained by landowners increased enormously (perhaps from 11 to 21 per cent of the value of agricultural production). (2) The landowners (and the government which received a higher share for nonstipendiary expenditures) tended to have a lower propensity to spend than the former ruling class. (3) Therefore, saving probably rose to a new higher level for the economy within a decade of the Restoration instead of starting from a low base in early Meiji and rising with reported increases in agricultural production as previously argued. (4) Most of the savings in agriculture were transferred out of the agricultural sector into the burgeoning commercial, financial, and industrial activities of the time.

[59] *Ibid.*, p. 271.
[60] Chung, Young-Iob, "The Role of Government in the Generation of Saving: The Japanese Experience, 1868-1893" (unpublished Ph.D. dissertation, Columbia University, 1965), Appendix B, p. 336.
[61] *Ibid.*, p. 139.

Comments on Capital Formation in Japan

The conclusions drawn in the last section suggest a reconsideration of the view that Japan's economic development took place with relatively little investment.[62] The most comprehensive and best documented source of data on capital formation in Japan is a study by Henry Rosovsky.[63] One finding of this study is that net domestic capital formation, excluding military expenditures, was at a low level ranging from 4.5 to 6.8 per cent of the net national product in overlapping ten-year periods from 1887-96 to 1907-16.

A second notable finding of Rosovsky's is that 43 per cent of domestic capital formation, exclusive of military construction and purchases of durable equipment, was public investment.[64] Net private investment would then be only 3 to 4 per cent of the net national product.

A conclusion that has been drawn based on Ohkawa's national income estimates and Rosovsky's capital formation data is that an exceptional feature of Japan's apparently exceptional growth was the lowest long-term marginal capital-output ratio of any presently developed nation at any stage of economic development. Simon Kuznets using the above data puts the ratio of marginal net domestic capital formation to marginal net domestic product at 1.6 for Japan for the period from 1885-89 to 1914-18.[65] The next lowest rate of 2.4, which is 50 per cent higher than Japan's, is that of Denmark.[66]

[62] One of the reasons for this view is that it was previously believed that there was very little surplus from which saving could be extracted.

[63] Henry Rosovsky, *Capital Formation in Japan, 1868-1940* (Glencoe, Illinois, 1961). This is a remarkably detailed study that will be mined for years for information and insight on the Japanese economy and capital formation. At the same time it has weaknesses in coverage. The author, aware of this, warns the reader about possible errors and understatement of capital formation at many points in the study.

[64] Computed from Rosovsky, *op.cit.*, p. 15.

[65] Simon Kuznets, "Quantitative Aspects of the Economic Growth of Nations: VI. Long-term Trends in Capital Formation Proportions," *Economic Development and Cultural Change*, IX, 4, Part 2 (July 1961), 17, Table 5, Column (6).

[66] *Ibid.*

A basic argument in this book is that Japan's growth was not exceptional and that it did not take place under the extraordinary circumstances claimed for it. If the growth rate is less than previously estimated and capital formation remains constant, the marginal capital-output ratio rises. Moreover, the coexistence of a high growth rate and a low marginal capital-output ratio is contrary to expectations. Other things being equal, a higher marginal capital-output ratio could be expected with a higher growth rate since the absorption of capital becomes increasingly difficult as more of it is taken in. In an underdeveloped economy where the rate of increase of know-how and skills tends to be low, the satiation threshold for absorption must necessarily be low.

The net investment rate of 4.5 to 6.8 per cent compared with other nations is extremely low if the Ohkawa growth rate of 4.0 per cent is accepted. One basis for this conclusion is that the Japanese rates recomputed by Kuznets for comparability are lower than the net investment rates of other economically advanced nations at a comparable stage in economic development.[67] This, of course, implies that the Japanese used capital more efficiently than other nations. Such a conclusion is hardly warranted. Japanese entrepreneurs were no less prone to errors in judgment, misuse of equipment,[68] and loss from external diseconomies than, say, their European counterparts at a comparable stage in growth; and Japan, too, required the building of an infrastructure which, moreover, took place in a shorter span of time than was the case in the West.

The 4.5 to 6.8 per cent net investment rates are, of course, much more plausible if the argument presented here is accepted that the growth rate was less than 2.8 per cent per year. However, if the investment rates were 4.5 to 6.8 per cent of the much higher estimates of production implicit in my argument, then Rosovsky has understated the absolute level of capital formation in Japan.

Are there bases for assuming that the Rosovsky data under-

[67] *Ibid.*, Table 1, Column (5).
[68] Smith, *Political Change and Industrial Development, op.cit.,* p. 39.

state capital formation? It may be inferred from the probable understatement of production in the secondary sector as argued in Chapter 6, that the production of capital goods was also understated. We also have Rosovsky's own statements cautioning the reader of the omission of some categories of capital. He excludes capital equipment which has a useful life of three years or less.[69] The fact that his estimates are obtained by adding investment by type makes further omissions unavoidable.[70] Excluded also are local government capital construction by voluntary cooperative effort.[71] Although Rosovsky believes that these omissions could hardly have been significant, he presents very little if any substantive evidence in support. In particular, it is probable that considerable local construction was produced by voluntary cooperative effort in the Meiji era[72] since such cooperation has had a long history in Japan.

Other factors also tend to impart a downward bias to Rosovsky's estimates. Rosovsky assumes that the ratio of gross nonresidential construction in agriculture to agricultural output was 1.0.[73] This assumption does not fully take into account the increase in mulberry fields and housing and equipment for silkworm egg incubation and silkworm nurture which accompanied the rapid expansion of sericulture. One further factor that probably gave a downward bias is the assumption that farm residential construction was a negligible factor.[74] Owing to the rapid expansion of agricultural land in Hokkaidō in the last two decades of the Meiji era, farm dwellings must have increased substantially in this period.

In view of the above evidence it is probable that capital formation in the Meiji era was understated in absolute terms.

[69] *Ibid.*, p. 311. It is probable that the useful life of capital equipment in the early stages of economic development was appreciably less than in later stages.

[70] *Ibid.*, p. 271. See also K. Ohkawa, "Capital Formation in Japan," *Economic Development and Cultural Change*, XII, 1 (October 1963), 110-11.

[71] Rosovsky, *op.cit.*, p. 158.

[72] Oshima, "Notes on an Alternative Method of Estimating the National Income and Expenditures of Japan, 1881," *op.cit.*, p. 247.

[73] Rosovsky, *op.cit.*, pp. 6-7.   [74] *Ibid.*, p. 6.

Summary

The primary purpose of this chapter was to reexamine the role of agriculture in the development of Japan's economy, particularly in respect to resource transfer, redistribution of income, transfer of saving, and capital formation.

Meiji resource transfer was a continuation of a Tokugawa period trend caused by an increase in agricultural production and the relative stability of population. This caused a diversion of resources away from agricultural production despite stringent effort by province rulers to retain resources in agriculture or, at the least, in the villages. Despite the flow, these efforts probably tended to overload labor in the rural areas, which may help to account for the growth of rural industrial production.

In the Meiji era the transfer gained momentum. Apparently the increment in the labor force was absorbed by the nonagricultural sector as the increase in agricultural production and imports and the probable existence of underemployed labor in agriculture made unnecessary additions to the agricultural labor force. The Meiji agricultural and nonagricultural labor force data do not accurately reflect the division of production between these sectors. The present data show an extraordinarily rapid increase in the nonagricultural labor force. It is argued here that the increase is partially due to the undercounting of industrial labor in the earlier years. This is consistent with the understatement of industrial production in the earlier years. A revision of labor force data by the use of a labor force participation rate is suggested. This procedure reduces the growth rate of the nonagricultural labor force to a level substantially less than that of previous estimates.

The conclusion that the growth rate of agricultural production was substantially less than previously estimated requires rethinking about how saving was generated in Japan. Most previous analysts have argued that agricultural saving came from the large increment in agricultural income. The argument here is that measures associated with the Meiji land reform caused a major redistribution of income from the samurai class to the landowning class. The redistribution probably caused a substantial increase in the rate of saving because the land-owning class was likely to have had a considerably higher propensity to save. If this source was the principal generator of saving in agriculture, it probably led to a rather abrupt rise in the rate of saving from a low to a higher level within the first decade after the Meiji Restoration. Most of this was probably transferred out of agriculture.

This review led to an examination of Rosovsky's capital formation data, and it was concluded that he understates capital formation in the Meiji period of his study. This finding is consistent with our previous finding that total production was seriously understated in the earlier years of Japan's post-Tokugawa development in that, then, there is no reason why capital goods production should not have been similarly understated.

These findings indicate that labor and capital inputs probably did not increase sharply in the second or the third decade after the Meiji Restoration.

APPENDICES
BIBLIOGRAPHY
INDEX

APPENDIX A

Tokugawa and Meiji Land Taxation

THE land tax[1] reform of the Meiji period and associated measures constituted the economic machinery that the Meiji leadership employed to destroy the old economic and social system and to create a new one. The main purposes of these acts were (1) to separate the daimyo from their hereditary sources of income and power and, therefore, to insure that their economic and social base for any move against the government would be weakened; (2) to obtain a source of stable money revenue; (3) to achieve a greater equity in the distribution of the tax burden; and (4) to institute a system of private property ownership that would help to improve the economic performance of the nation.

The cornerstone of these various measures was the tax revision that took place early in the Meiji era. The purpose of this Appendix is to examine some of the land tax law changes that occurred beginning in the Tokugawa period and into the Meiji era. Particularly close attention will be given to those provisions which were designed to achieve tax equity,[2] but which thereby provided opportunity and incentive for land tax evasion.

For the first few years of the Meiji era the Tokugawa land tax was carried over by the new leadership pending the formulation of a new tax system. The major reform legislation was enacted in 1873 and will be referred to as the Land Tax Revision Act of 1873. A few major changes were incorporated in the Land Tax Law of 1884 which abolished the 1873 act; in

---

[1] The term "land tax" will be used generically to denote the tax on produce, income, rent, or value of agricultural land. For systematic examination of the various uses of the term, see Haskell P. Wald, *Taxation of Agricultural Land in Underdeveloped Economies* (Cambridge, Mass., 1959), pp. 7-41.

[2] It will become apparent from the discussion to follow that tax equity among landowners was believed to be achieved by a proportional tax on land wealth.

most basic respects, the two laws were similar, however. All three taxes had in common the following two characteristics: (1) the land tax was the major source of revenue, and (2) the cadastre was the basis for land tax assessment and collection. In most other respects the Tokugawa land tax differed from the other two. It will also be seen that there were three basic forms of the Tokugawa land tax.

The carryover of the tax system from the Tokugawa period was provided by a law[3] promulgated in 1868, which provided revenue for the transitional period while a new tax system was being devised. Under it taxes continued to be collected on the same basis as in the past except in situations where they constituted an exceptionally heavy burden. The Meiji government, however, did not have fiscal control over the entire nation until the fiscal year 1872.[4] During the Tokugawa period only a part of the land was under the direct jurisdiction of the shogunate, and the rest was held by daimyo who enjoyed a high degree of autonomy. Thus, until the domains of the daimyo were abolished in 1871, only the territories that had been directly held by the shogunate were under the fiscal control of the Meiji government. During this period the taxes in the territories of the daimyo continued to be assessed, collected, and disbursed by the daimyo as they had been during the Tokugawa period.[5]

Owing to the existence of many independent fiscal authorities in the Tokugawa period, the tax system that the Meiji government had inherited was highly diverse.[6] The levies can be broadly classified under three headings: the land tax, the supplementary taxes, and the corvée. The latter two classes

[3] *Fukoku 612* (August 7, 1868).

[4] In fiscal 1871 (October 1870 through September 1871) the total revenue of the Meiji government was 22.1 million yen; in fiscal 1872 (October 1871 through December 1872) the total was 50.4 million. (*MZS*, Vol. 3, pp. 180, 185.)

[5] Ministry of Finance, *Meiji-Taisho zaisei shi* [The financial history of the Meiji-Taisho period] (20 vols., Tokyo, 1937), Vol. 6, p. 2.

[6] *DNSS, passim.* See also Yosaburo Takekoshi, *The Economic Aspects of the History of the Civilization of Japan* (3 vols., London, 1930), Vol. 3, pp. 386-407.

were relatively unimportant as revenue producers. By supplementary taxes is meant all the many levies other than the land tax or the corvée. The land tax, overwhelmingly the most important of the three, differed widely in character and application in different domains. Three basic types of this tax, all of which can be characterized as a produce tax principally paid in kind, existed. One can be described as the modified variable assessment system[7] in which the tax on agricultural land was generally determined as follows:[8]

1. All registered village agricultural land was identified, classified, measured, and graded by means of a cadastral survey that took place infrequently. Methods of grading varied, but each was some variant of a superior-medium-poor classification.

2. Each year the output of brown rice[9] per *tan* from superior grade paddy field was estimated by sampling. The output per *tan* from each inferior grade paddy field was assumed to be 0.2 *koku* less than the next higher grade paddy field as a rule. The superior grade upland field was usually assumed to yield 0.4 *koku* less in brown rice value than the superior grade paddy field. The output from each inferior grade upland field was assumed to be 0.2 *koku* less in brown rice value than the next higher grade upland field as a rule. It is seen that the output of upland fields was quoted in *koku* of rice, a monetary unit of the time.

3. The total output of a field was estimated by multiplying the area of that field by the estimated output per *tan* of that grade of field.

4. The tax for that field was determined by multiplying the estimated total output by a uniform tax rate which was a proportion of the total output.

5. The tax was levied on the village, and it was held responsible for the payment of the total village assessment, which

[7] *DNSS*, Vol. 2, pp. 339-40. The Japanese called this system the *kemi-hō*. (*Ibid.*)

[8] Taken primarily from *Nihon keizaishi jiten, op.cit.*, pp. 546, 997, 1603-04. See also *DNSS*, Vol. 2.

[9] The Japanese term *genmai* is translated as brown rice. *Genmai* is rice from which the outer husk has been removed.

was, of course, the sum of the taxes on all fields within the village.

This system appears to have been used widely, though not exclusively during the first century of the Tokugawa Shogunate. The tax was conceptually a proportional tax on gross farm produce, or farm produce net of certain costs.[10] Because the relative taxable productivity of each field was fixed when each was graded, the tax per unit area on each field was proportional to its grade relative to others. Since the harvest need not be proportional to the grade of a field,[11] the tax per unit area on each field was not necessarily proportional to the harvest from that field. Although under this system fields would have to be regraded periodically so that adjustments could be made as changes in land productivity occurred, regrading occurred infrequently. The inequitable taxation which resulted was a serious weakness of this method of assessment.

The second type of Tokugawa land tax can be described as a variable assessment system.[12] Under it every field is inspected annually to determine its harvest. In this respect it differs from the modified variable assessment system under which all yield estimates were based upon a sample survey of superior grade paddy fields. The variable assessment system was instituted around the middle of the eighteenth century as a replacement for the modified system.[13] But it was not universally adopted. Of the three basic types of Tokugawa land tax, this clearly was the costliest to administer.

A third type that also appears to have been used during the second half of the Tokugawa period in place of the modified variable assessment system can be called the fixed assessment system.[14] The distinguishing feature of this system is that the assessment remained fixed for a varying number of years de-

[10] Where gross produce was taken, it is probable that the tax rates were lower. Seed and fertilizer costs were sometimes deducted.

[11] For example, some fields would tend to do better in wet years, others in dry years.

[12] The Japanese term for the variable assessment system is *arige-dori.* (*DNSS*, Vol. 2, p. 342.)

[13] *Ibid.*, p. 341.

[14] The Japanese term for this type is *jōmen-dori.* (*Ibid.*, p. 329.)

pending on the policy of the daimyo. The fixed assessment was determined by reference to the normal produce over a certain period of time. One way to determine the fixed assessment was to average the taxes based on the variable assessment system over a number of years.[15] This method of averaging taxes can be used only when the fixed assessment system replaces the variable assessment system. For subsequent reassessment some form of the variable assessment system must be used. The fixed assessment system commended itself because it was easier to administer than the variable systems. In principle the assessment was altered periodically, but in some cases it remained unchanged for centuries.[16] Although the fixed and the variable assessment systems predominated during the latter half of the Tokugawa Shogunate and the modified variable assessment system prevailed in the earlier half, none was used exclusively in either period.

The coexistence of the three systems of taxation implies that land productivity tended to rise more rapidly in provinces where the fixed assessment system prevailed since under the latter the incremental production will accrue to the cultivator. Where the cultivator was a tenant a fixed rent would have had the same effect. But a fixed rent was not likely over the long run, and in most cases the rent tended to be a proportion of the year's harvest. Therefore, in provinces where the incidence of landowner-cultivators was high, the effect of a fixed assessment system on productivity would have tended to be more pronounced. These comments assume that Japanese cultivators acted rationally in the management of their farms—a sound assumption, at least over the longer term.

Regardless of which system was used, wide differences existed in tax rates applied, surtaxes imposed, land and harvest measurement practices, and other administrative practices, and these resulted in great differences in the burdens borne by different taxpayers, villages, and provinces. These inequities carried over into the Meiji era, although some attempts were

[15] *Nihon keizaishi jiten, op.cit.*, p. 1604.
[16] *MZZKSS*, Vol. 7, p. 301. In this event the tax rate as a proportion of the reported harvest tended to fall as land productivity rose.

made to adjust intolerable injustices.[17] The Meiji leaders recognized that a thorough reform of the tax system was necessary. But as stated earlier, the objectives of the Meiji leadership extended much beyond equity needs, and the other objectives were not always consistent with tax equity.

The major laws that created the new land tax system and brought in a new set of land relations constituted the Land Tax Revision Act of 1873.[18] Under the new system the land tax continued to be the principal source of revenue. However, it was planned to add various commodity taxes to the tax system over a period of time to reduce the burden on the agricultural sector.[19] The corvée, a highly unpopular levy, was abolished as a national levy.

The salient features of the new land tax follow:

1. It established individual responsibility for tax payment in lieu of village responsibility.[20]

2. The tax base was to be land value instead of the annual harvest, or the average annual harvest.

3. The tax was to be paid in money rather than in kind.

4. The tax rate was set at 3 per cent of land value but with the proviso that the rate was to decrease to 1 per cent as revenue from other sources increased.

The establishment of individual responsibility for tax payment was preceded by a set of laws that established private property ownership rights by abolishing feudal land relations and restrictions. They accomplished the following: (a) established the principle that farmers were the owners of land;[21]

---

[17] The government attempted to make taxes uniform in those areas formerly held by the Tokugawa family. (Ōkurashō 505 [July 1870].)

[18] What is here called the Land Tax Revision Act of 1873 consists of the following five documents: (1) Jōyu (July 1873); (2) Dajōkan fukoku 272 (July 1873); (3) Dajōkan fukoku 272 besshi: chiso kaisei jōrei (July 1873); (4) Dajōkan fukoku 272 besshi: chiso kaisei kisoku (July 1873); (5) Dajōkan fukoku 272 bessatsu: chihōkan kokoroesho (July 1873).

[19] Dajōkan fukoku 272 besshi: chiso kaisei jōrei (July 28, 1873), Article 6.

[20] For a study of village cooperation and responsibility during the Tokugawa period, see Smith, op.cit., Chapters 5, 12.

[21] Gyōseikan fukoku 1096 (December 18, 1868).

(b) established the right to choose one's vocation which rendered meaningless regulations that tied the peasant to the land;[22] (c) established the right of free cropping;[23] (d) ordered the distribution of land ownership certificates for all land;[24] (e) abolished restrictions on the sale and purchase of land;[25] and (f) made the transfer of land ownership certificates a condition of the sale of land.[26] In the transition from village to individual responsibility for tax payments, the establishment of clear ownership rights probably eliminated some of the confusion that would have attended the change.

The change from payment in kind to payment in money was a logical development of the change from a harvest tax to a land value tax. A harvest tax is a proportion of the harvest and is assessed as so many units by volume, weight, or piece of the crop harvested, whether the actual assessment is determined annually or is a constant based on some past estimate of a normal harvest. Therefore, payment in kind is more readily understood and least likely to involve disputes. If payments are made in money in lieu of kind, the problem arises of converting the tax share of the crops into money which involves pricing difficulties. Therefore, in this case for administrative simplicity, a land value tax payable in money would be desirable. Payment in money is also desirable for economy. Collection in kind involves storage and sale of the commodities which makes tax collection enormously expensive and very wasteful of resources.[27] The Tokugawa period taxes were paid either in money or in rice which may be considered a form of money of the time. That is, taxes on crops other than rice were not paid as a rule in kind but in money or its equivalent in rice mainly because the other crops were much less negotiable than

[22] *Dajōkan fukoku 654* (December 18, 1871).

[23] *Ōkurashō 47* (September 7, 1871).

[24] *Ōkurashō 83* (July 4, 1872).

[25] *Dajōkan fukoku 50* (February 15, 1872).

[26] *Ōkurashō 25* (February 24, 1872).

[27] In the Tokugawa period, collection in kind entailed less transportation because domains collected and disposed of commodities mainly within their borders except for a few provinces which produced large rice surpluses.

rice.[28] In view of the preference for payments in rice when not made in money, it is probable that uneconomical use of land for rice production occurred. On the other hand, conversion to money payments would tend to encourage more efficient use of land.

The provision[29] in the Land Tax Revision Act of 1873 which stipulated that the land tax rate would be reduced to 1 per cent in time was an admission by the government that it regarded the tax on the agricultural sector to be unduly heavy relative to that on other sectors. It was explained in the law that the 3 per cent rate was temporarily necessary until other taxes were established. As soon as revenues from taxes on tea, tobacco, lumber, etc., should exceed 2,000,000 yen, the tax on land was to be gradually reduced. The tax rate did decrease to 2.5 per cent in 1877,[30] but this occurred in response to landowners' pleas for relief because the rice price had fallen in 1876.[31] The national land tax rate did not drop below this level for more than 60 years. The Land Tax Law of 1884,[32] which abolished the Land Tax Revision Act of 1873, did not incorpo-

[28] The preference for payment in rice of taxes on other crops is indicated by the income of the Shogunate in 1863. It included gold, silver, and copper, plus the following: 744,001 koku of rice; 445 koku of wheat; 4,448 koku of other grains; and 632 koku of salt. Less than 1% of the volume of payments, exclusive of payment in gold, silver, and copper, was paid in commodities other than rice. (Takekoshi, op.cit., Vol. 2, p. 228.)
The use of rice to pay taxes on other agricultural crops explains why many peasants consumed little or no rice. If a peasant farmed both irrigated and dry land, growing rice on the former and barley on the latter, he would be required to pay a rice tax on both the rice and barley harvests, leaving little, if any, for his own consumption depending on the relative size of the two types of cultivated land.

[29] Dajōkan fukoku 272 besshi: chiso kaisei jōrei (July 28, 1873), Article 6.

[30] Dajōkan fukoku 1 (January 4, 1877).

[31] The price fell from 7.28 yen per koku in 1875 to 5.01 yen in 1876 at the Tokyo Fukagawa wholesale markets. (Ministry of Agriculture and Commerce, Food Bureau, Beikoku tōkei: nihon no bu [Rice statistics: Japan] [Tokyo, 1924], p. 30.) The prices in the provinces tended to be lower than in Tokyo.

[32] Dajōkan fukoku 7 (March 15, 1884).

rate the provision promising a decrease in the land tax rate.
The change of policy occurred due to price inflation which
effectively reduced the tax burden and the increasing revenue
needs of the government.

One consequence of making the established land value the tax
base was that the revenue was generally not subject to annual
fluctuations, thus conforming with the tax revision objective of
obtaining a stable money revenue. In the Tokugawa period,
revenues necessarily fluctuated in localities where they were
dependent on the annual harvest, but they were also subject
to downward revisions in times of crop failure even where the
tax was a fixed charge.[33] In a country which is subject to an
unusual number of natural disasters[34] this type of flexibility
appears to be a necessity in a sector of the economy living close
to the subsistence level. In Meiji Japan, despite the stable revenue objective, some downward flexibility also existed due to
this factor.[35]

The thorniest problem of the Meiji land tax revision was land
valuation. Where value is defined as the market value as it is
here,[36] the valuation of land that has been recently sold is simple; the sale value is a reasonable approximation to the current
market value. But since land was rarely sold, the recent sale
price of a given piece of land was seldom available. Furthermore, a recent sale price was hardly reliable; since the buyer
was likely to be aware that the sale price would become the
land value and, therefore, the tax base, he would be tempted to

[33] *DNSS*, Vol. 2, p. 329.

[34] Because Japan lies along the East Asiatic typhoon belt, severe wind
and flood damage is a common occurrence. Japan also lies in one of the
world's most active earthquake belts and is subject to severe earth damage and the *tsunami*. Typhoons and earthquakes can ruin irrigation systems, upon which Japan's all important rice crop is based, and otherwise
severely damage crops.

[35] Much of the Meiji tax relief to disaster areas was granted by special
legislation for each situation. In 1901, however, legislation was enacted
to cover crop failure resulting from floods. Two years later, coverage was
extended to crop failure from all forms of natural disaster. (*Meiji-Taisho
zaisei shi, op.cit.*, Vol. 6, pp. 594-98.)

[36] The Japanese term *chika* is translated as "the market value of land,"
which in the usage above is shortened to "land value."

underreport the sale price in collusion with the seller.[37] Even knowing the correct price of a recently sold plot would not necessarily provide a measure for the revaluation of other village land. The value per *tan* so derived cannot be applied equally to all land because such factors as fertility, location, and the irrigability of land—all of which affect value—tend to vary from plot to plot. Moreover, the sale price is a reasonable approximation of the market price before, not after, the tax revision. Equity, under these circumstances, required that some procedure be worked out to obtain appropriate valuation of each plot of land and to account for the change in value resulting from the tax change.

In its effort to attain fair land valuation the Finance Ministry ordered a costly and time-consuming cadastral survey,[38] which was not completed for all classes of private land until 1881 although the survey of arable land was almost wholly completed by the end of 1876.[39] The information required for each plot of land included the name of the owner, number assigned to it, classification, area, normal harvest, and value. On land for which land ownership certificates had been issued, the value recorded on the certificate[40] was taken as the land value with the proviso that a plot would be revalued if the valuation on

[37] Instructions issued by the Finance Ministry on July 4, 1872, required the recording of the land value on the land ownership certificate. (*MZZKSS*, Vol. 7, p. 206.) The Land Tax Revision Act of 1873 also required the recording of land value on the certificates. (*Dajōkan fukoku 272 besshi: chiso kaisei shikō kisoku* [July 1873], Article 15.) From the perspective of the tax collector, land ownership certificates identified the person responsible for land tax payments on the land for which it was issued.

[38] Cadastres were also the basis of land taxation in the Tokugawa period. They were incomplete and inaccurate because cadastral surveys had not been undertaken at periodic intervals to keep them up to date. For a criticism of the Tokugawa land system, see Kōhei Kanda proposal for land tax reform in *MZZKSS*, Vol. 7, p. 301.

[39] Ono, *Meiji zenki tochi seido shiron, op.cit.*, pp. 103-04.

[40] The value entered was the "estimated current market value" that was required to be reported to the relevant government office. (*MZZKSS*, Vol. 7, p. 206.) Not all certificates issued earlier had the value entered therein. Some had the rent; some, the harvest and rent; and some required no indication of the value of the holding. (*Ibid.*, pp. 202-05.)

the certificate was no longer equivalent to the market value because land values had changed, or if the area of the plot had changed since the certificate was issued.[41] The responsibility for the original survey in rural areas was charged to the village, but the owner's approval was required for the value assigned to a plot.[42] When disagreement as to land value arose between the owner and the village, procedures leading to the sale of the land by auction were to be followed and land ultimately sold to the highest bidder if the owner persisted in rejecting the village valuation.[43]

The Finance Ministry officials who were assigned to the land survey were required to check the written reports submitted by the villages and to conduct personal inspections of the villages to check their accuracy.[44] Because land valuation is largely a subjective matter and because the officials required an objective basis for checking the valuations submitted by the villages, a procedure to obtain what was called the *standard value* was worked out as a guide for the officials to estimate the value of cultivated land.[45]

The *standard value* was the capitalized value of net farm income. Net farm income is defined as the gross value of farm output minus the cost of seeds and fertilizers, the national land tax, and the local surtax on land. The interest rate used to obtain the capitalized value was to be the prevailing rate in the area concerned.[46]

[41] For example, the area of a paddy field could and did increase owing to conversion of an adjoining part of a nonirrigated tract of land or the restoration of flood-damaged land.

[42] *Dajōkan fukoku 272 besshi: chiso kaisei shikō kisoku* (July 1873), Article 16. In assigning responsibility to the village the Meiji authorities were following Tokugawa period practice. It was also sensible because it enabled the literate individuals in the village to take charge of a project that required literacy to complete successfully.

[43] *Ibid.*

[44] *Dajōkan fukoku 272 bessatsu: chihōkan kokoroesho* (July 1873), Article 4.

[45] *Ibid.*, Article 12.

[46] *Dajōkan fukoku 272 besshi: chiso kaisei shikō kisoku* (July 1873), Article 1.

The equation described can be put into the following form:

$$(1) \quad V = \frac{R-C-T-T'}{i}$$

where V = *standard value* of land
R = value of gross output
C = cost of seeds and fertilizers
T = national land tax
T' = local surtax on land
i = prevailing interest rate

This appears to be circular reasoning because the object is to obtain the value of the land as a basis for computing the land tax, and the value of land in the above equation is dependent on the land tax. This apparent difficulty is bypassed because both the national and local taxes are a proportion of the land value. The equation can then be written:

$$(2) \quad V = \frac{R-C-tV-t'V}{i}$$

where t = national land tax rate
t' = local surtax rate on land

Then the following transformations can occur:

$$iV = R-C-(t+t')V$$

$$(3) \quad V = \frac{R-C}{i+t+t'}$$

Thus if the tax rates are obtainable, the land value can be calculated. It is also possible to obtain the national land tax directly from the following equation:

$$(4) \quad T = t\frac{R-C}{i+t+t'}$$

Equation (3) shows that the following five variables affect the *standard value* of each plot of land: the cost of seeds and fertilizers, the national land tax rate, the local surtax rate on land, the interest rate, and the total revenue from the plot. The last of these, however, is dependent on the area of the plots, the yield per unit area, and the prices of the crops, making a total of seven basic determinants of the *standard* value of cultivated land. The valuation of these determinants is, of course, important to both the government and the landowners. In order to minimize controversy, the values of many of these variables were arbitrarily defined by law. The cost of seeds and fertilizers was defined as 15 per cent of the value of gross output.[47] The national land tax rate was fixed at 3 per cent of the land value by law.[48] The local surtax rate on land was arbitrarily set at one-third of the national tax rate for the purpose of computing the *standard value*.[49] The prices of crops were generally established as those prevailing in the nearest local market averaged over a five-year period, although the time periods varied in early 1874.[50] The interest rate was stated to be the prevailing rate of return on land in each locality,[51] but it was primarily determined by edict. The law stated that the rate was not to exceed 7 per cent.[52] The records indicate that the norm was 6 per cent,[53] and the general tenor of the instructions to field officials point to 6 per cent as the norm that the government

[47] *Dajōkan fukoku 272 bessatsu: chihōkan kokoroesho* (July 1873), Article 18.

[48] *Dajōkan fukoku 272* (July 1873). The national land tax rate was decreased to 2.5% in 1877. (*Dajōkan fukoku 1* [January 4, 1877].)

[49] *Dajōkan fukoku 272 bessatsu: chihōkan kokoroesho* (July 1873), Article 18.

[50] Some vacillation occurred in early 1874 in determining the period over which the rice price was to be averaged. For a brief period an 18-month average was taken; then a 10-month average. The final decision was a five-year average determined in June, 1874. (*MZZKSS*, Vol. 7, Document 46, p. 338; Document 49, pp. 339-40; Document 51, p. 340. See also Ono, *Meiji zenki tochi seido shiron, op.cit.*, pp. 79-80.) The average prefectural rice price for land valuation ranged between 2.426 yen in Akita Prefecture and 5.450 yen per *koku* in Gumma Prefecture. (*MZZKSS*, Vol. 7, Appendix 8, p. 442.)

[51] *Dajōkan fukoku 272 besshi: chiso kaisei shikō kisoku* (July 1873), Article 1.

[52] *Dajōkan fukoku 272 bessatsu: chihōkan kokoroesho* (July 1873), Article 19.

[53] The rates for the various prefectures and districts within prefectures varied closely around 6% with many prefectures reporting a flat 6% rate. (*MZZKSS*, Vol. 7, Appendix 7, p. 442.)

expected the officials to establish.[54] As for the other two variables—the areas of cultivated plots and the yield per unit area of
each plot—the landowner and the village were responsible for
determining both. The area was to be obtained by measurement and the yield by reference to past records. Both were
subject to challenge by government officials.

An alternative method of determining the land value was
to capitalize the value of the rent.[55] To the extent that the rent
varies with changes in land productivity this modification does
not violate the spirit of the law: namely, the implication that
the tax should vary with productivity. But land income net
of seed, fertilizer, and land tax costs is not the same as the
money rent. Since money rent as defined by the law was net
of the income retained by the tenant as well as net of taxes
and costs of seeds and fertilizers, it is a smaller figure than land
income. Capitalizing the value of the rent would yield a lower
land value, other things remaining equal. The tax authorities
resolved the problem by lowering the interest rate by which
the capitalized value of rented land was to be computed. The
general rule appears to have been to assume that the income
of the tenant was one-third and the rent was two-thirds of farm
income net of taxes and the costs of seeds and fertilizers. With
this assumption the proper interest rate to be used to capitalize
the value of rent was judged to be two-thirds of the interest
rate to be used when net farm income was capitalized. The
suggested interest rate for tenant land was 4 per cent when
the rate on owner-cultivated land was 6 per cent. With the
assumptions given above, the land value would turn out to be
identical on the same property whether that property was
owner-cultivated or tenant-cultivated.[56] With respect to the

[54] *Dajōkan fukoku 272 bessatsu: chihōkan kokoroesho* (July 1873),
Articles 12, 15.

[55] *Ibid.*, Article 12.

[56] Assume that on a plot of owner-cultivated land the farm income
net of taxes and costs of seeds and fertilizers is 300 yen. Capitalized at
6%, the income yields a land value of 5,000 yen. Suppose the same land
had been tenanted. Out of the above income the tenant retains 100 yen
and the owner obtains 200 yen as rent. The rent capitalized at 4% yields
the same land value, 5,000 yen.

valuation of paddy fields it appears that the equation for obtaining the capitalized value of the net farm income was used almost exclusively.[57]

The fact that the villages were responsible for the original valuation gave them an opportunity to understate production and land values. Although officials could check the area estimates for accuracy, they had little basis for challenging the production reports except by reference to Tokugawa period records with which they were equipped. This may account in part for the fact that the average cadastral survey yields of 1.32 *koku* per *tan*[58] were about equal to the average Jōkyō (1684-88) yields of 1.3 *koku*.[59]

In theory the agricultural land tax as established by the Land Tax Revision Act of 1873 was a tax on the market value of land; in practice, the market value was assumed to be the capitalized value of the net farm income, or of the rent capitalized at a lower interest rate. If the tax base was to be the actual market value, conformity with the law would require that a plot be reassessed whenever its market value changed. If the market value was assumed to be the capitalized value of the normal net farm income, reassessment would also be required whenever the normal net farm income changed. Ideally annual reassessments would be required in either case since the tax was levied annually. The original act of 1873 did not provide specifically for reassessments. In 1874 the 1873 law was amended to provide a quinquennial revaluation of land beginning in 1880.[60]

[57] This conclusion derives from the fact that follow-up instructions on how to value irrigated land deal only with the treatment of variables associated with the equation. See *e.g.*, MZZKSS, Vol. 7, Document 46, pp. 338-39; Document 49, pp. 339-40; Document 51, p. 340. The following documents are fairly lengthy discussions, *pro* and *con*, of various aspects of land valuation where the formula is discussed: *ibid.*, Document 88, pp. 364-67; Documents 92-94, pp. 380-406; Document 97, pp. 406-12.

[58] Hideichi Horie, "The Agricultural Structure of Japan in Meiji Restoration," *Kyoto University Economic Review*, XXXI, 2 (October 1961), 15.

[59] See Chapter 4, p. 76n.

[60] *Dajōkan fukoku* 53 (May 12, 1874).

In 1884 the policy of periodic revaluation, which was never carried out in practice, was abandoned. The Land Tax Law of 1884 which abolished the Land Tax Revision Act of 1873 stipulated that the assessed value of land would remain unchanged except when land was reclassified.[61] It defined assessed value as the "value entered in the land ownership certificate,"[62] in contrast to market value as defined by the 1873 law, and thus escaped the responsibility for periodic revaluation implicit in making the land value dependent on productivity or market value. The main reason for the change of policy was that it became clear that periodic revaluation would be costly and time-consuming and provoke political friction.[63]

Reclassified plots were reassessed by using the equation developed in the 1873 law[64] with modifications. If the 1873 formula were used without modification, the land values determined after 1884 would tend to differ for the same quality land in the same locality owing to changes in the independent variables. To avoid this inequality, and because the intention of the lawmakers was to maintain the general level of land values at the levels determined during the land survey of the 1870's, it was made clear that the value of a reclassified field was to be determined with reference to the values of nearby fields.[65]

The practice of computing the assessed value by capitalizing what was assumed to be the net farm income did not necessarily determine the true market value. Even if the net farm income was estimated honestly and with tolerable accuracy, the value based on the market price and that based on net farm income would still tend to differ because of the existence of

[61] *Dajōkan fukoku 7 bessatsu: chiso jōrei* (March 15, 1884), Article 7.

[62] *Ibid.*, Article 1. Land ownership certificates constituted proof of ownership and also fixed the responsibility for the payment of land taxes. After 1889 the quotation was amended to read the "value entered in the land register." (*Hōritsu 30* [November 29, 1889], Article 1.) Registration in the land register became proof of ownership after 1889.

[63] *MZZKSS*, Vol. 7, Documents 87-90, pp. 361-79.

[64] *Ōkurashō tasshi gogai: chiso jōrei toriatsukai kokoroesho* (April 5, 1884), Article 14.

[65] *Ibid.*, Articles 12, 13.

tangible and intangible factors which make a given piece of land more or less desired than another producing the identical net revenue. Suppose, however, that the net farm income was systematically underreported, a practice that farmers and other businessmen almost universally engage in. In this event, the market value and the capitalized value can diverge widely.

When the Land Tax Law of 1884 was promulgated, the market value concept was abandoned and a value maintenance policy was adopted. This transformation is notable because the tax thereafter was not dependent in principle on productivity. The tax would depend solely on the tax rate assigned to the class of land, and thus would not dampen the incentive to increase productivity.[66] However, the market value concept need not have lowered the incentive to raise productivity if the farmers were able to underreport production with impunity as was apparently true.

The adoption of the value maintenance policy probably has two less problematic effects. It would cause the emergence of increasingly greater inequities in land valuation as over time some land values would increase and others would decrease owing to the differential impact of natural calamities, population growth, urbanization, improved transportation facilities, and changes in demand for agricultural products. It would also tend to decrease the incentive to underreport yield as apparently it did from around the turn of the century when further land revaluation was abandoned as stated below.

The agricultural land valuation policy established in 1884 remained unchanged in principle during the Meiji era. A com-

[66] In the Tokugawa period the following combination of tax policies prevailed in most provinces: severe taxes on arable land; reluctance to lower established taxes; and a highly favorable treatment of newly reclaimed land to encourage reclamation. These policies together sometimes led to the abandonment of highly productive but heavily taxed land in favor of reclamation of undeveloped land. The effect was probably an overall decline in productivity, although the tax burden may have been lightened sufficiently so that the peasant was better off than previously. Moreover, the severe land taxes (confiscatory taxes to keep the peasants at the subsistence level of living) had two probable effects. It may have inhibited the peasant's will to raise productivity and encouraged him and the village to falsify village reports.

plete revaluation of one class of private land, *takuchi*, did take place in 1910.[67] Some sentiment also existed for a complete revaluation of agricultural land,[68] but it was not until the 1930's that this occurred.[69] However, piecemeal changes in the value of agricultural land did take place under special legislation. There were four land revaluations in all; the first two for the purpose of making intraprefectural value adjustments (i.e., to make value adjustments between villages or districts within prefectures), and the last two for making interprefectural adjustments. The first intraprefectural revaluation took place from 1880 to 1886,[70] the second in 1887.[71] Both of these were minor adjustments accounting for total land tax changes of 423 thousand yen and 333 thousand yen, respectively.

During this period of intraprefectural value adjustments the need for a general revaluation to adjust interprefectural injustices was being discussed. One result of the discussion was the revaluation of 1889[72] which reduced arable land values by 129,531 thousand yen and arable land taxes by 3,242 thousand yen, a decline of about 10 per cent. This reduction was regarded as a partial remedy allowable within the restrictions imposed by budget requirements. The second and last interprefectural revaluation took place in 1898-99[73] following the passage of a revaluation bill which in one form or another had been introduced annually into the Diet since its establishment in 1890. The decrease in land value attributable to this revaluation was 148,598 thousand yen. This means a decline in arable land taxes of 3,715 thousand yen at the 2.5 per cent tax rate which prevailed from 1877 to 1898. The land value reductions for the two revaluations were accomplished by reducing the

[67] See *Hōritsu 3* (March 15, 1910).

[68] Yoshiharu Yanagi, *Saishin chiso hō yōgi* [Commentary on the recent land tax laws] (Tokyo, 1934), p. 15.

[69] Revaluation was based on *Hōritsu 45* (March 31, 1926). But use of the new value as the tax base was not authorized until 1931 by *Hōritsu 28* (March 31, 1931).

[70] *MZS*, Vol. 5, pp. 403-10.

[71] *Ibid.*, pp. 623-60.

[72] *Ibid.*, pp. 660-83.

[73] *Ibid.*, pp. 683-726.

nominal yield per *tan* and the value of rice per *koku*. During the interprefectural value reductions, changes were not allowed in two prefectures, Yamaguchi and Miyagi, which it was believed fared better during the cadastral survey of the 1870's than other prefectures in respect to land valuation.

The fact that the government continued to be troubled by the land valuation problem is evidence that the tax equity goal[74] of the Meiji government was not achieved in either the land survey of the 1870's or the 1880's. The first survey failed to achieve this objective owing to widespread concealment, misclassification, and undermeasurement of land and underreporting of yield as indicated in Chapters 2, 3, and 4. The objective of the second survey was apparently limited to the elimination of concealment and misclassification of land. A serious attempt never appears to have been made to remedy land undermeasurement, probably because it was the least conspicuous of the tax evasion practices. The four land revaluations that occurred after the first land survey probably made the tax burdens increasingly more equitable. But after the last revaluation of 1898-99—which fixed land values until the 1930's except where land class change occurred—a departure from tax equity once again became inevitable since changes in land productivity would tend to occur and the same class of land was subject to uniform tax rates. Although tax equity proved to be an elusive goal[75] as it has for all governments faced with a need

[74] The functional distribution of income changed enormously from the Tokugawa period to the Meiji era. This question is discussed in Chapter 7.

[75] Of the three other goals of the land reform and associated measures, two were generally attained. The separation of the daimyo from their hereditary sources of income and power was achieved judging from the original intent of the Meiji leadership which was to prevent a successful counterrevolution. Where the daimyo continued to remain the focal point of political power, it was within the framework of the new political institutions. No one can doubt that the goal of improving the economic performance of the nation by instituting a private property system was accomplished. There is no question that this system provided greater incentive for individual economic effort than the feudal system offered in both agriculture and the economy as a whole.

The final goal of a stable money revenue from the land tax was techto raise revenue, when this goal was abandoned in respect to land taxes, it may have had two desirable effects: the dampening of the incentive to underreport production and the raising of the incentive to increase land productivity.

---

nically attained. A stable money revenue was sought because the preceding system of a tax in kind provided a revenue that fluctuated widely in money value as crop prices changed. But the real implied goal was, of course, an adequate revenue which it was believed a stable revenue would provide. This goal was not attained as the Meiji government was obliged to print and borrow money and seek new, unplanned sources of revenue.

APPENDIX B

Agricultural Land Improvement Policy

THE 1890's are an important period in Japanese agricultural history, since it was during this period that Japan changed from a nation self-subsistent in food[1] to one dependent on foreign sources for a part of its food supply. This appendix is a study of the change in agricultural policy that then occurred, and the effect of this change on agricultural production. We will find that the timing of that effect is consistent with my view that the growth rate of agricultural production was probably greater after 1918-22 than before it.

Until 1890, owing to the relative abundance of domestically produced agricultural products, the nation had understandably neglected agriculture relative to other industries. In fact, undue attention to agriculture at this time would have undermined the objective of creating an economically strong nation because it would have impeded the flow of resources from agriculture to nonagriculture, a necessary condition of Japan's economic growth. It was not a case of total neglect, however. The fact that agricultural products were the most important elements in Japan's imports and exports in early Meiji and that agriculture was the principal source of government revenue served to direct a certain amount of attention to it. For example, it was in this period that the government imported foreign seeds, livestock, fertilizers, agricultural implements, and the like owing to the belief that things Western were superior. The long-term need to increase arable land area was also recognized in early Meiji as is evident in the favorable tax treatment of newly reclaimed land in the land tax laws.

But when it became evident that agriculture was not supplying the nation's food needs in the 1890's, a clearly marked change in agricultural policy took place. The more important events in the 1890's that indicate the shift in policy are: (1) the increasing stress placed on accuracy in reporting production

[1] A small net export of rice occurred until the 1890's.

and the rise in the number of crops reported; (2) in 1893, the formal establishment of agricultural experimental stations; (3) in 1894, the enactment of legislation for the establishment of prefectural experimental stations; (4) in 1896, the enactment of legislation to establish the Hypothec Bank and agricultural and industrial banks; (5) in 1899, the enactment of the following laws: the Arable Land Adjustment Law, a law creating and subsidizing the agricultural association, and a law subsidizing the prefectural experimental stations. These are not the only laws or issues that will be discussed. They have been enumerated to indicate that beginning in the 1890's agriculture started to obtain increasingly more benefits from government expenditures and that these benefits were closely related to the need for increased agricultural production.

Of the various government measures directed toward this end, those concerned with agricultural land development (including the extension of the arable land area and the improvement of existing arable land) received the greatest attention and the largest funds. This appendix is primarily an attempt to show the probable effect of such measures on agricultural production.[2]

Gauged by the area of land affected, the most important of the many land development laws of pre-World War II Japan was the Arable Land Adjustment Law.[3] The original purpose of this law was to achieve a more efficient use of existing arable land. Over time, however, the objective was broadened to include all forms of arable land development. More attention will be given to this law than to others as it has a longer history and clearly shows that interest in arable land development deepened over time.

The specific purpose of the Arable Land Adjustment Law of 1899 was arable land consolidation and rationalization. This

[2] The role of experimental stations in increasing agricultural production was discussed in Chapter 4.

[3] Arable Land Adjustment Law is the translation that has been adopted here for *Kōchi seiri hō*. This law was originally passed as *Hōritsu 82* (March 22, 1899). Ten years later it was completely revised by *Hōritsu 30* (April 12, 1909). The descriptive designation *Kōchi seiri hō* was retained for the revised law.

was prompted by a characteristic feature of Japanese cultivated fields—fragmentation into lots too tiny and irregular for efficient operation even with the techniques used in Japan, which are adapted to small-scale operations. The average farmer cultivates a number of noncontiguous plots, which are typically scattered widely throughout the village, comprising a total area of about one *chō*. It was estimated that in 1926 the number of lots of arable land was 93.9 million.[4] The number of agricultural households in that year was 5,555 thousand.[5] Each farm household, then, held an average of almost 17 lots. Furthermore, the roads, paths, and ridges between fields, irrigation ditches, and canals tend to turn and twist causing a further waste of cultivated land.

The obvious inefficiency of this land structure led to efforts to rationalize it long before the Meiji era. Theoretically, the ideal solution for the improvement of fragmented and irregularly shaped land is consolidation into larger rectangular units which requires the straightening of roads, paths, ridges, canals, etc. But the independent consolidation of land owned by a single owner is impossible if his holdings are scattered, as they generally were. Therefore, a rational adjustment first requires a redistribution of arable land among all owners in a district done in such a way that the land value of each landowner's holdings remains proportionally the same before and after the redistribution.[6] Moreover, ideally each farmer would emerge from such an undertaking with two pieces of contiguous land,[7] one of which is a paddy field and the other an upland field. Despite the many difficulties involved, attempts to rationalize arable land were made before the Meiji era and did achieve limited success.[8]

[4] Ministry of Finance and Bank of Japan, *Statistical Yearbook of Finance and Economy of Japan—1948* (Tokyo, 1948), p. 182.

[5] *NRT*, p. 4.

[6] The exact value of a landowner's holding changes because land consolidation increases the productivity of land and, therefore, the total real value also increases.

[7] Each paddy field or upland field may in practice have to be divided into two or more pieces owing to terrain or other problems.

[8] Izutarō Suehiro, *et al.*, eds., *Gendai hōgaku zenshū* [Collected studies

Ultimately the nation turned to legislation—the Arable Land Adjustment Law of 1899—in the effort to rationalize cultivated land structure. But the law came only after efficient land use became imperative when Japan became a net food importer in the 1890's. However, no thoroughgoing land consolidation was achieved under the 1899 law and its amendments or the 1909 law and its amendments. It was the failure of the original aim of the adjustment law that led to the amendment of 1905, the revision of 1909, and the subsequent amendments of the latter, most of which broadened the purpose of the law to include many other forms of arable land improvement. As we examine the changes that occurred, it will become clear that the nation's legislators went to great lengths to encourage arable land improvement.

The purpose of the 1899 law was given in an explanatory statement[9] as follows:

> In examining the condition of the nation's agricultural land, we find that agricultural development and management are being seriously impaired because some land is not being efficiently used, and time and labor is being wasted owing to excessive fragmentation of land; misshapen plots; and the lack of regularity in the arrangement of roads, of ridges and paths between fields, and of waterways for irrigation and drainage purposes. In recent years some attempts have been made to restructure paddy fields and ridges and paths, and the government has also tried to encourage improvement by conferring special benefits such as the principle that such improvement cannot be the basis for an increase in land value. But improvement has been slow. Since arable land adjustment cannot be undertaken without the cooperation of all landowners involved, the purpose of this law is to enforce

---

of contemporary law] (39 vols., Tokyo, 1928-31), Vol. 31, p. 399.

According to one source there was only one truly successful land consolidation project. This occurred during the Tokugawa period under the direction of Yugaku Ohara. (Seiichi Tōbata, *An Introduction to the Agriculture of Japan* [Tokyo, 1958], p. 21.)

[9] *NNHS*, Vol. 4, p. 214.

the mandatory participation of a dissenting minority; by pro-
tecting the equity and other rights of third parties; by maintaining the principle that adjustment will not change land
value; by bestowing on the participants without charge public land no longer publicly required; by exemption of participants from the land registration and building registration
taxes; and by facilitating the collection of funds to defray the
costs of adjustment.

The law's treatment of land taxes was one of its most attractive features. The key phrase in the above statement is "the
principle that adjustment will not change land value."[10] By
"land value" is meant the assessed land value for tax purposes
and not the market value. The latter tends to increase with
adjustment as explained below. But if the market value increases and the assessed value remains constant for adjusted
land, then such land is obtaining a *de facto* tax reduction.

The initiation and execution of adjustment was facilitated by
conferring very great powers on those who undertook the
projects.[11] The two most important of these have been mentioned in the explanatory statement. They were the authority,
when necessary to carry out the objectives of the adjustment
project, to enforce the participation of a dissenting minority,[12]
and the power to collect funds to defray the costs of adjustment.[13] Other powers or rights granted included the authority
to trespass on, measure, and make alterations on property and
to examine confidential government records without payment
of fees.[14]

The scope and purpose of the 1899 law was extended considerably by amendment in 1905. The 1899 law had defined
land adjustment as follows:[15]

[10] The principle was originally established in 1897 in *Hōritsu* 39
(March 30, 1897).
[11] For a full discussion of powers conferred, see Suehiro, *et al.*, *op.cit.*,
Vol. 31, pp. 415-18.
[12] *Hōritsu* 82 (March 22, 1899), Article 3.
[13] *Ibid.*, Article 65.
[14] *Ibid.*, Articles 6, 8, and 21.
[15] *Ibid.*, Article 1.

Land adjustment, whose purpose is to promote the agricultural utilization of land, means in this law the exchange, division, and consolidation of land; the transformation of its boundaries and terrain; and the alteration, removal, and construction of canals, ditches, roads, and ridges and paths between fields.

The 1905 amendment broadened the definition so that the latter part of the definition was changed to read:[16] ". . . the alteration, removal, and construction of roads, levees, canals, ditches, reservoirs, and ridges and paths between fields; and the concomitant arrangements and construction that are associated with irrigation and drainage."

In 1909 the nation's legislators further broadened the law by a thorough revision of the 1899 act.[17] The main objective of the 1899 law was land improvement by consolidation of fragmented plots and the more rational arrangement of other features of arable land, and particularly of paddy fields. The 1909 law retained all important features of the 1899 law. The broadening took two paths. One was achieved by expanding the definition of adjustment to include projects whose purpose was not so much land improvement through rearrangement and consolidation of lots but through reclamation of undeveloped land[18] or by conversion of upland fields to paddy fields.[19] This meant that these land improvement measures could be undertaken on a community basis by interested parties over the protests of a dissident group if the projects were undertaken by an incorporated body, as all of the larger projects were. In this case agreement by 50 per cent of the members of the proposed corporation of the adjustment district

[16] Suehiro, *et al., op.cit.,* Vol. 31, p. 401.

[17] *Hōritsu 30* (April 13, 1909). The laws will be distinguished wherever necessary by dating as the 1899 law or the 1909 law. The 1909 law was amended in 1910, 1914, 1919, and 1933, but the main objective and spirit of the law was established at the beginning.

[18] Undeveloped land was defined to include forests, *genya,* ponds and bogs, and miscellaneous land. Developed land was defined to include paddy fields, upland fields, *takuchi,* salt fields, and mineral spring sites. (*Dajōkan fukoku 7 bessatsu: chiso jōrei* [March 15, 1884] Article 3.)

[19] *Ibid.*

was sufficient to carry the project provided that the 50 per cent owned two-thirds of the area and value of the land involved.[20]

The second path along which the broadening took place was in concessions with respect to land valuation and tax liability. The 1909 law retained the following concessions made in the 1899 law: (1) the principle that land value would not be changed as a result of improvements deriving directly from arable land adjustment;[21] (2) exemption from land registration or building registration taxes where the need for registration arose out of the adjustment process;[22] and (3) the free grant of public land to participants where such public land was freed from use as roads, waterways, levees, reservoirs, etc.[23] To clear the way for the new concessions, the 1909 law specified that provisions in the Land Tax Law of 1884 regarding changes in land value and taxes do not apply to land class changes which have occurred under its (1909 law) provisions. The types of land class changes specified were (1) reclamation of undeveloped private land; (2) change in classification of developed private land (particularly conversion of upland fields to paddy fields); and (3) changes in classification of other classes of land owing to alterations in the boundaries or terrain of fields or owing to the alteration, removal or construction of roads, levees, waterways, or reservoirs.[24] The 1909 law then provided its own specifications as to what treatment was to be accorded to the above classes of land.

It is desirable to obtain an understanding of why land revaluation was needed and how it was accomplished before

[20] *Hōritsu 30* (April 12, 1909), Article 50. The 1899 law differed here in detail. It required the approval of two-thirds of the members who represented two-thirds of the area and value of the land involved. (*Hōritsu 82* [March 22, 1899], Article 20.)

[21] *Hōritsu 30* (April 12, 1909), Article 13.

[22] *Ibid.*, Article 10.

[23] *Ibid.*, Article 11. When private land was converted to public use, this was also done without compensation if public land converted to private use was at least an equal exchange in value. If conversion to public use exceeded in value conversion to private ownership, then compensation was made. (*Ibid.*)

[24] Specifically, the 1909 law states that Articles 10, 11, and 16-19 of the Land Tax Law of 1884 do not apply. (*Ibid.*, Article 12.)

examining the specifications. Land adjustment is a process of at least partially destroying the surface structure of land[25] and reconstructing it in a manner designed to increase the efficient use of arable land and of land facilities, including roads, and irrigation and drainage systems. Before adjustment the public records show the identification number, classification, valuation, and ownership of each lot within the adjustment district. After the restructuring of the district a new set of public records has to be created. Each lot must be assigned a new identification number, classification, valuation, and owner.[26] Valuation of the new lots—a valuation for tax purposes distinct from the market value—is necessary as one of the bases upon which an owner can be assigned to it,[27] and as the base on which the land tax is to be levied.

In cases where land adjustment occurred in an area entirely devoted to paddy fields, the valuation problem was relatively simple. The original total assessed value of the fields in the adjustment district was allocated to the new fields by application of the previously mentioned principle that the total assessed land value would remain the same in the district. This meant that the total assessed value of private land in the district would not increase despite an increase in area. The area of private land can increase due to remeasurement of undermeasured area or a reduction in the area of public land owing to a more rational arrangement of publicly owned roads, levees, waterways, and reservoirs. If the area of private land increases, the tax burden per unit area must decline since the total assessed value of private land remains constant. The lot by lot

---

[25] Adjustment as defined in the 1899 law would have required almost a total alteration of the surface features of the district such as ridges and paths between fields, roads, irrigation ditches, reservoirs, etc., to consolidate the minute lots.

[26] Also requiring transfer are liens against fields, tenancy rights, and other obligations or rights. (*Ibid.*, Articles 17-25, 30.) Every one of the land improvement operations authorized under the adjustment laws usually requires the alteration of some of the lots within the district.

[27] The basic requirement for the assignment of fields was that they be similar in respect to area, class, quality, and value to what was previously held. (*Ibid.*, Article 30.)

valuation was the legal responsibility of the chief of the tax office in whose jurisdiction the adjustment district was located. In practice, the detailed valuation was formulated by the responsible officials of the adjustment cooperative and passed by the general membership of the cooperative.[28] It was then forwarded to the tax office chief for approval.

The land valuation and tax treatment described above dealt with situations that the 1899 law also provided for. In the following discussion we take up those provisions of the 1909 law and its amendments which deal with reclamation of undeveloped private land, improvement through conversion to another class of developed private land, treatment of land reclaimed or converted before the adjustment, and reclamation of undeveloped public land and publicly owned bodies of water.

When undeveloped private land was reclaimed for agricultural purposes or when developed private land was converted to agricultural use or from one agricultural use to another (*e.g.*, upland fields to paddy fields), if the total area of such changes did not exceed 20 per cent of the total area of private land in the adjustment district, the total assessed value of the land in the district remained unchanged.[29] That is, the community, in effect, was told that the area of cultivated land or of improved cultivated land could increase by 20 per cent of the area of private land in the adjustment district without incurring additional tax liability for the district as a whole. If the reclaimed or converted land exceeded the stipulated percentage, the increase in the assessed value of the district would be based on the increased value of the reclaimed or converted land as estimated immediately after the completion of the adjustment project.

The procedure for computing the increased value when the

[28] Suehiro, *et al.*, *op.cit.*, Vol. 35, p. 227. Where the adjustment project was operated on a partnership basis, the unanimous consent of the partners was required in setting land values. *Ibid.*

[29] *Hōritsu 30* (April 12, 1909), Article 14. A 1914 amendment of the article makes this point more explicit. (*Hōritsu 30* [March 30, 1914], Article 1.)

improved land exceeded the stipulated amount follows. First, the pre-adjustment value of the land to be reclaimed or converted was obtained. Second, the value of improved land was estimated directly after the adjustment.[30] Third, the difference between the two values is divided by the area of the improved land to determine the average increase per unit area in the value of the land. Fourth, the average increase in value is multiplied by that part of the area of the improved land which exceeds the 20 per cent allowance. The product is then added to the old assessed value of the district to obtain the new assessed value.

The new assessed value of the district is less than the sum of the old assessed value of the land in the district whose classifications have not changed and the new assessed value of the improved land—owing to the 20 per cent allowance. This means that the assessed value of land that was not improved would have to be reduced. Therefore, adjustment involving land improvement gave tax relief to the entire district. The new assessed value of improved land remained as determined, but it has been stated that this value tended to be lower than for comparable land when the improved land became fully productive. Furthermore, the value for taxation purposes reverted to the pre-adjustment value for up to 40 years[31] for reclaimed land and 6 years for converted land from the date when reclamation or conversion started. Because the assessed values of undeveloped land, upland fields, and paddy fields tended to differ greatly, it follows that reversion to pre-adjustment assessed values of reclaimed or converted land meant a very substantial land tax reduction for an extended period.[32]

[30] The significance of reassessment of improved arable land immediately following the adjustment is that the land value tended to be estimated considerably lower than would have been true if the revaluation occurred after the land became fully productive.

[31] The 40-year tax relief became effective in 1919. (*Hōritsu 45* [April 9, 1919], Article 14.) The 1909 law had provided a 20-year relief, and the 1914 amendment had liberalized it to 20 to 30 years.

[32] The Arable Land Adjustment Law of 1909 could have forced some communities to adjust on a community basis because otherwise its benefits would have been monopolized by a few and the benefits may not

The 1909 adjustment law did not provide for special treatment of cultivated land reclaimed from public bodies of water or from undeveloped public land lying within the adjustment districts. However, in the 1914 amendment fields reclaimed from public bodies of water were totally exempted from the land tax for up to 50 years, and those reclaimed from public undeveloped land were similarly exempted up to 10 years.[33] In

have been fully realized. Let us assume that there are 100 landowners in a community each with 2 *chō* of land, 1 *chō* of which in each case is a paddy field and the other *chō* is undeveloped land. Let us further assume that 40 landowners own undeveloped land that can be fully converted to paddy fields, and that none of the others can be developed at all. If the 40 landowners develop their own land independently they will end with 80 *chō* of paddy fields. When the adjustment project is completed the reclaimed land will be revalued. The average per *chō* difference in the pre- and post-adjustment values of the reclaimed land will be determined. The product of this average difference and that area of the reclaimed land which exceeds 20% of the 80 *chō* of land (in this case 24 *chō*) will be added on to the old assessed value of the 80 *chō* to become the new "assessed" value. The new "assessed" value, however, is not the new tax base and will not be for the next 40 years because the newly reclaimed land will continue to be taxed at its undeveloped valuation for 40 years. There has also been a downward revision of the value of the original 40 *chō* of paddy fields because the 16 *chō* of reclaimed land (20% of 80 *chō*) was added without an increase in the old total assessed value, thus a redistribution of assessed values has taken place. Therefore, the actual tax on the 80 *chō* of land for the 40-year period is lower than the tax before the adjustment occurred.

Suppose now that the entire community had undertaken the project. In this event, because the reclaimed land amounts to only 20% of the total private land in the project, there will be no increase in the assessed land value for the entire project. But the old assessed value will be redistributed among the 200 *chō* of land in the district. Because the assessed value of reclaimed land has increased, the assessed value of all other land whose classifications have not changed will be reduced. As for the reclaimed land its land value for tax purposes will continue to be the pre-adjustment value for 40 years. The entire community will have gained in this case; the full benefit of the adjustment law will have been realized; and, in this particular case, the 40 owners do not suffer any loss from community participation. If the total area reclaimed had been less than 20% of the project's private land area, the 40 owners whose land was reclaimed would have suffered a loss from community participation, since the tax benefits would have been distributed more thinly than the optimum for the 40 owners.

[33] *Hōritsu 32* (March 30, 1914), Part 2 of Article 14.

1919 the exemption period was made a full 60 years and a full 20 years, respectively, for the two types of reclamation.[34] The assessed values of these lands were to be determined after the expiration of the exemption periods subject to the proviso that if the reclamation had not been successfully accomplished an additional period of exemption would be granted.

As events proved, the main accomplishment of the adjustment program was land improvement in the form of reclamation, conversion of developed land into cultivated land, conversion of upland fields into paddy fields, and improvement of drainage and irrigation facilities.[35] Only limited success was attained in land consolidation.

There are a number of reasons for the comparative failure of consolidation. One serious impediment was the difficulty in obtaining a consensus on the relative value of the lots that would have to be exchanged. This is exemplified by the typical landowner who places a higher value on his plot of land than on another of the same quality and size.

A second barrier to land consolidation was the need to protect the rights of all persons affected, including the tenants.[36] Some of the problems involving rights can be best illustrated by putting them in their extreme forms. First, suppose that all landowners own one lot each. In this event, if no landowner is to be deprived of his land, consolidation is impossible, although the straightening of the interstitial elements is possible. Second, suppose that a big landowner rents each of his many lots to a different individual. If the cultivation rights of each tenant are to be protected, consolidation cannot take place. Finally, suppose that a landowner has a number of lots, and that each is mortgaged to a different money lender. The first mortgage right of each mortgage can be best protected by maintaining the same number of lots.

A final important reason for the comparative failure of consolidation was that the original idea borrowed largely from the

---

[34] *Hōritsu 45* (April 9, 1919), Part 2 of Article 14.

[35] *NNHS*, Vol. 4, pp. 213-22.

[36] Forty-two per cent of the total area adjusted under the Arable Land Adjustment Law was leased land. (*Ibid.*, p. 172.)

West was more applicable to the agricultural land situation in Western Europe which differed immensely from the one existing in Japan.[37] In contrast to Western Europe, Japan was characterized by a high proportion of tenant farmers, small farms, high man-land ratio, a high proportion of irrigated land, and hilliness of the terrain. Even in Europe, land consolidation was a difficult and time-consuming undertaking, despite the clear economies of scale that could be obtained.[38] Consolidation in Japan meant that each farmer would ideally have a paddy field and an upland field, each averaging about an acre in area. Western innovations designed to obtain economies of scale were not suitable for such minute areas. Moreover, they were not applicable as a rule to irrigated land. The abundance of labor made labor-saving, which was the principal gain from consolidation, less attractive than where labor was scarce. Consolidation of irrigated fields is a much more expensive operation than that of upland fields, and if the slope is relatively steep, it would also mean the removal or the partial loss of topsoil which would tend to affect land productivity. Moreover, where there is much hilly land, such factors as the direction that the land faces, the nearness of trees, the possibility of flood damage, etc., tend to cause differences in land value making agreement on land valuation difficult.

Some of the more important gains that were realized from land adjustment were:[39] 1) increase in the area of arable land and irrigated land; 2) increase in land productivity; 3) improvement of the drainage system; 4) better utilization of water; 5) increase in land value; 6) greater availability of credit owing to the increase in land value; 7) increase in labor productivity; 8) increased rent on leased land; 9) greater con-

[37] NNHS, Vol. 4, pp. 197-203. Japan had its own theory of land consolidation developed during the Tokugawa period. (*Ibid.*, Vol. 1, pp. 153ff.)

[38] *Ibid.*, Vol. 4, pp. 197-203.

[39] Suehiro, *et al.*, *op.cit.*, Vol. 31, pp. 407-08. Also see NNHS, Vol. 6, pp. 159-70. It is evident that land adjustment also benefits the community as a whole owing to the increase in community income, improvement of transportation facilities, better control of water, etc. (Suehiro, *et al.*, *op.cit.*, Vol. 31, pp. 408-09.)

venience and time saving in transportation; and 10) more frequent and efficient use of animals in cultivation. Some of these
gains require further explanation. It is to be noted that adjustment normally occurs in districts where paddy fields constitute
the largest class of land.

Although most of the increase in the area of arable land was
accounted for by land reclamation, some of the increase resulted from consolidation, even though consolidation occurred
on a limited scale. The more a given paddy field is subdivided,
the greater the amount of space that will be occupied by ridges
and paths between fields. Consolidation, then, tends to increase
productive land area by reducing the area of land classes not
in direct productive use.[40] The area of productive land also
tends to increase when roads, waterways, paths, ridges, and
other necessary parts or interstitial elements of cultivated land
are straightened.

The improvement of the drainage system has three important
consequences. The first is that by permitting the drainage after
harvest of those paddy fields which previously remained inundated the year around, or were inadequately drained,[41] it is
possible in the southern half of Japan to plant a second crop
on the same field. The second consequence is that adequate
drainage makes possible an increase in the fertility of soil because better methods of cultivation and fertilizer use become
possible.[42] The third result is that the improvement of the
drainage system and the concomitant rationalization of the
irrigation system makes possible a more effective control of
paddy field inundation which also increases land productivity.

Increase in labor productivity, greater convenience and time-
saving in transportation, and the more frequent and effective
use of animals in cultivation derive from the consolidation of
land. If a farmer has even one less plot than he previously had,

[40] The paths and ridges between fields are often utilized for productive
purposes; therefore, any increase in their area need not be a total loss.

[41] In 1953 over 11% of paddy fields were inundated the year around
and over 20% were inadequately drained. Kayo, *op.cit.*, p. 64.

[42] *NNHS*, Vol. 1, pp. 461-68. A schematic comparison of the efficiency
of fields flooded the year around and those effectively drained is made
to the advantage of the latter in *ibid.*, pp. 465-67.

he will waste less time shifting from one plot to another. Larger plots also make possible the use of animals where previously the plots were too small for efficient use. In either case a labor-saving innovation or modification of farm operation occurs. Moreover, the use of animals makes possible a more effective working of the soil itself.

The gain in productivity from land improvement and better control of water is impressive. One estimate of the total gain in per *tan* yield of rice in paddy fields from 1900 to 1935 is 0.39 *koku*. Of this gain 0.24 *koku* is credited to land adjustment.[43] Because by 1940 nearly one million *chō* of paddy fields had been involved in land adjustment,[44] the annual yield in 1940 tended to be nearly 2.4 million *koku* greater than it was in 1900, owing to gains in productivity from land adjustment alone.

The response to the Arable Land Adjustment Law is shown in Table B-1.[45] Beginning in 1905 when a substantial broadening of the law occurred, the area approved[46] remained at high levels. About this time three other events occurred which probably had an impact on land adjustment projects. In 1905 the Russo-Japanese War ended releasing resources tied to the war effort. In 1906 the Agriculture and Commerce Ministry in order to induce prefectural encouragement of adjustment projects, made funds available to subsidize prefectural expenses of conducting surveys, preparing plans, and supervising adjustment.[47] In the same year the Land Adjustment Section of the Agriculture and Commerce Ministry was established to accelerate the program.[48] Apparently in response to these stimuli and to the broadening of the law, the area approved climbed steeply in 1906 to 33 thousand *chō*. The following two years saw a 25 per

[43] *NNHS*, Vol. 6, pp. 159-60.

[44] *MAF Yearbook*, Vol. 17, p. 6.

[45] The law became effective on January 15, 1900. *Chokurei* 4 (January 12, 1900.)

[46] The area approved does not include the area of projects abandoned nor that for which approval was revoked by the end of 1939. Kayō, *op.cit.*, p. 80.

[47] *Nōshōmushō rei* 18 (June 1, 1906).

[48] *NNHS*, Vol. 4, p. 223. The Japanese name for the section is *Kōchi seiri ka*.

TABLE B-1

AREA OF ARABLE LAND ADJUSTMENT PROJECTS APPROVED, 1900-40
(1000 *chō*)

Year	Approved[a] area	Cumulated approved area	Year	Approved area	Cumulated approved area
1900	0.8	0.8	1920	39.3	558.7
1901	2.3	3.1	1921	42.7	591.5
1902	3.3	6.4	1922	32.1	623.6
1903	5.5	11.9	1923	37.8	661.3
1904	7.8	19.7	1924	44.4	705.8
1905	10.0	29.8	1925	45.8	751.6
1906	33.0	62.8	1926	40.3	791.9
1907	24.2	87.0	1927	44.4	835.3
1908	25.1	112.1	1928	38.0	873.2
1909	37.2	149.3	1929	38.8	912.0
1910	40.7	190.0	1930	35.1	947.2
1911	57.3	247.3	1931	48.1	995.2
1912	39.0	286.3	1932	36.0	1031.2
1913	37.1	323.4	1933	42.1	1073.3
1914	44.8	368.2	1934	26.9	1100.2
1915	37.7	405.9	1935	26.8	1127.0
1916	28.5	434.4	1936	22.3	1149.3
1917	26.5	460.9	1937	28.2	1177.5
1918	26.1	486.9	1938	21.1	1198.6
1919	32.5	519.5	1939	13.0	1211.6
			1940	26.7	1238.3

SOURCE: Nobufumi Kayō, *Nihon nōgyō kiso tōkei* [Basic statistics of Japanese agriculture] (Tokyo, 1958), p. 80.

NOTE: [a] Approved area does not include the area of projects abandoned nor that for which approval was revoked by the end of 1940.

cent decline from the 1906 figure, but in 1909 the area reached a new high and two years later attained a peak of 57 thousand *chō*. The increase in 1909 can be attributed to the more liberal adjustment law which became effective on June 1, 1909. From that year on, the area approved did not drop below 32 thousand *chō* except during World War I and after Japan had become deeply involved in military actions against the Chinese in the

1930's. By the end of 1940 the cumulated area approved was 1,238 thousand *chō*.

A considerable change in the registered area of all land and of arable land in the adjustment districts also occurred. The total pre-adjustment area of the districts was 1,238 thousand *chō*. The post-adjustment area of the same districts was 1,303 thousand *chō*, a gain of 5.6 per cent. Almost all of this increase was probably due to the correct measurement of undermeasured land.[49] The area of arable land increased from 970 thousand to 1,143 thousand *chō*, a gain of 18 per cent. The increase in arable land was more than entirely accounted for by paddy fields whose area rose from 770 to 958 thousand *chō*, a gain of 187 thousand *chō*, while the upland area declined from 199 to 185 thousand *chō*, a loss of 15 thousand *chō*.[50] Some part of this gain in arable land area was probably due to the reclassification of arable land classified as other land classes, and a small part was due to correct measurement. However, reclamation and conversion to cultivated land probably accounted for most of the gain.

An important instrument used by the government to promote increased agricultural production was the subsidy. A variety of subsidies were provided, most of which probably helped to raise production, directly or indirectly. An important early subsidy was given to the agricultural association, a quasi-official organization, which was to raise agricultural productivity. But by far the largest subsidies were given for arable land improvement, including land improvement under the Arable Land Adjustment Law.

The earliest direct monetary subsidies for reclamation were granted by prefectures with the liberality of the grants differing among them.[51] Direct national subsidies to individuals or groups engaged in agricultural land improvement were pro-

[49] Not all undermeasurement was eliminated, however. (See Chapter 3, pp. 55ff.)

[50] Area data in this paragraph are from *MAF Yearbook*, Vol. 17, p. 6.

[51] *NNHS*, Vol. 5, pp. 312-13; also *ibid.*, Vol. 4, pp. 217-18. Gumma Prefecture, for example, enacted legislation in 1901 to bear 25% of the reclamation costs. (*Ibid.*, p. 218.)

vided by law in 1919.[52] These subsidies were given annually to
each eligible participant from the year work was started on the
improvement to four years after completion.[53] It paid up to 6
per cent of the cumulated costs of the improvement in a given
year.[54] The average total payment to each participant was
about 40 per cent of the total cost of the improvement.[55]
Projects eligible for these subsidies included the reclamation of
undeveloped land and bodies of water and the conversion of
developed land into paddy fields.[56] The total area reclaimed
under the provisions of this law through 1940 was 96 thousand
chō.[57] In addition, from 1923 to 1940 there were 540 subsidized
projects involving 520 thousand _chō_ of cultivated land for the
improvement of irrigation and drainage facilities.[58]

The encouragement and subsidization of agricultural land
reclamation and development continued during the war and
postwar years. During the war years as overseas sources of food
supply became uncertain or failed, the tempo of aid was accelerated. In 1941 the Agricultural Land Development Law
was enacted to speed the development of new cultivated land
and the improvement of existing cultivated land.[59] One of the
purposes of this act was to provide the legal basis for the
creation of land development corporations.[60] A five-year plan
was instituted the same year which called for a 200 thousand
chō increase in paddy fields, a 300 thousand _chō_ increase in upland fields, and an improvement of 1,720 thousand _chō_ of existing cultivated land.[61] Despite these efforts, owing to wartime
shortages of labor and materials, the land area under cultivation
continued to decline.[62] In 1943 the government made further

[52] _Hōritsu_ 42 (April 5, 1919).   [53] _Ibid.,_ Article 2.
[54] _Ibid._   [55] Suehiro, _et al., op.cit.,_ Vol. 25, p. 244.
[56] _Hōritsu_ 42 (April 5, 1919), Article 1.
[57] Kayō, _op.cit.,_ p. 81. The law was abolished in 1941 (_Hōritsu_ 65
[March 12, 1941], Article 74).
[58] Kayo, _op.cit.,_ p. 82.
[59] _Hōritsu_ 65 (March 12, 1941), Articles 1 and 2.
[60] _Ibid.,_ Article 4. They were called _Nōchi kaihatsu eidan._
[61] _NNHS,_ Vol. 9, p. 528.
[62] The reported area of cultivated land declined from 6,078 thousand
chō in 1940 to 4,986 thousand _chō_ in 1946. (_NRT,_ p. 10.) Some of this
decline was fictitious.

efforts to encourage agricultural production, introducing what were called "Measures to increase the food supply."[63] To increase incentive, subsidies for land improvement were raised from 40 per cent of costs to 65 per cent of costs at this time.[64] In the postwar period three important factors contributed to continued subsidization of agricultural land development. They were the food shortage of the years immediately following the war, the need to conserve foreign exchange, and the need to provide work for the millions added to the labor force after the war through demobilization and repatriation of overseas Japanese. In November 1945, following the disastrously low rice harvest of the year, an emergency five-year plan[65] was approved by the cabinet. This called for reclamation of 1.55 million *chō* of land, the improved drainage of 100 thousand *chō*, and the improvement of 2.1 million *chō* of cultivated land. The food objective was the production of 14 million additional *koku*[66] of grains. These strenuous efforts to increase and improve cultivated land continued although the achievements always fell short of the goals.

The area of addition to cultivated land from 1941 to 1945 inclusive is 115 thousand *chō*, including Hokkaidō.[67] During the same period 747 thousand *chō* of cultivated land was improved.[68] In the postwar period from 1946 to 1955 inclusive, the additions to cultivated land owing to reclamation was 516 thousand *chō* including Hokkaidō, and 328 thousand *chō* excluding it.[69] Agricultural land improvement occurred on 1,490 thousand *chō*.[70]

Agricultural subsidies by the national government did not attain appreciable proportions until after the enactment of the law to subsidize land reclamation and improvement in 1919. Beginning in 1919, however, they climbed steeply, increasing by nearly 30 times in 15 years. An important reason for the

[63] The Japanese called it the "*Shokuryō zōsan taisaku.*" (*NNHS*, Vol. 9, p. 527-28.)
[64] *Ibid.*   [65] *Ibid.*, p. 544.
[66] One *koku* is equal to 4.96 bushels. See Appendix E for conversion table.
[67] Kayō, *op.cit.*, p. 83.   [68] *Ibid.*   [69] *Ibid.*, p. 84.
[70] *Ibid.*, p. 85.

increase was to quiet the rural unrest that had started in the early 1920's and had culminated in the assassination of Prime Minister Inukai on May 15, 1932. Five-year averages of agricultural subsidies by the national government (including assistance in natural disaster areas) follow:[71]

	million yen
1917-21	1,045
1922-26	4,908
1927-31	12,282
1932-36	30,123

The final important government measure to promote agricultural production was to make long-term, low-cost loans available to landowners for arable land development. Loans of this type were not always available. It was not until about the turn of the nineteenth century that significant contributions toward a solution of the nation's agricultural credit problem were made, although the problem received some attention in the early Meiji era.[72] In 1897 the Hypothec Bank of Japan was established to serve as a central real estate mortgage bank. Its purpose was to provide long-term, low-cost financing to agriculture directly through its branches or indirectly through the prefectural agricultural and industrial banks to which it supplied funds. The agricultural and industrial banks for which enabling legislation was passed in 1896 (the same year as for the Hypothec Bank), which were hardly more than branch banks of the Hypothec Bank, made agricultural loans for much the same purposes and under much the same terms as the Hypothec Bank.[73] Credit associations were another financial

[71] Computed from *NNHS*, Vol. 8, p. 74.

[72] Except where otherwise noted the discussion of financial institutions and their practices is dependent on Ono, *Nōson shi, op.cit.*, pp. 449-67. See also Harold G. Moulton, *Japan: An Economic and Financial Appraisal* (Washington, 1931), pp. 172-86.

[73] Hypothec Bank loans for arable land adjustment outstanding in 1923 totalled 55 million yen. Another 133 million yen were loaned to farmers and a part of these loans were undoubtedly used for long-term purposes. (Kamekichi Takahashi, *Meiji taishō nōson keizai no hensen* [Change in agricultural economy during the Meiji and Taishō eras] (Tokyo, 1926), p. 170).

institution designed for the extension of low-cost credit to agriculture, including long-term credit. The latter were of particular importance to the rural community because they provided loans to the small landowners who usually were not sufficiently good risks for loans from the Hypothec Bank or the agricultural and industrial banks.

Low-cost agricultural credit became available only from around the turn of the century, but it increased very rapidly thereafter. Illustrative are the agricultural loans of the Hypothec Bank which increased as follows (end of year figures):[74]

	million yen
1907	18,408
1917	116,278
1927	336,214
1937	522,720

Let us briefly review the accomplishments of the arable land development program. The Arable Land Adjustment Law accounted for over 1.2 million *chō* of land approved for adjustment, the completion of adjustment projects on over 700 thousand *chō* through 1940,[75] and a gain of nearly 200 thousand *chō* in the area of paddy fields. Because the adjustment program did not start until 1900 and the approved area remained under 200 thousand *chō* through 1910, the impact of adjustment on agricultural output could scarcely have become significant before that time. This point is even clearer when data on completed projects are examined. In 1910 the area of completed projects was 43 thousand *chō*; in 1914 it had increased to 129 thousand *chō* and by the end of 1918, to 219 thousand. These figures indicate that appreciable effect on agricultural production could not have been expected before World War I. The fact that subsidization of land reclamation and improvement by the national government on a noteworthy scale began

[74] Ōkurashō Kinyū Seido Chōsa Kai, *Kinyū kikan hattatsu shi* [History of the development of financial institutions] (Tokyo, 1949), pp. 105-06.

[75] *MAF Yearbook*, Vol. 17, p. 5. By completion of adjustment projects is meant the completion of the physical land changes that had been approved.

The enthusiastic farmer response to the adjustment law made possible a substantial decline in misclassification and undermeasurement of land.

only after 1919 places substance under the above conclusion. We have further noted that the land development program was strengthened in the war and postwar years relative to the prewar program.

The national government's arable land reclamation and improvement program began at around the turn of the century and it gained strength as Japan became increasingly dependent on foreign sources for its food. It has been shown that the vast bulk of the land development took place after World War I. It has also been shown that land improvement increased labor and land productivity. These findings are consistent with our view that the growth rate of agricultural production was greater from 1898-1902 to 1918-22 than from 1878-82 to 1898-1902, and from 1918-22 to 1955-61 than from 1878-82 to 1918-22.

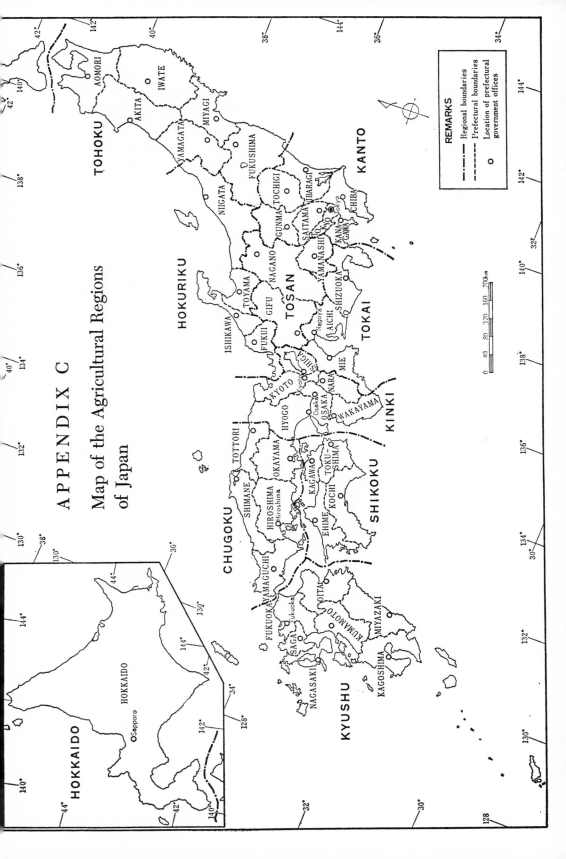

APPENDIX C

Map of the Agricultural Regions of Japan

REMARKS
— · — Regional boundaries
— · · — Prefectural boundaries
○ Location of prefectural government offices

0 40 80 120 160 200 km

HOKKAIDO

HOKKAIDO
○ Sapporo

TOHOKU
AOMORI
IWATE
AKITA
YAMAGATA
MIYAGI
FUKUSHIMA
NIIGATA

KANTO
TOCHIGI
IBARAGI
GUNMA
SAITAMA
TOKYO
Tokyo
CHIBA
KANAGAWA

HOKURIKU
TOYAMA
ISHIKAWA
FUKUI

TOSAN
NAGANO
GIFU
YAMANASHI
SHIZUOKA

TOKAI
AICHI
Nagoya
MIE

KINKI
SHIGA
KYOTO
Kyoto
NARA
OSAKA
Osaka
HYOGO
WAKAYAMA

CHUGOKU
TOTTORI
SHIMANE
OKAYAMA
HIROSHIMA
Hiroshima
YAMAGUCHI

SHIKOKU
KAGAWA
TOKU-SHIMA
EHIME
KOCHI

KYUSHU
FUKUOKA
Fukuoka
SAGA
NAGASAKI
OITA
KUMAMOTO
MIYAZAKI
KAGOSHIMA

APPENDIX D

Selected Period and Era Names and Dates

Period	Era	Years
Yamato		300-710
Nara		710-794
Heian		794-1185
Kamakura (Minamoto)		1185-1333
Muromachi (Ashikaga)		1333-1573
Momoyama		1573-1603
	Bunroku	(1592-1596)
Tokugawa (Edo)		1603-1868
	Jōkyō	(1684-1688)
	Genroku	(1688-1704)
	Kyōhō	(1716-1736)
	Meiwa	(1764-1772)
	Tempō	(1830-1844)
	Keiō	(1865-1868)
Gendai (Modern)		1868——
	Meiji	(1868-1912)
	Taishō	(1912-1926)
	Shōwa	(1926——

APPENDIX E
Tables of Measures

Square Measure:

1 *tsubo*	equals 3.95 square yards	
30 *tsubo* equal 1 *se*	equals 119 square yards	
10 *se* equal 1 *tan*	equals 0.245 acres	
10 *tan* equal 1 *chō*	equals 2.45 acres	

Capacity (converted in English measure):

1 *gō*	equals 0.318 pints
10 *gō* equal 1 *shō*	equals 3.18 pints
10 *shō* equal 1 *tō*	equals 3.97 gallons
10 *tō* equal 1 *koku*	equals 4.96 bushels

APPENDIX F

TAXED PADDY FIELD AREA, 1878-1922

(1000 *chō*)

Year	Nation	Hokkaidō	Nation less Hokkaidō	Year	Nation	Hokkaidō	Nation less Hokkaidō
	(1)	(2)	(3)		(1)	(2)	(3)
1878	...	...	...	1903	2806	4	2802
1879	...	...	...	1904	2818	4	2814
1880	2623	...	2623	1905	2823	4	2819
1881	2631	...	2631	1906	2835	5	2830
1882	2631	1	2630	1907	2836	5	2831
1883	2644	1	2643	1908	2844	5	2839
1884	2642	1	2641	1909	2852	5	2847
1885	2641	1	2640	1910	2842	5	2837
1886	2653	1	2652	1911	2849	5	2844
1887	2698	1	2697	1912	2851	5	2846
1888	2777	1	2776	1913	2961	5	2856
1889	2752	1	2751	1914	2855	5	2849
1890	2752	...	2752	1915	2872	6	2866
1891	2532	0	2532	1916	2892	7	2885
1892	2602	...	2602	1917	2889	7	2882
1893	2734	0	2734	1918	2909	8	2901
1894	2744	0	2744	1919	2914	9	2905
1895	2748	0	2748	1920	2922	10	2912
1896	2732	0	2731	1921	2927	12	2915
1897	2739	0	2738	1922	2935	13	2922
1898	2735	0	2735				
1899	2745	2	2743				
1900	2764	3	2761				
1901	2780	4	2776				
1902	2800	4	2796				

SOURCE: Computed from *Tōkei nenkan*. Okinawa data is not included.

NOTES: Data for Aichi, Gifu, and Mie Prefectures are missing in 1891, and those for Aichi and Gifu are missing in 1892 owing to a severe earthquake which occurred in 1891.

Up to and including 1899, the date of record is December 31, and from 1901 it is January 1. To maintain an unbroken series, January 1 data are taken to be those of the previous calendar year.

Areas of less than 500 *chō* is designated by "0"; datum not entered in the *Tōkei nenkan* is indicated by "...".

STATISTICAL APPENDIX: TABLE 1B

Taxed Upland Field Area, 1878-1922

(1000 *chō*)

Year	Nation	Hokkaidō	Nation less Hokkaidō	Year	Nation	Hokkaidō	Nation less Hokkaidō
	(1)	(2)	(3)		(1)	(2)	(3)
1878	...	...	...	1903	2324	21	2303
1879	...	...	...	1904	2334	25	2309
1880	1847	...	1847	1905	2344	27	2317
1881	1855	...	1855	1906	2358	30	2328
1882	1876	8	1868	1907	2358	30	2328
1883	1883	9	1874	1908	2356	28	2328
1884	1882	10	1872	1909	2358	28	2330
1885	1886	12	1874	1910	2349	28	2321
1886	1894	13	1881	1911	2347	30	2317
1887	1987	14	1973	1912	2345	30	2315
1888	2274	14	2260	1913	2343	30	2313
1889	2291	14	2277	1914	2324	31	2293
1890	2278	0	2278	1915	2337	35	2302
1891	2150	1	2149	1916	2367	41	2326
1892	2174	...	2174	1917	2361	41	2320
1893	2279	1	2278	1918	2402	68	2334
1894	2285	1	2284	1919	2447	110	2337
1895	2289	1	2288	1920	2496	155	2341
1896	2277	1	2276	1921	2550	206	2344
1897	2282	1	2281	1922	2597	253	2344
1898	2257	1	2256				
1899	2286	16	2270				
1900	2299	16	2283				
1901	2307	16	2291				
1902	2334	19	2315				

SOURCE and NOTES: See same for Table 1A.

STATISTICAL APPENDIX: TABLE 1C

Taxed Arable Land Area, 1878-1922
(1000 *chō*)

Year	Nation	Hokkaidō	Nation less Hokkaidō	Year	Nation	Hokkaidō	Nation less Hokkaidō
	(1)	(2)	(3)		(1)	(2)	(3)
1878	...	...	...	1903	5130	25	5105
1879	...	...	...	1904	5152	29	5123
1880	4470	...	4470	1905	5167	31	5136
1881	4486	...	4486	1906	5193	35	5158
1882	4507	10	4497	1907	5194	35	5159
1883	4527	10	4517	1908	5200	33	5167
1884	4524	12	4512	1909	5210	33	5177
1885	4527	13	4514	1910	5191	33	5158
1886	4547	14	4533	1911	5196	35	5161
1887	4685	15	4670	1912	5196	35	5161
1888	5051	15	5036	1913	5204	35	5169
1889	5043	15	5028	1914	5179	36	5143
1890	5030	0	5030	1915	5209	41	5168
1891	4682	2	4680	1916	5259	48	5211
1892	4776	...	4776	1917	5250	48	5202
1893	5013	2	5011	1918	5311	76	5235
1894	5029	2	5027	1919	5361	119	5242
1895	5037	2	5035	1920	5418	165	5253
1896	5009	2	5007	1921	5477	218	5259
1897	5021	2	5019	1922	5532	266	5266
1898	4991	2	4989				
1899	5031	17	5014				
1900	5063	19	5044				
1901	5088	21	5067				
1902	5134	23	5111				

Source: Columns (1) and (2) computed from Statistical Appendix: Tables 1A and 1B.

STATISTICAL APPENDIX: TABLE 2

ANNUAL PERCENTAGE CHANGES[a] IN TAXED PADDY FIELD, UPLAND FIELD,
AND ARABLE LAND AREA, EXCLUDING HOKKAIDŌ, 1878-1922
(unit=per cent)

Year	Paddy field	Upland field	Arable land	Year	Paddy field	Upland field	Arable land
	(1)	(2)	(3)		(1)	(2)	(3)
1878	...	...	...	1903	0.2	—0.5	—0.1
1879	...	...	...	1904	0.4	0.3	0.4
1880	...	...	...	1905	0.2	0.3	0.2
1881	0.3	0.4	0.4	1906	0.4	0.5	0.4
1882	0.0	0.7	0.3	1907	0.1	0.0	0.0
1883	0.5	0.3	0.4	1908	0.2	0.0	0.2
1884	—0.1	—0.1	—0.1	1909	0.3	0.1	0.2
1885	0.0	0.1	0.0	1910	—0.4	—0.4	—0.4
1886	0.5	0.4	0.4	1911	0.3	—0.2	0.1
1887	1.7	4.9	3.0	1912	0.1	—0.1	0.0
1888	2.9	14.5	7.8	1913	0.3	—0.1	0.2
1889	—0.9	0.8	—0.2	1914	—0.2	—0.8	—0.5
1890	0.0	0.0	0.0	1915	0.6	0.3	0.5
1891	—8.0	—5.7	—6.9	1916	0.6	1.1	0.8
1892	2.8	1.2	2.0	1917	—0.1	—0.3	—0.2
1893	5.1	4.8	4.9	1918	0.7	0.6	0.6
1894	0.4	0.3	0.3	1919	0.2	0.1	0.2
1895	0.1	0.2	0.2	1920	0.2	0.2	0.2
1896	—0.6	—0.5	—0.6	1921	0.1	0.1	0.1
1897	0.3	0.2	0.2	1922	0.3	0.0	0.2
1898	—0.1	—1.1	—0.6				
1899	0.3	0.6	0.5				
1900	0.6	0.6	0.6				
1901	0.5	0.3	0.4				
1902	0.7	1.1	0.9				

SOURCES: Columns (1), (2), and (3) computed from Statistical Appendix:
Tables 1A, 1B, and 1C, respectively.
NOTE: [a] The figure for any year is the change from the previous year.

STATISTICAL APPENDIX: TABLE 3A

AREA PLANTED TO PADDY RICE ACCORDING TO GOVERNMENT
STATISTICS, 1878-1922
(1000 *chō*)

Year	Nation	Hokkaidō	Nation less Hokkaidō	Year	Nation	Hokkaidō	Nation less Hokkaidō
	(1)	(2)	(3)		(1)	(2)	(3)
1878	2490	...	2490	1903	2772	16	2756
1879	2536	...	2536	1904	2790	18	2772
1880	2558	...	2558	1905	2800	19	2781
1881	2544	...	2544	1906	2810	20	2790
1882	2559	...	2559	1907	2820	22	2798
1883	2583	0	2583	1908	2831	27	2804
1884	2573	1	2572	1909	2843	31	2812
1885	2573	1	2572	1910	2850	35	2815
1886	2588	2	2586	1911	2868	40	2828
1887	2608	2	2606	1912	2885	46	2839
1888	2659	2	2657	1913	2903	50	2853
1889	2695	2	2693	1914	2902	44	2858
1890	2713	2	2711	1915	2924	55	2869
1891	2717	2	2715	1916	2935	59	2876
1892	2708	2	2706	1917	2945	64	2881
1893	2724	3	2721	1918	2953	67	2886
1894	2681	3	2678	1919	2961	74	2887
1895	2725	4	2721	1920	2978	82	2896
1896	2730	5	2725	1921	2986	91	2895
1897	2720	6	2714	1922	2990	102	2888
1898	2745	7	2738				
1899	2763	9	2754				
1900	2749	9	2740				
1901	2762	12	2750				
1902	2758	16	2742				

SOURCE: Ministry of Agriculture and Forestry, Agriculture and Forestry Economics Bureau, Statistical Section, *Nōrinshō ruinen tōkeihyō, 1868-1953* [Historical statistics of the Ministry of Agriculture and Forestry, 1868-1953], p. 10.

STATISTICAL APPENDIX: TABLE 3B

ARABLE LAND AREA IN HOKKAIDŌ, 1878-1922

(1000 chō)

Year	Arable land	Paddy field	Upland field	Year	Arable land	Paddy field	Upland field
	(1)	(2)	(3)		(1)	(2)	(3)
1878				1903	286	15	271
1879				1904	329	17	312
1880				1905	344	21	323
1881	12	1	11	1906	346	21	325
1882	15	1	14	1907	410	22	388
1883	23	1	22	1908	436	28	408
1884	27	1	26	1909	510	38	472
1885	26	2	24	1910	538	38	500
1886	25	2	23	1911	580	44	536
1887	31	2	29	1912	618	49	569
1888	35	2	33	1913	632	56	576
1889	41	2	39	1914	654	58	596
1890	45	2	43	1915	683	60	623
1891	52	2	50	1916	717	63	654
1892	56	3	53	1917	747	67	680
1893	66	3	63	1918	795	71	724
1894	79	3	76	1919	816	74	742
1895	97	4	93	1920	839	84	755
1896	115	5	110	1921	855	93	762
1897	143	6	137	1922	853	94	759
1898	170	7	163				
1899	216	9	207				
1900	241	10	231				
1901	266	13	253				
1902	289	19	270				

SOURCE: Columns (1) and (2). Kayō, Nobufumi, ed., *Nihon nōgyō kiso tōkei* [Basic statistics of Japanese agriculture] (Tokyo, 1958), p. 607. Column (3) is the difference between Columns (1) and (2).

STATISTICAL APPENDIX: TABLE 4

UNDERMEASUREMENT INDEX OF PADDY FIELDS AND UPLAND FIELDS
BY PREFECTURES, 1956

Prefecture	Paddy field UI	Upland field UI	Prefecture	Paddy field UI	Upland field UI
Aomori	1.143	1.086	Ōsaka	1.012	0.987
Iwate	1.139	1.068	Hyōgo	1.112	1.078
Miyagi	1.117	1.199	Nara	1.024	0.998
Akita	1.024	1.046	Wakayama	1.040	1.038
Yamagata	1.072	1.056	Tottori	1.067	1.084
Fukushima	1.073	1.054	Shimane	1.038	1.047
Ibaragi	1.067	1.008	Okayama	1.044	1.043
Tochigi	1.019	0.999	Hiroshima	1.096	1.084
Gumma	1.045	1.021	Yamaguchi	1.013	1.007
Saitama	1.037	1.027	Tokushima	1.046	1.041
Chiba	1.047	1.031	Kagawa	1.093	1.064
Tokyo	1.054	1.054	Ehime	1.035	1.041
Kanagawa	1.009	1.010	Kōchi	1.112	1.118
Niigata	1.139	1.090	Fukuoka	1.042	1.009
Toyama	1.047	1.024	Saga	1.088	1.094
Ishikawa	1.055	1.045	Nagasaki	1.103	1.048
Fukui	1.065	1.000	Kumamoto	1.089	1.094
Yamanashi	1.037	1.024	Ōita	1.075	1.056
Nagano	1.087	1.061	Miyazaki	1.093	1.051
Gifu	1.058	1.026	Kagoshima	1.079	1.056
Shizuoka	1.078	1.070			
Aichi	0.998	0.995	Nation		
Mie	1.085	1.045	(minus		
Shiga	1.071	1.019	Hokkaidō)	1.069	1.049
Kyōto	1.090	1.030			

SOURCE: Taken from a 1956 mimeographed worksheet provided by Kōichi Hatanaka of the Crop Statistics Section of the Ministry of Agriculture and Forestry.

YIELD PER TAN OF SELECTED CROPS ACCORDING TO GOVERNMENT STATISTICS, 1879-1922

Year	Paddy rice	Wheat	Barley	Naked barley	Sweet potatoes	White potatoes	Foxtail millet	Barnyard millet	Soy beans	Buckwheat
	koku	koku	koku	koku	kan	kan	koku	koku	koku	koku
1879	1.249	0.521	0.814	0.687	167	91	0.824	0.996	0.516	0.470
1880	1.223	0.630	0.969	0.885	163	99	0.770	0.954	0.551	0.447
1881	1.169	0.566	0.874	0.696	175	83	0.682	0.885	0.509	0.439
1882	1.173	0.650	0.965	0.897	184	142	0.702	0.962	0.543	0.436
1883	1.177	0.639	0.964	0.754	173	140	0.717	0.934	0.505	0.452
1884	1.047	0.679	0.998	0.858	209	119	0.643	1.095	0.530	0.425
1885	1.312	0.606	0.896	0.775	…	…	…	…	…	…
1886	1.426	0.797	1.174	0.974	…	…	…	…	…	…
1887	1.524	0.779	1.135	0.987	253	172	1.058	1.265	0.698	0.705
1888	1.444	0.767	1.124	0.874	…	…	…	…	…	…
1889	1.216	0.739	1.134	0.836	…	…	…	…	…	…
1890	1.576	0.536	0.834	0.478	…	…	…	…	…	…
1891	1.392	0.831	1.249	1.007	…	…	…	…	…	…
1892	1.513	0.707	1.042	0.932	234	184	1.260	1.250	0.701	0.714

Year										
1893	1.354	0.753	1.099	0.939	...	...	...	...	...	...
1894	1.547	0.898	1.315	1.105	208	215	0.912	1.187	0.675	0.698
1895	1.450	0.888	1.306	1.044	209	190	0.943	1.196	0.734	0.678
1896	1.310	0.803	1.206	0.882	284	175	1.027	1.214	0.680	0.637
1897	1.196	0.832	1.255	0.946	256	202	0.957	1.081	0.712	0.569
1898	1.701	0.898	1.351	1.081	268	92	1.069	1.165	0.645	0.663
1899	1.414	0.890	1.295	0.968	247	172	0.929	1.124	0.749	0.567
1900	1.482	0.908	1.345	1.087	279	188	1.012	1.192	0.778	0.761
1901	1.669	0.898	1.386	1.072	265	190	1.122	1.316	0.859	0.719
1902	1.315	0.817	1.262	0.936	257	128	0.885	0.805	0.673	0.572
1903	1.649	0.399	1.134	0.627	265	162	1.048	1.302	0.784	0.702
1904	1.817	0.841	1.370	0.994	236	173	0.927	1.440	0.830	0.701
1905	1.339	0.794	1.275	0.950	263	231	0.892	1.109	0.711	0.681
1906	1.616	0.894	1.410	0.993	278	242	1.127	1.223	0.763	0.747
1907	1.707	1.003	1.539	1.085	315	251	1.160	1.344	0.777	0.743
1908	1.798	0.981	1.466	1.100	317	253	1.133	1.325	0.785	0.746
1909	1.808	0.994	1.472	1.124	308	257	1.146	1.389	0.785	0.810
1910	1.600	0.968	1.498	0.994	284	262	1.104	1.329	0.710	0.838
1911	1.762	1.004	1.568	1.125	342	265	1.072	1.391	0.755	0.805
1912	1.703	1.044	1.637	1.162	334	264	1.030	1.262	0.738	0.680

STATISTICAL APPENDIX: TABLE 5 (*continued*)

Year	Paddy rice	Wheat	Barley	Naked barley	Sweet potatoes	White potatoes	Foxtail millet	Barnyard millet	Soy beans	Buckwheat
	koku	*koku*	*koku*	*koku*	*kan*	*kan*	*koku*	*koku*	*koku*	*koku*
1913	1.689	1.081	1.705	1.274	337	250	1.196	0.921	0.630	0.687
1914	1.920	0.938	1.549	0.991	322	280	1.037	1.630	0.789	0.847
1915	1.862	1.045	1.721	1.160	343	278	1.227	1.567	0.809	0.814
1916	1.934	1.107	1.674	1.156	353	271	1.332	1.531	0.804	0.787
1917	1.810	1.194	1.708	1.277	322	283	1.199	1.514	0.830	0.655
1918	1.807	1.134	1.579	1.220	350	245	1.211	1.512	0.799	0.625
1919	1.996	1.160	1.841	1.179	372	313	1.343	1.757	0.915	0.829
1920	2.056	1.103	1.531	1.225	371	238	1.312	1.709	0.897	0.876
1921	1.794	1.083	1.707	1.059	347	275	1.304	1.698	0.875	0.868
1922	1.980	1.142	1.735	1.160	345	242	1.316	1.682	0.821	0.873
1923	1.800	1.064	1.590	1.041	345	235	1.270	1.705	0.807	0.864
1924	1.869	1.123	1.759	1.055	331	248	1.252	1.120	0.793	0.765
1925	1.926	1.306	1.933	1.415	348	267	1.319	1.630	0.909	0.901

SOURCE: Ministry of Agriculture and Forestry, Agriculture and Forestry Economics Bureau, Statistical Section, *Nōrinshō ruinen tōkeihyō, 1868-1953* [Historical statistics of the Ministry of Agriculture and Forestry, 1868-1953].

NOTE: National data were not compiled for the crops indicated in years marked by " .... ".

STATISTICAL APPENDIX: TABLE 6

ESTIMATION OF INDEX OF DRYLAND CROP YIELD IN 1915-1925
(1879-84=100)

Crop	Average area planted 1918-22 (1000 *chō*)	(1) as % of total	Ratio of 1915-25 yield to 1879-84 yield	Weighted yield increase[b] (2) × (3)
	(1)	(2)	(3)	(4)
Wheat	535	15.5	1.85	28.5
Barley	528	15.4	1.83	28.2
Naked barley	648	18.8	1.48	27.8
Sweet potatoes	311	9.0	1.94	17.5
White potatoes	123	3.6	2.35	8.5
Soy beans	450	13.1	1.60	21.0
Foxtail millet	142	4.1	1.77	7.3
Barnyard millet	48	1.4	1.63	2.3
Buckwheat	134	3.9	1.79	7.0
Cocoon[a]	523	15.2	2.50	38.0
Total	3442	100.2		186.3

SOURCES: Column (1) computed from Ministry of Agriculture and Forestry, Agriculture and Forestry Economics Bureau, Statistical Section, *Nōrinshō ruinen tōkeihyō, 1868-1953* [Historical statistics of the Ministry of Agriculture and Forestry, 1868-1953].
Column (3) computed from Statistical Appendix: Table 5, except for the cocoon yield ratio.

NOTES: [a] A problem with estimating the cocoon yield ratio was in obtaining the area planted in 1879-84. It was assumed that this was 230 thousand *chō*. The average cocoon production at this time was 11.8 million *kan*. The average yield per *chō* of mulberries is 50 *kan*. The average yield in 1915-25 was 125 *kan* (area = 512 thousand *chō* and yield = 65.9 million *koku*) computed from same source as Column (1). The ratio of 125 to 50 is 2.50. The assumption of 230 thousand *chō* planted to mulberries is probably an overstatement. Any lower estimate will, of course, reduce the increase in the per *tan* cocoon yield, therefore lower the growth rate of dryland crops. The *kan* is equal to 8.27 pounds.

[b] Since I do not accept the yield index computed here, but reduce it to a level close to that of corrected rice yields, the use of highly refined techniques in computing the upland crop yield index is not warranted. However, some comments on biases in the weighting used here should be provided.

I have used the area planted to crops instead of value of crops as the weight in determining the above index of yield for 1918-22 (1879-82 = 100). This expedient was taken because using value weights (Ministry of Agriculture and Forestry values appearing in *Nōrinshō ruinen tōkeihyō: 1873-1929*) would have given undue weight to cocoons, the crop whose yield increased considerably more than any other crop used in obtaining the yield, and also because prices were distorted during the war. Reliable value data are not obtainable for earlier years. The undue weighting of cocoons results from the unusual rise in the price of cocoons during the war years. Using value weights would have given cocoons a weight of 47% instead of the above weight of 15%. The actual value of cocoon production in the 1918-22 period was about 26% of the value of agricultural production after deduction of the value of paddy rice production because the value of crops not used in determining the yield index was 80% of the value of crops used. I assume that the increase in the yield of crops not used in determining the yield index more closely approximated the yield increases of crops used other than cocoons. Moreover, in earlier years the value of cocoon production as a proportion of total value of agricultural production less paddy rice seems to have run about 20% or less. For the above reasons the use of area planted weights appears reasonable.

The use of 1918-22 planted area as weights biases the index upward. If 1878-82 area weights had been used, the relative weights of cocoons, sweet potatoes, and white potatoes whose recorded yields increased more rapidly than those of other crops would have been unduly underweighted because their areas were relatively much smaller than in 1918-22. The same argument applies to value weights.

STATISTICAL APPENDIX: TABLE 7

AVERAGE YIELD PER TAN OF SELECTED CROPS AND INDEX OF YIELD, 1879-1922

	Paddy field rice	Index	Wheat	Index	Barley	Index	Naked barley	Index
	koku	%	koku	%	koku	%	koku	%
1879-1884	1.173	100	.614	100	.931	100	.796	100
1885-1889	1.384	118	.738	120	1.093	117	.889	112
1883-1887	1.297	111	.700	114	1.033	111	.870	109
1888-1892	1.428	122	.716	117	1.077	116	.825	104
1883-1897	1.371	117	.835	136	1.236	133	.983	123
1898-1902	1.516	129	.882	144	1.328	143	1.029	129
1903-1907	1.626	139	.786	128	1.346	145	.930	117
1908-1912	1.734	148	.998	163	1.528	164	1.101	138
1913-1917	1.843	157	1.073	175	1.671	179	1.172	147
1918-1922	1.927	164	1.124	183	1.679	180	1.169	147

	Sweet potatoes	Index	White potatoes	Index	Soy beans	Index
	kan	%	kan	%	koku	%
1879-1884	179	100	112	100	.526	100
1894-1898	245	137	175	156	.689	131
1899-1902	263	147	154	138	.741	141
1903-1907	271	151	212	189	.773	147
1908-1912	317	177	260	232	.755	144
1913-1917	335	187	272	243	.772	147
1918-1922	357	199	263	235	.861	164

	Foxtail millet	Index	Barnyard millet	Index	Buckwheat	Index
	koku	%	koku	%	koku	%
1879-1884	.723	100	.971	100	.450	100
1894-1898	.982	136	1.168	120	.649	144
1899-1902	1.003	139	1.120	115	.656	146
1903-1907	1.031	143	1.284	132	.715	159
1908-1912	1.097	152	1.339	138	.776	172
1913-1917	1.198	166	1.433	148	.758	168
1918-1922	1.297	179	1.672	172	.814	181

SOURCE: Computed from Statistical Appendix: Table 5.

BIBLIOGRAPHY

A. BOOKS AND MONOGRAPHS IN JAPANESE, INCLUDING JAPANESE GOVERNMENT PUBLICATIONS

Andō, Hiroshi. *Tokugawa bakufu kenji yōryaku* [Outline of the provincial administration of the Tokugawa Shogunate]. Tokyo, 1915.

Ario, Keichō. *Hompō chiso no enkaku* [A history of Japan's land tax]. Privately printed by the monthly conference of the Hypothec Bank of Japan, 1914.

Asakura, Kōkichi. *Meiji zenki nihon kinyū kōzō shi* [History of the structure of early Meiji finance]. Tokyo, 1961.

Bureau of Statistics. *Tōkei nenkan* [Statistical yearbook]. Tokyo, 1882-84. Cited as *Tōkei nenkan*.

Cabinet Bureau of Statistics. *Dai nihon teikoku tōkei nenkan* [Statistical yearbook of the greater Japanese empire]. Tokyo, 1937-40. Cited as *Tōkei nenkan*.

———. *Nihon teikoku tōkei nenkan* [Statistical yearbook of the Japanese empire]. Tokyo, 1885-1936. Cited as *Tōkei nenkan*.

Furushima, Toshio. *Kinsei nihon nōgyō no tenkai* [Agricultural development in the Tokugawa period]. Tokyo, 1963.

Hemmi, Kenzo. "Nōgyō jinkō no koteisei" [Stability of agricultural population]. *Nihon no keizai to nōgyō* [Japanese economy and agriculture]. Eds. Seiichi Tobata and Kazushi Ohkawa. Tokyo, 1956.

Hōgetsu, Keigo. *Chūsei ryōseishi no kenkyū* [A study of the feudal weight system]. Tokyo, 1961.

Jiji Tsūshinsha. *Jiji Almanac, 1963.* Tokyo, 1962.

Kayō, Nobufumi, ed. *Nihon nōgyō kiso tōkei* [Basic statistics of Japanese agriculture]. Tokyo, 1958.

Kikkawa, Hidezō. *Shizoku jusan no kenkyū* [Study of the economic rehabilitation of the Samurai]. Rev. edn., Tokyo, 1953.

Kondo, Yasuo. *Nihon nōgyō no tōkeiteki bunseki* [Statistical analysis of Japanese agriculture]. Tokyo, 1953.

Meiji Zaisei Shi Hensankai [Committee for the compilation of Meiji financial history]. *Meiji zaisei shi* [History of Meiji public finance]. 15 vols. Tokyo, 1904-05. Cited as *MZS*.

Ministry of Agriculture and Commerce, Food Bureau. *Beikoku tōkei: nihon no bu* [Rice statistics: Japan]. Tokyo, 1924.

Ministry of Agriculture and Forestry, Agriculture and Forestry Economics Bureau, Statistics Section. *Nōrinshō ruinen tōkeihyō, 1868-1953* [Historical statistics of the Ministry of Agriculture and Forestry, 1868-1953]. Tokyo, 1955. Cited as *NRT*.

——. *Nōsakumotsu ruinen tōkeihyō: ine, 1881-1956* [Agricultural crop statistics: rice, 1881-1956]. Tokyo, 1957. Cited as *NRTHI*.

——. *Statistical Yearbook of the Ministry of Agriculture and Forestry.* Cited as *MAF Yearbook*.

Ministry of Agriculture and Forestry, Secretariat, Statistics Section. *Meiji rokunen naishi Shōwa yonen nōrinshō ruinen tōkeihyō* [Historical statistics of the Ministry of Agriculture and Forestry, 1873-1929]. Tokyo, 1932.

Ministry of Finance. *Dai nihon sozei shi* [Annals of taxation in Japan]. 3 vols. and supp. Tokyo, 1926. Cited as *DNSS*.

——. *Meiji zenki zaisei keizai shiryō shūsei* [Collection of financial and economic materials of early Meiji]. 21 vols. Tokyo, 1932-36. Cited as *MZZKSS*.

Ministry of Finance and Bank of Japan. *Statistical Yearbook of Finance and Economy of Japan—1948.* Tokyo, 1948.

Nakazawa, Benjirō. *Nihon beika hendō shi* [History of fluctuations in Japan's rice prices]. Tokyo, 1933.

Nihon Gakujutsu Shinkōkai. [Japan association for the advancement of science]. *Beikoku nisshi, 1912-1934* [Rice diary, 1912-1934]. Tokyo, 1935.

Nihon keizai shi jiten [Encyclopedia of Japanese economic history]. Compiled by Nihon Keizai Shi Kenkyūshō [Institute for research in Japanese history]. 3 vols. Tokyo, 1940.

Niwa, Kunio. *Meiji ishin no tochi henkaku* [Land reform of the Meiji Restoration]. Tokyo, 1962.

Ohkawa, Kazushi. *Nōgyō no dōtai bunseki* [Dynamic analysis of agriculture]. Tokyo, 1954.

——. *Nōgyō no keizai bunseki* [Economic analysis of agriculture]. Tokyo, 1955.

Okazaki, Yōichi. *Meiji shonen iko Taishō kunen ni itaru danjo nenreibetsu jinko suikei ni tsuite* [Population estimates by sex and age from 1870's to 1920]. Institute of Population Problems Research Series No. 145, February 1, 1962. Tokyo, 1962.

Ōkurashō Kinyū Seido Chōsa Kai. *Kinyū kikan hattatsu shi* [History of the development of financial institutions]. Tokyo, 1949.

Ono, Takeo, ed. *Kinsei jikata keizai shiryō* [Provincial economic materials of the Tokugawa period]. 10 vols. Tokyo, 1932.

——. *Meiji zenki tochi seido shiron* [Treatise on early Meiji land system]. Tokyo, 1948.

——. *Nōson shi* [History of rural Japan]. Tokyo, 1941.

Ōta, Kasaku. *Meiji-Taishō-Shōwa beika seisaku shi* [Rice value policy of Meiji, Taishō, Shōwa eras]. Tokyo, 1938.

Prime Minister's Office, Statistics Bureau. *Nihon tōkei nenkan* [Statistical yearbook of Japan]. Tokyo, 1949————. Cited as *Tōkei nenkan*.

Sekiyama, Naotarō. *Kinsei nihon no jinkō kōzō* [Structure of Tokugawa period population]. Tokyo, 1958.

Suehiro, Izutarō, *et al.*, eds. *Gendai hōgaku zenshū* [Collected studies of contemporary law]. 39 vols. Tokyo, 1928-31.

Takahashi, Kamekichi. *Meiji-Taishō nōson keizai no hensen* [Change in agricultural economy during Meiji and Taishō eras]. Tokyo, 1926.

Takimoto, Seiichi. *Nihon hōken keizai shi* [History of Japan's feudal economy]. Tokyo, 1930.

Tōa Keizai Chōsa Kyoku, ed. *Hompō ni okeru kome no jūkyū* [Supply and demand for rice in Japan]. Tokyo, 1932.

Tōbata, Seiichi. *Nihon nōgyō no tenkai katei* [Process of Japan's agricultural development]. Rev. and enl. edn. Tokyo, 1947.

Tōbata, Seiichi, and Toshitarō Morinaga, eds. *Nihon nōgyō hattatsu shi* [History of Japan's agricultural development]. 10 vols. and 2 supp. vols. Tokyo, 1953-59. Cited as *NNHS*.

Tōbata, Seiichi, and Kazushi Ohkawa, eds. *Nihon no keizai to nōgyō* [Japanese economy and agriculture]. Tokyo, 1956.

Tsunematsu, Seiji. "Nōgyō to zaisei no sayō" [Agriculture and public finance]. *Nihon no keizai to nōgyō* [Japanese economy and agriculture]. Eds. Seiichi Tōbata and Kazushi Ohkawa. Tokyo, 1956.

Umemura, Mataji. *Chingin-koyō-nōgyō* [Wages-employment-agriculture]. Tokyo, 1961.

————. "Sangyō rōdō idō to sono kōka" [Inter-industrial labor movement and its effect]. *Nihon no keizai to nōgyō* [Japanese economy and agriculture]. Eds. Seiichi Tōbata and Kazushi Ohkawa. Tokyo, 1956.

Yamada, Moritarō. *Nihon shihon shugi bunseki* [An analysis of Japanese capitalism]. 7th rev. edn. Tokyo, 1955.

Yamada, Yūzō. *Nihon kokumin shotoku suikei shiryō* [Materials for the estimation of Japan's national income]. Tokyo, 1951.

Yamaguchi, Kazuo. *Meiji zenki keizai no bunseki* [An analysis of early Meiji economy]. Tokyo, 1956.

Yanagi, Yoshiharu. *Saishin chiso hō yōgi* [Commentary on the recent land tax law]. Tokyo, 1934.

B. BOOKS AND MONOGRAPHS IN ENGLISH

Allen, George C. *A Short Economic History of Modern Japan*. 2nd rev. edn. London, 1962.

Beasley, William G. *The Modern History of Japan.* New York, 1964.

Bellah, Robert N. *Tokugawa Religion.* Glencoe, Illinois, 1962.

Bennett, M. K. *The World's Food.* New York, 1954.

Chambliss, William J. *Chiaraijima Village: Land Tenure, Taxation, and Local Trade, 1818-1884.* Tucson, 1965.

Cohen, Jerome B. *Japan's Economy in War and Reconstruction.* Minneapolis, 1948.

Craig, Albert C. *Chōshū in the Meiji Restoration.* Cambridge, 1961.

Crawcour, E. S. "Japan's Economy on the Eve of Modernization." *The State and Economic Enterprise in Japan.* Ed. William W. Lockwood. Princeton, 1965.

Dore, R. P. *Land Reform in Japan.* London, 1959.

———. "The Legacy of Tokugawa Education." *Changing Japanese Attitudes toward Modernization.* Ed. Marius B. Jansen. Princeton, 1965.

Farnsworth, Helen. "The Role of Wheat in Improving Nutritional Status and Labor Productivity in Lesser Developed Countries." *International Wheat Surplus Utilization Conference Proceedings.* Brookings, South Dakota, 1958.

Food and Agriculture Organization of the United Nations. *Cadastral Surveys and Records of Rights in Land: An FAO Land Tenure Study.* FAO Agricultural Studies, No. 18. Rome, March 1953.

Gerschenkron, Alexander. "Economic Backwardness in Historical Perspective." *The Program of Underdeveloped Countries.* Ed. Bert Hoselitz. Chicago, 1952.

Gleason, Alan H. "Economic Growth and Consumption Levels in Japan." *The State and Economic Enterprise in Japan.* Ed. William W. Lockwood. Princeton, 1965.

Hagen, Everett E. *On the Theory of Social Change: How Economic Growth Begins.* Homewood, Illinois, 1962.

Hoselitz, Bert, ed. *The Program of Underdeveloped Countries.* Chicago, 1952.

Jansen, Marius B., ed. *Changing Japanese Attitudes toward Modernization.* Princeton, 1965.

Johnston, Bruce F. *Japanese Food Management in World War II.* Stanford, 1953.

Law School of Harvard University, The International Program in Taxation. *Papers and Proceedings of the Conference on Agricultural Taxation and Economic Development.* Cambridge, 1954.

Lewis, W. Arthur. *The Theory of Economic Growth.* London, 1955.

Lockwood, William W. *The Economic Development of Japan.* Princeton, 1954.

———, ed. *The State and Economic Enterprise in Japan.* Princeton, 1965.

Moulton, Harold G. *Japan: An Economic and Financial Appraisal.* Washington, D.C., 1931.

Nasu, Shiroshi. *Aspects of Japanese Agriculture.* New York, 1941. (mimeographed)

Norman, E. Herbert. *Japan's Emergence as a Modern State.* New York, 1940.

Ogura, Takekazu. *Agricultural Development in Modern Japan,* Tokyo, 1963.

Ohkawa, Kazushi *et al. The Growth Rate of the Japanese Economy Since 1878.* Tokyo, 1957.

Ohkawa, Kazushi and Henry Rosovsky. "A Century of Japanese Economic Growth." *The State and Economic Enterprise in Japan.* Ed. William W. Lockwood. Princeton, 1965.

Oshima, Harry T. "Meiji Fiscal Policy and Economic Progress." *The State and Economic Enterprise in Japan.* Ed. William W. Lockwood. Princeton, 1965.

Passin, Herbert. *Society and Education in Japan.* New York, 1965.

Robertson Scott, J. W. *The Foundations of Japan.* London, 1922.

Rosovsky, Henry. *Capital Formation in Japan, 1868-1940.* Glencoe, Illinois, 1961.

Sansom, George. *A History of Japan, 1334-1615.* Stanford, 1961.

———. *The Western World and Japan.* New York, 1951.

Sawada, Shujirō. "Innovation in Japanese Agriculture, 1880-1935." *The State and Economic Enterprise in Japan.* Ed. William W. Lockwood. Princeton, 1965.

Sheldon, Charles D. *The Rise of the Merchant Class in Tokugawa Japan.* Locust Valley, New York, 1958.

Smith, Thomas C. *Agrarian Origins of Modern Japan.* Stanford, 1959.

———. *Political Change and Industrial Development in Japan: Government Enterprise, 1868-1880.* Stanford, 1955.

Taeuber, Irene B. *The Population of Japan.* Princeton, 1958.

Takekoshi, Yosaburo. *The Economic Aspects of the History of the Civilization of Japan.* 3 vols. London, 1930.

Tōbata, Seiichi. *An Introduction to the Agriculture of Japan.* Tokyo, 1958.

Tranter, A. Victor. *Evasion in Taxation.* London, 1929.

Tsuru, Shigeto. *Essays on Japanese Economy.* Tokyo, 1958.

United States, Department of State, Office of International Research. *Japan's Food, Beverage and Tobacco Position, 1928-36.* Office of International Research Report No. 4126. 1948. (mimeographed)

Wald, Haskell P. *Taxation of Agricultural Land in Underdeveloped Economies.* Cambridge, 1959.

Wickizer, V. D., and M. K. Bennett, *The Rice Economy of Monsoon Asia.* Stanford, 1941.

C. ARTICLES AND PAPERS IN JAPANESE

Hatanaka, Kōichi. "Kōchi tōkei no kakuritsu" [Establishment of reliable arable land statistics]. *Nōrin tōkei chōsa* [Survey of agriculture and forestry statistics], VII, 10 (October 1957), 10-16.

———. "Waga kuni ni okeru sakuzuke to kōchi ni kansuru tōkei chōsa no genkyō" [Present state of statistical reporting on crop and arable land area in Japan]. *Nōgyō tōkei kenkyū* [Agricultural statistics research] III, supp. (February 1956), 1-10.

Hayami, Yūjiro. "Hiryō tōka ryō no suikei" [Fertilizer consumption estimates]. *Nōgyō Sōgō Kenkyū* [Quarterly Journal of the National Research Institute of Agriculture], XVII, 1 (January 1963), 247-325.

Hijikata, Seibi. "Shokugyobetsu jinkō no hensen wo tsūjite mitaru shitsugyō mondai" [Unemployment problem viewed from the perspective of changing structure of industrial labor force]. *Shakai Seisaku Jihō* [Social Policy Review] CVIII (September 1929), 76-87.

Ishikawa, Shigeru. "Nihon no keiken wa tekiyō kanō ka" [Is the Japanese experience applicable?]. *Keizai Kenkyū* [The Economic Review], XIV, 2 (April 1963).

Kampō [Official Gazette]. Tokyo, 1890———.

Kojima, Toshihiro. "Meijiki nōgyō tōkei no mondai ishiki" [Meiji problems revealed in agricultural statistics]. *Nōgyō Sōgō Kenkyū* [Quarterly Journal of the National Research Institute of Agriculture], XII, 4 (October 1958), 77-109.

Nakayama, Seiki. "Shokuryō shōhi suijun no chōki henka ni tsuite" [Long-run trend of food consumption in Japan, 1878-1955]. *Nōgyō Sōgō Kenkyū* [Quarterly Journal of the National Research Institute of Agriculture], XII, 4 (October 1958), 13-37.

Yamada, Saburo. "Nōgyō sanshutsu gaku no suikei" [Estimation of the value of agricultural production], *Keizai Kenkyū* [The Economic Review], XV, 1 (January 1964), 71-76.

Yasuba, Yasukichi. "Nihon no kōgyō seisan shisu" [Japan's industrial production index]. Paper presented at the third conference of the Tokyo Keizai Kenkyū Center, January 1965.

Yokoi, Jikei. "Nōkai ni tsuite" [In regard to the Agricultural Association]. *Teikoku Nōkai Hō* [Bulletin of the Imperial Agricultural Association], IV, 4 (April 1914), 1-10.

D. ARTICLES AND PAPERS IN ENGLISH

Beasley, W. G. "Feudal Revenue in Japan at the Time of the Meiji Restoration." *Journal of Asian Studies*, XIX, 3 (May 1960), 255-72.

Borton, Hugh. "Peasant Uprisings in Japan." *Transactions of the Asiatic Society in Japan*, 2nd series, XVI (May 1938), 1-219.

Bronfenbrenner, Martin. "Some Lessons of Japanese Economic Development, 1853-1938." *Pacific Affairs*, XXXIV, 1 (Spring 1961).

Chung, Young-iob. "The Role of Government in the Generation of of Savings: The Japanese Experience, 1868-1893" (unpublished Ph.D. dissertation, Columbia University, 1965).

Crawcour, E. S. "Changes in Japanese Commerce in Tokugawa Period." *Journal of Asian Studies*, XXII, 4 (August 1963), 387-400.

Dore, R. P. "Agricultural Improvement in Japan, 1870-1900." *Economic Development and Cultural Change*, IX, 1, Part 2 (October 1960), 69-91.

———. "Meiji Landlord: Good or Bad?" *Journal of Asian Studies*, XVIII, 3 (May 1959), 343-55.

Edgeworth, F. Y. "Stationary State in Japan." *Economic Journal*, V (September 1895), 480-81.

Fei, J. C. H. and Gustav Ranis. "Capital-Labor Ratios in Theory and in History: Reply," *American Economic Review*, LIV, 6 (December 1964), 1063-69.

———. "Innovation, Capital Accumulation, and Economic Development," *American Economic Review*, LIII, 3 (June 1964), 213-313.

Hall, John W. "The Castle Town and Japan's Modern Urbanization." *Far Eastern Quarterly*, XV, 1 (November 1955), 37-56.

Harootunian, Harry D. "The Economic Rehabilitation of the Samurai in the Early Meiji Period." *Journal of Asian Studies*, XIX, 4 (August 1960), 433-44.

Hobsbaum, E. J. "The British Standard of Living, 1790-1850." *Economic History Review*, 2nd series, X, 1 (April 1957), 46-68.

Horie, Hideichi. "The Agricultural Structure of Japan in Meiji
    Restoration." *Kyoto University Economic Review*, XXXI, 2
    (October 1961).
Ike, Nobutaka. "Taxation and Landownership in the Westernization
    of Japan." *Journal of Economic History*, VII, 2 (November
    1947), 160-82.
Johnston, Bruce F. "Agricultural Productivity and Economic De-
    velopment of Japan." *Journal of Political Economy*, VII, 2
    (November 1947), 160-82.
————. "Agricultural Development and Economic Transformation:
    A Comparative Study of the Japanese Experience." *Food
    Research Institute Studies*, III, 2 (November 1962), 223-76.
Johnston, Bruce F. and John W. Mellor. "The Role of Agriculture in
    Economic Development." *American Economic Review*, LI,
    4 (September 1961), 566-93.
Kuznets, Simon. "Quantitative Aspects of the Economic Growth of
    Nations: 1. Levels and Variability of Rates of Growth."
    Economic Development and Cultural Change, V, 1 (October
    1956), 1-94.
————. "Quantitative Aspects of the Economic Growth of Nations:
    VI. Long Term Trends in Capital Formation Proportions."
    Economic Development and Cultural Change, IX, 4, Part 2
    (July 1961), 1-124.
Morris, Morris David. "The Problem of the Peasant Agriculturist in
    Meiji Japan, 1873-1885." *Far Eastern Quarterly*, XV, 3 (May
    1956), 357-70.
Nakamura, James I. "The Role of Meiji Land Reform in the Eco-
    nomic Development of Japan." Paper presented at the Con-
    ference on Land and Tax Reform in the Less Developed
    Countries, University of Wisconsin, Milwaukee, Wisconsin,
    August 26-28, 1963.
Nelson, Richard R. "Growth Models and the Escape from the Low-
    Level Equilibrium Trap: The Case of Japan." *Economic De-
    velopment and Cultural Change*, VIII, 4, Part 1 (July 1960),
    378-88.
Ohkawa, Kazushi. "Capital Formation in Japan." *Economic De-
    velopment and Cultural Change*, XII, 1 (October 1963),
    110-11.
————. "Economic Growth and Agriculture." *Annals of the Hitotsu-
    bashi Academy*, VII, 1 (October 1956), 46-60.
Ohkawa, Kazushi and Henry Rosovsky. "The Role of Agriculture in
    Modern Japanese Economic Development." *Economic De-*

velopment and Cultural Change, IX, 1, Part 2 (October 1960), 43-67.

Oshima, Harry T. "National Income Statistics of Underdeveloped Countries," *Journal of American Statistical Association,* LII (June 1957), 162-74.

———. "Notes on an Alternative Method of Estimating the National Income and Expenditures of Japan, 1881," *Keizai Kenkyū* [The Economic Review], VIII, 3 (July 1957).

———. "The Role of Land Taxes in Japanese Development (1867-1912) and Its Relevance to Underdeveloped Countries." Paper presented in Philippines to the Joint Legislative-Executive Tax Committee, Summer 1960.

Patrick, Hugh T. "Lessons for Underdeveloped Countries from the Japanese Experience of Economic Development." *Indian Economic Journal,* IX, 2 (October 1961).

Ranis, Gustav. "The Financing of Japanese Economic Development." *Economic History Review,* XI, 3 (April 1959), 440-54.

Reubens, E. P. "Capital-labor Ratios in Theory and in History: Comment," *The American Economic Review,* LIV, 6 (December 1964), 1052-62.

———. "Foreign Capital in Economic Development: The Japanese Experience, 1868-1913" (unpublished Ph.D. dissertation, Columbia University, 1952).

Shishido, Toshio. "Japanese Agriculture: Productivity Trend and Development of Technique." *Journal of Farm Economics,* XLIII, 2 (May 1961), 285-95.

Smith, Thomas C. "Landlord's Sons in the Business Elite." *Economic Development and Cultural Change,* IX, 1, Part 2 (October 1960), 93-107.

———. "The Land Tax in the Tokugawa Period." *Journal of Asian Studies,* XVIII, 1 (November 1958), 3-19.

Watanabe, Tsunehiko. "Economic Aspects of Dualism in the Industrial Development of Japan." *Economic Development and Cultural Change,* XIII, 3 (April 1965), 293-312.

Index

Tables are indexed by page number with "t" following.

ous thinking, 141; increase in, 142, 146; and level of income, 136; loss of employment outlets, 152; measurement of, 153; non-agricultural, 146; and number of households, 144; plausibility of changes in, 149; and population, 144-48, 145t, 147t, 148t; primary sector, 144, 145t; samurai in, 154, 158; secondary sector, 144, 145t, 146; tertiary sector, 144, 145t, 146; underreporting of, 14, 147. See also Hemmi agricultural labor force estimates; Hijikata labor force estimates; Ohkawa estimates, labor force; gainfully occupied population.

labor force participation rate, 146, 147t, 148

labor input, 141-42, 152

labor migration, 138, 139, 151, 153, 154, 158, 183

labor productivity, 17, 21, 125, 151; Tokugawa period, 16; increase in, 61, 141, 159, 209, 210-11; growth rate of, 140; denial of rapid growth, 141

labor supply, 15, 140, 149, 150, 151

labor surplus, 164

labor transfer, to agriculture, ix; from agriculture, 77, 78, 138, 144-49, 150; causes of, 150; effects of, 154; previous hypotheses on, 149, 150; rate of, 149, 153; Tokugawa period, 138n, 140

land, alienation of, 158; investment in, 165n; ownership by cultivator, 158; restoration of ruined, 29, 35; subsidy for improvement, 40; supply of, 15. See also arable land; cultivated land; genya; paddy fields; salt fields; takuchi; upland fields; woodland; and concealment; misclassification; undermeasurement

land adjustment. See arable land

adjustment; Arable Land Adjustment Law

land classification, 59, 179, 204

land consolidation, 198, 199, 200, 202, 208-09, 210

land conversion, 202, 208, 213

land fragmentation, 199, 200

land holdings, change in size, 75n

land improvement, xiii, 59-61, 62n, 154

land maps, 24, 32

land measurement, 4, 9, 53, 55, 179, 181, 190

land ownership certificate, 23, 183, 186, 186n, 192, 192n

land price, underreporting of, 186

land productivity, 48-52, 77, 117n, 137, 209, 211

land reclamation, 25n, 29, 35, 37, 40, 49, 60, 202, 205-08, 213

land reclassification, 213

land records, Tokugawa period, 22

land redistribution, 199

land reform, 162, 169

land register, 24

land registration, 23, 34-35; of concealed land, 25, 27, 30, 54, 55; tax, 201, 203

land revaluation, 10, 65, 194-95; under special legislation, 65, 66, 67, 68, 73, 82; quinquennial, 191, 192

land survey, of 1873-79, 8, 22, 23, 25, 54-55, 64, 65, 67, 68n, 69, 73, 74n, 90, 91, 103, 121, 163, 186, 186n; of 1886-89, 23-24, 25, 30, 31, 32, 33, 39, 55; of 1956, 56; and the village, 8, 59, 187; landowner resistance to, 32

land tax, 159, 160, 162n, 163, 168, 177n, 178, 182, 183, 187; decline in, 194-95; treatment in Arable Land Adjustment Law, 201, 203, 204-08. See also Tokugawa land tax

land tax burden, 53

land tax evasion. See tax evasion